16.95

THE NEW COMPLETE
ENGLISH SPRINGER SPANIEL

A sensational flush by Double National Amateur Field Champion Gwibernant Gefni ("Fire"), owned by Dr. John Riepenhoff. Fire won two Amateur Opens and National Amateur Championship in a four week period. —*Somerville.*

THE NEW COMPLETE

English
Springer Spaniel

by
CHARLES S. GOODALL

and
JULIA GASOW

THIRD EDITION
First Printing—1984

HOWELL BOOK HOUSE Inc.
230 Park Avenue, New York, N.Y. 10169

Library of Congress Cataloging in Publication Data

Goodall, Charles S.
   The new complete English springer spaniel.

   Bibliography: p. 288
   1. English springer spaniels.   I. Gasow, Julia.
II. Title.
SF429.E7G66   1984   636.7′52   84-9048
ISBN 0-87605-118-2

Contents

SECTION II

SHOW and OBEDIENCE SPRINGERS
by Julia Gasow

Heather Schaefer, 10 years old, and her year-old English Springer, "Trapper". This photo (together with a 50-word essay) was the first winner (in 1983) of the annual "Search for the Great American Dog" contest by Purina Dog Chow that offers $25,000 and an appearance in the annual Macy's Thanksgiving Day parade as first prize.

GLOSSARY OF SPRINGER
HUNTING AND FIELD TRIAL TERMS

Blink: An extremely serious fault whereby a dog deliberately avoids game, often due to too much pressure in training.

Bolter: A Spaniel that departs from his handler and goes self-hunting (hunts for himself and not for, or with, his handler).

Cast: Has several meanings, but usually means the distance or depth which a hunting Spaniel penetrates the cover when quartering.

Cover: Vegetation in the area where one is hunting or working his dog.

Hard Mouth: A fault by a dog which injures game while in the act of retrieving.

Heel: The traditional command ordering a Spaniel to walk at handler's left heel if handler is a right-handed gunner.

Honor: Steadiness to both wing and shot of game flushed by brace mate in a trial or while hunting.

Hup: The traditional command ordering a Spaniel to sit.

Objectives: Clumps of brush or gamey looking cover which a good hunting Spaniel should investigate.

Pattern: The degree of perfection, or lack of same, which a Spaniel demonstrates while quartering.

Potter: Lingering or remaining too long on stale scent.

Punch Out: Action of a Spaniel with a poor hunting pattern which hunts straight out and away from his handler, instead of quartering.

Quartering: The desirable back-and-forth, windshield-wiper-like, design to both sides of his handler of the hunting Spaniel.

Runner: Game which chooses to run rather than flush. Often a cripple with broken wing.

Steady to Wing or to Flush: A Spaniel that stops instantly and remains motionless when it flushes game, or if a stray bird passes overhead.

Steady to Shot: The act whereby a Spaniel stops instantly (preferably sits) when gun is discharged.

Wild Flush: A bird that flushes or lifts some distance in front or to the side of a dog, usually out of gun range.

Work a Line, Trail Out, etc: Following the body or foot scent in cover or on ground to locate moving game.

SECTION I

Gun and Field Springers

by

Charles S. Goodall

CHARLES S. GOODALL

The following tribute, written by William F. Brown, editor of *The American Field,* appeared in the introduction to Mr. Goodall's book, *How To Train Your Own Gundog,* (1982):

Charles S. (Chuck) Goodall is one of Nature's noblemen, a superb sportsman with an unrivalled background in gun dogs, including the pointing breeds, spaniels and retrievers. He has been a hunter and amateur trainer of gun dogs for more than forty years. He grew up in Southern Illinois and dates his addicition to upland game and waterfowl hunting with dogs from his early youth. He confesses he was frequently in trouble with school authorities who had the temerity to schedule classes on opening day of quail, pheasant, duck and dove seasons.

Chuck Goodall's dedication to good dog work stems from the fact that early-on he became convinced that 95% of the excitement and appeal of hunting came from observing the actions of home-trained pointing dogs, spaniels or retrievers in finding and retrieving game.

He became interested in field trials when he witnessed several American Field Futurities held near his Southern Illinois home in the 1930s. After graduation from the University of Illinois he found that field trials enabled him to utilize and enjoy spending time with his dogs in the field for eight or ten months each year instead of just during the ever-decreasing open hunting seasons.

It's evident that he was a successful amateur trainer because he placed home-trained dogs in field trials more than 150 times! He has also served as a field trial judge for the several breeds in sixteen states on more than one hundred occasions. Many hunting trips to a dozen or more states, Mexico and Canada helped to broaden his knowledge of canine behavior as well as that of many species of upland game and waterfowl.

His experience embraces distinguished service as a club official, as a lecturer for sportsmen's clubs, and a reporter of significant trials. Indeed, Chuck Goodall is one of America's outstanding authorities on hunting dogs and field trials, uniquely equipped to author this excellent book. He is preeminently qualified to tell others how to train their gun dogs.

—William F. Brown

Mr. Brown's salute has been echoed in many honors bestowed upon Mr. Goodall through the years. Notable among them was the first Martin Hogan Memorial Award (1952), for "the individual who contributed most to gun dogs and the sport of field trials in the Middle West."

The long list of Mr. Goodall's services to dogdom include membership on the Board of Trustees of the Morris Animal Foundation from 1967 to 1977, and Chairman of its Canine Division for four years. He was a Governor of the English Springer Spaniel Field Trial Association for 27 years, and secretary of the English Springer Spaniel Field Trial Club of Illinois for 28 years. Additionally, he was a founder and officer of the Illinois River Retriever Club and secretary of the North Arkansas Bird Dog Club for six years.

A prolific writer, he has written three other books on gun dog training, and over 200 articles and stories on gun dogs and related subjects.

Reproduction after etching by Ben Marshall (1767-1835), a noted British artist. Spaniels such as these were the early ancestors of present-day Springers, and were known at the time as Norfolk Spaniels, Springing Spaniels, and by other names appropriate to the locality or use.

Preface

T HE AUTHOR of the gun dog section of this book is pleased to be associated with co-author Mrs. Fred Gasow who very graciously accepted the publisher's invitation to write the show and Obedience sections of this book. Her long time interest and personal experience in successfully breeding, showing, and judging English Springer Spaniels on the bench more than qualifies her for the difficult literary task which she has performed so successfully.

The English Springer Spaniel is a magnificent gun dog, well qualified as the leading contender for the title of all around gun dog conferred on him by such recognized authorities as David Michael Duffy, the late Henry Davis and other American and British authorities.

The breed's early ancestors were recognized as top hunting dogs and described as such by two ancient books—*Livre De Chase,* circa 1387, and *Of Englishe Dogges,* written in 1576. Obviously, the early type spaniels did not spring into existence the year the books were published and must have been around for a long time. We had personal confirmation of this fact in the 1930s from the late British authority, Freeman Lloyd, who told us he had seen a tapestry woven in the first century A.D. which depicted a typical spaniel dog. It is obvious that the intense hunting desire of the present day Springers were programed into the breed's ancestors more than 600 years ago when they were used extensively in the Middle Ages to flush game for the falcons and to start game for the gaze and trail hounds. But those ancient ancestors through selective breeding with some characteristics preserved and others modified in their transaction from half-wild flush and chase dogs to their present level of intensely, but programed trainable, gun dogs. In 1901 the largest breed of flushing, sporting spaniels known under several names were recognized by the English Kennel Club as English Springer Spaniels. British sportsmen, who kept Springers for hunting, organized field trials for the breed in keeping with its original skills and talents in this earliest of all human canine relationships. But all admirers of

13

the breed's pleasing temperament and disposition were not hunters, and they organized bench shows in which the dogs were competitively judged on their cosmetic excellence of physical conformation. The same sequence of events occurred in the United States and Canada in the early 1920s, with breed recognition by both American and Canadian Kennel Clubs followed by the inauguration of field trials and bench shows in both countries, modeled somewhat on earlier British versions.

The show and field competition each increased in quantity and quality and it soon became apparent with Springer Spaniels, as it had earlier for Pointers and English Setters, that the physical and mental characteristics for each type were so far apart that it would be virtually impossible to consistently combine them in individual Springers. The superior hunting dog requires a dozen or more action characteristics of physical and mental skills. The show Springer requires a dozen or more characteristics to achieve desirable cosmetic levels of conformation excellence, none of which are necessary in a superior gun dog. And none of the gun dog attributes can enhance the show dog's conformation. It is genetically possible to breed Springers with four dozen necessary characteristics, but obviously much more difficult than to breed one with half this number. Also, any hunter knows that the absence or even below average quantities of any of the necessary hunting characteristics will eliminate that individual as a superior gun dog. In fact, if he has subnormal trainability characteristics he may not even qualify as an acceptable house pet.

It is often difficult for the prospective new dog owner to know or even comprehend existence and/or the difference between the two types of Springer.

We beg the indulgence of informed readers who are aware of it. Our reason for the emphasis is to encourage prospective buyers of Springers to avoid disappointment and select a puppy from the breed type most suitable to his purpose. Our firm conviction is based not only on knowledge of the great variation in type and use of horses, cattle, swine, and sheep, but also of the existence of the 125 breeds of purebred dogs, all of which have been programed for specific action or use by selective breeding. Also, our experience in observing 20,000 or more trained gun dogs of the several breeds, and in field training effort expended personally on approximately 200 show-bred dogs and an equal number of field dogs, has made us rather wary of anyone who proposes to consistently breed dual type Springers (or Pointers, or English Setters) which qualify as an acceptable type of both show and field dog. The exceedingly rare one which occurs is the exception which proves the rule.

It is physically impossible to acknowledge the contributions of pictures, ideas and factual information contributed by scores of Springer fanciers from all sections of the country. But it would be unfair not to express the appreciation of the publishers and the author for those who went out of their way to contribute extra time and effort to make this book possible. We do therefore gratefully acknowledge the contributions of the following:

The American Kennel Club
The English Kennel Club
Bufkin Spaniel Society
Robert C. Brown
Donald P. Cande
Dr. Janet Christensen
Edmonton Springer Spaniel Club
Patrick Fischer
Mrs. Peter ("Billie") Garvan
Les Girling
Cliff and Rex Hankins

John Isaacs
Mrs. James (Syphie) Kineon
Richard Kloss
David Lorenz and family
Talbot Radcliffe and John DeMott
John Seyman
Andy Shoaff
Mr. and Mrs. Tom Vail
Ed. Whitaker
Mr. and Mrs. E. W. Wunderlich
Mrs. M. Goodall

— CHARLES S. GOODALL

At the 1950 US National Championship Field Trial, a 17-inch snowfall on the first day presented many problems for Springers and handlers. Pictured are the top winners. L. to r.: The late Phil Armour with the National trophy, Steve Studnicki with National winner FC Whitlemore George; judges Bucky Moore and the late Dr. Harry Shoot; Ruffy Eakin, professional trainer with C. M. Kline's Flyer's Ginger of Shady Glen, which placed 2nd; and author Chuck Goodall with FC Square Peg, 3rd place winner and Best Dog handled by an Amateur award winner.   —*Photo, Evelyn Shafer.*

Print from *The Gentleman's Recreation*, England, 1686.

1

Origin, History and Development of the English Springer Spaniel

***

THE ENGLISH SPRINGER SPANIEL, leading contender for the title of best all-around gun dog, is an ancient and respected breed whose ancestors can be traced back into the dim and distant reaches of time. Thus the sportsman who would be thoroughly equipped to train and use these fine dogs in the field should have basic knowledge of the breed's origin and early history as a means of attaining complete utilization of their many and great hunting talents.

There are several theories as to where the ancient parent stock of spaniel-type dogs originated. Some say they originated in Great Britain. The majority opinion, however, holds that they first came from Spain, as the breed name implies. This position is sustained by eminent authorities, the first of which was the French nobleman, Gaston de Foix (often called Gaston Pheobus). He wrote *Livre de Chasse* in 1387, most of which was reproduced in *The Master of Game,* written between the years 1406 and 1413 by Edward, second Duke of York, who wrote that spaniels were good hounds for the hawk and that even though they came from Spain, there were many in other countries. Further evidence of their distribution throughout Europe may be found in the statement of the late Freeman Lloyd, a 20th century sportsman-writer of note, who told the author (about 1934) that he had seen an Italian tapestry circa the 1st century A.D., which depicted a spaniel-type dog fawning at its master's feet.

Another noted authority who held with the Spanish origin theory was the excellent 16th century British scholar, Dr. John Caius, whose book *"Of Englishe Dogges"*, a short treatise written in Latin and published in 1576, states: "Of gentile dogges serving the hauke, and first of the Spaniell called in Latine Hispaniolus, there be two sorts:

1. The first findeth game on the land.
2. The other findeth game on the water."

The good Doctor described the land spaniel as "one which spryngeth the birde and betrayth flight by pursuite." He elaborated further by adding, "the first kinde of such serve the Hauke, the second the net, or traine. The first kinde have no peculier names assigned unto them save onely that they be denominated after the byrde which by naturall appointment he is alloted to take, for the which consideration, some be called Dogges

1. For the Falcon
2. The Pheasant
3. The Partridge
4. And such like.

The common sort of people call them by one generall word, namely Spaniells, as though these kinde of Dogges came originally and first of all out of Spaine."

Dr. Caius then distinguished between the two kinds of land spaniels of that day, one of which flushed game and the other of which set or pointed its game. He described this type, which is generally considered to be the early ancestors of our present day Setters, by the Latin name of *"Index"*. Dr. Caius' work was translated into English by Abraham Fleming at a later date.

Most of the reliable 20th century authorities on Spaniels attribute the origin of the breed to Spain. Such serious students of Spaniels as Maxwell Riddle, Henry Ferguson, Clarence Pfaffenberger, C. A. Phillips and R. Claude Cane held with the Spanish origin theory. The late 19th century British writer, J. R. Walsh, who used the nom de plume "Stonehenge", wrote that he had no doubt that the sport of Hawking was known and practiced by the early Britons, but that the Roman invaders under Caesar in 55 B.C. were totally ignorant of the science. He stated further that the Romans, who began their occupation of the Isles in 43 A.D., learned the sport of Hawking from Britons and improved upon it by introducing the Land Spaniel, if not the Water Spaniel, too, to the country. Further evidence of the Spaniel's early residence in Britain is to be found in an ancient Welsh law of 300 A.D. and 942 A.D. which referred to them by breed name. Regardless of whether one accepts the Spanish origin theory, it's not too difficult to imagine the sports-minded rugged adventurers of Caesar's Roman legions "liberating" a few Spaniels in their conquest of Spain and taking them to Britain, even as soldiers in the great wars of the 20th century and earlier have done.

Numerous ancient authorities considered Spaniels as belonging to one of two distinct types. The larger group comprised the *Land Spaniels* (some flushed and some pointed their game). The flushers beat out, flushed and chased game for the Hawks or Hounds. If the mounted hunters were slow in arriving at the scene of the Hawks' kill, the Spaniels were known to attack and even eat the hawk and the kill. The setting types crouched to enable the hunter to cast or drop his net over the game, and occasionally the dog, too. The second type were the *Water Spaniels* which retrieved waterfowl and, sometimes, the arrow which missed its mark. These facts are well documented in early literature and art objects as the principal methods of hunting in the 14th, 15th, and 16th century.

This was all to change, however, with an invention of great significance in which the wheel lock firearm was replaced by the flintlock. This notable event occurred in France about 1630, and since it reduced the time lag between the trigger pull and the discharge of the projectiles from the muzzle, made it possible for sportsmen to engage in "flying shooting" (wing shooting). This piece was introduced into Britain in the late 17th century and without doubt was the beginning of the art of fine gun dog training. Trying to shoot over one or several couples of wild, uncontrolled Spaniels with any kind of gun would have been useless then as now. As a consequence Spaniels during the next 300 years were transformed from untrained, wild beaters, to smooth, polished gun dogs which must hunt within gun range and retrieve with a tender mouth in order to save the game for the table.

The Springer's evolution from a variety of local types, used exclusively to start game for the Hawk or Hound, to a gun dog which would accept training kindly, was an evolutionary one. Early type Spaniels were described by one 17th century writer as being of 13 different kinds. Those called Land Spaniels came in a variety of colors, sizes, and shapes, as we have seen in their manner of handling game. And it was not unusual to find two or even three types in the same litter. Small ones (under 25 pounds) came to be called *cocking spaniels,* while the larger ones were called *springing spaniels* or *setting spaniels.* The setting Spaniels undoubtedly were the ancestors of present day Setters.

Much was written about the middle age practice of crossing spaniel types with hounds, terriers, and even "mungrels". These early sportsmen were able, however, to maintain the basic hunting desire in their dogs. Markham, for instance, points it out in his *"Art of Fowling",* written in 1621. He says, ". . . it is the nature of every spaniell to hunt all manner of byrdes (though some with more earnestness and greediness) . . . and there then remaineth nothing but the accustoming the Dogge thereunto, and acquainting him with your hinde and determination. . . " Thomas Bewicke (1752-1828) confirmed Markham's opinion, and was, incidentally, the first writer to use the words Springer and Cocker in referring to specific type Spaniels. His beautiful woodcuts of the 25 different "breeds" of hunting dogs of his day illustrate Springers and Cockers in great detail.

The impact of the advent of the flintlock on Spaniels was tremendous; just as some hunted with more desire than others (Markham), some were more tractable and quickly learned to hunt to the gun and not for themselves. This is highly important and one reason why modern field strains outshine their bench-bred brothers. The hunting strains through the ages have been selected and bred not only for hunting desire, but also for their ability to accept training kindly.

The first real attempt to standardize the physical and mental characteristics of the Springer was made by the Boughey family, whose stud book dates back to 1812. Many present day Springers can be traced to Mop I, Mop II, and Frisk—early inmates of the Boughey's Aqualate Kennels in Shropshire.

Organized competitive sport for Spaniels began with the founding of The Spaniel Club in England in the late 19th century. They drew up standards for bench show (physical conformation) competition and shows were held. But as often happens where qualities other than working or functional abilities are the sole measure of perfection, much controversy arose because the show dogs could not face cover or hunt properly because of their short legs and long backs. As a consequence another club, The Sporting Spaniel Society, was organized to test Spaniels for their hunting ability. Soon both clubs were holding trials (the first one in January 1899). At the third or fourth event a Springer dog named Tring beat a Clubber named Beechgrove BEE (after two previous losses to Bee) to become the first Springer trial winner.

In 1902, the English Kennel Club recognized the English Springer Spaniel officially as a breed. The first Springer field champion in the world was C. A. Phillips' Rivington Sam, whose blood still flows through the veins of many present day Springers. Sam was probably half Cocker.

The late, well informed U.S. sportsman, Edward D. Knight, summed up the early development of the breed as follows, "It can readily be seen that the fountainheads of Springerdom logically fall into four distinct classes:

1. Individuals of relatively pure ancestry whose pedigrees had been privately maintained for generations.
2. Similar individuals which came from strains which had been bred for years by private families concerning which no records had been maintained.
3. Individuals of unknown ancestry which had been picked up purely on the basis of type or performance.
4. Individuals resulting from planned matings where blood of other breeds was frankly infused for a definite purpose."

During the first quarter of the 20th century six great pivotal sources or fountainhead strains of Springer bloodlines were established in England, according to the late eminent Scotch authority, C. Mackay Sanderson. The patriarch to which each strain owes its origin is listed below. Most of the top field dogs in Britain and America today have one or more of these great stud dogs in their pedigree.

Eng. TC Rivington Sam, the first Springer Spaniel ever to become a field trial champion in any country. Many of the great field dogs are direct descendants of Sam, who was owned by C. A. Phillips, and trained by James Thompson, both of Scotland.

1. F. C. Velox Powder, whelped in 1903, by Randle ex Belle.
2. E. F. C. Rivington Sam, whelped in 1911, by Spot of Hagley ex Rivington Riband.
3. Denne Duke, whelped in 1908, by Bosh ex Daisy.
4. Dash of Hagley, whelped in 1905, by Dash ex Beulas.
5. Caistor Rex, whelped in 1908, by Bob ex Lively.
6. Cornwallis Cavalier, whelped in 1914, by Spot ex Beaney.

Sanderson reported to the author that in 1948 the line from Rivington Sam was the top line in Great Britain, in that half of the British Field Champions were direct descendants of Sam as well as a score of gun dogs. He considered the bloodlines of Dash of Hagley as runner-up to Sam in the production of Field Champions and gun dogs, with Cornwallis Cavalier in number three position.

In the second quarter of the 20th Century dozens of names of British Springer owners, breeders, trainers, handlers and shooting people may be found in the gun dog literature of the day, some of whom were known to the author personally or by reputation. Some of these who contributed the most to the furtherance of the breed, either by perpetuating old or establishing new bloodlines, and by testing the quality of their breeding efforts through training Springers for the gun or the competitive sport of field trials, are most deserving of mention. They include: C. A. Phillips, James Colin, Ethel Thompson, William Humphrey, The Duke of Hamilton, Lorna Countess Howe, Selwyn Jones, Joe Greatorex, John

Talbot Radcliffe, England's outstanding and perhaps its record-breaking breeder of great Springers that could win field trials. In the 1960s, he predicted he would produce a strain of Springer blood with great native ability to scent, drive and run—dogs that would be trainable and would handle. The U.S. win record for Saighton-bred Springers of 10 National wins, 9 Seconds, 7 Thirds, and 6 Fourths indicates that his forecast was remarkably accurate. In addition, many other Saighton-bred Springers have won field championships in England and the U.S.

Kent, John Forbes, Tom Laird, H. S. Lloyd, R. R. Kelland, Colonel F. H. B. Carrell, Captain Traherne, George Curle, Mason Prime, A. E. Curtis, George Clark, W. D. Edwards, Edgar Winter, L. D. Wigan, Miss D. Morland Hooper, and A. L. Trotter.

In the third quarter of the 20th century Britishers who contributed substantially to the continued development of the breed must include the names of Mr. and Mrs. R. B. Weston-Webb, who bred four Field Champions, plus a number of fine gun dogs. Both handled their own Springers for shooting and/or trials. Talbott Radcliffe, another prominent amateur handler and trainer, has bred four Field Champions as well as exporting a number of fine Springers to America to increase the number of Champions from his blood. Hal Jackson, R. N. Burton, and F. Thomas were other amateurs who made their mark during this period. F. George, Dr. Tom Davidson, and Major Peacock also attained prominence for their contribution to the sport and breed. The Messrs. E. and M. Ainsworth were the owners, and D. Munro the breeder, of the outstanding British stud dog of the period. Their great male Field Champion, Rivington Glensaugh Glean, sired eight or more in England plus several others which acquired the title in the U.S. The late W. G. Sheldon bred five Field Champions and was an earnest competitor in trials. Mrs. Margaret Pratt and Mrs. P. M. Badenach-Nicolson are distinguished members of the distaff in British Springer circles. Jack Davey bred and exported to America Wivenwood Willey, who won the U.S. National in 1966.

The encouragement given by British sportsmen to professional trainers accounts in part for the development of the Springer with great drive, speed and enthusiasm for hunting, with nose to match the speed and temperament to handle kindly. There have always been fine professionals in England and the present group continues this great tradition. Joe Greatorex probably heads the list during this period with almost 20 Field Champions—a half dozen National Champions and several Brace Championships to his credit. Andrew Wylie and his brother, J. S. Wylie, have produced a score of fine gun dogs and their share of Field Champions. The same applies to John MacQueen and his son, John, Jr., who are cousins of Larry MacQueen, a top U.S. professional. Jack and Keith Chudley, another team of brothers, developed winning ways at their Harpersbrook Kennels and delighted many owners with their smooth polished results. Way up in North Wales, Keath Erlandson has made a fine reputation in a dozen years. He handled five Springers to the field title and bred many good ones including a double U.S. National Field Champion and a double U.S. Amateur National Field Champion (Gwibernant Ganol and Gwibernant Gefni). Another fine professional who loves Springers, but trains all breeds of gun dog, is also most handy with the pen. Peter Moxon writes a column on Springers and has produced a fine book on gun dog training.

The great producing British bitch, Layerbrook Dusty Susan, owned by British professional Mike Scales. Five of her offspring, each with Layerbrook prefix—Beau, Jet, Smudge, Solo and Crystal—became U.S. field champions. Another, NAFC Sunray of Chrishall, won back-to-back National Amateurs and placed 2nd in another for owner Dr. Warren Wunderlich. —Isaacs.

Three well-known British Springer men. L. to r.: Jack Davey, breeder and trainer of U.S. National Open Champion Wivenwood Willie; Jim Lock, exporter to U.S. of several top Springer winners; and Mike Scales, breeder of U.S. National Amateur Champion Sunray of Chrishall and of five Layerbrook Springers which have won U.S. championships, and breeder/handler of British National Champion (1980) Layerbrook Michelle. —*Photo, John Isaacs.*

Following is a complete list of winners and their owners of the English Kennel Club's Championship Field Trial, held each January for Spaniels of any variety except Cocker Spaniels. This trial is emblematic of the British National Championship. Spaniels to qualify must place first or second in a trial held during the current shooting season.

The famous British professional handlers, Keith and Jack Chudley, with four of their many trial winning Springers.

THE BRITISH NATIONAL FIELD CHAMPION SPRINGER SPANIELS

Spaniel:	*Owner:*
1914 Champion Denne Duke	C. Eversfield
1915 to 1921—No trials were held because of World War I.	
1922 FC Flush of Avendale	The Duke of Hamilton
1923 FC Dan of Avendale	The Duke of Hamilton
1924 FC Firecall	Dr. Wilson
1925 FC Reece of Avendale	The Duke of Hamilton
1926 FC Banchory Bright	Mrs. Quintin Dick
1927 FC Banchory Bright	Mrs. Quintin Dick
1928 FC Rivington Rollo	C. A. Phillips
1929 FC Nithsdale Rover	Col. C. Brooks
1930 FC Peter O'Vara	Selwyn Jones
1931 FC Banchory Boy	Lorna Countess Howe
1932 FC Bee of Blair	G. Clark
1933 FC Maida of Barncleuch	Lorna Countess Howe
1934 FC Dalshangan Maida	H.H. The Maharaja of Patiala
1935 FC Spy O'Vara	Selwyn Jones
1936 FC Beeson of Blair	G. Clark
1937 FC Style O'Vara	Selwyn Jones
1938 FC Sally O'Vara	Selwyn Jones
1939 FC Bobble	Cadet Calvert
1940 thru 1947—No trials were held because of World War II.	
1948 Breckonhill Bee	G. Curle
1949 Rivington Glensaugh Glean	E. and M. Ainsworth
1950 FC Spurt OVara	Selwyn Jones
1951 Criffel Daisy Belle	T. B. Laird
1952 FC Ludlovian Darkie	W. G. Sheldon
1953 FC Acheron Pat.	R. N. Burton
1954 FC Scramble O'Vara	Selwyn Jones
1955 FC Scramble O'Vara	Selwyn Jones
1956 FC Gwen of Barnacres	H. Jackson
1957 FC Griffle Snip	T. B. Laird
1958 FC Willy of Barnacres	H. Jackson
1959 FC Micklewood Slip	Capt. R. W. Corbett
1960 FC Harpersbrook Reed	F. George
1961 FC Markdown Muffin	F. Thomas
1962 FC Ruffin Tuff	J. M. Kelvey
1963 FC Berrystead Freckle	Charles Williams
1964 FC Saighton's Stinger	Talbot Radcliffe
1965 FC Medowcourt Della	Ronald Weston-Webb
1966 FC Hamer's Hansel	B. Dalton
1967 No trial held	
1968 Joss of Barnacres	H. Jackson
1969 FC Layerbrook Michelle	Mike Scales
1970 FC Layerbrook Michelle	Mike Scales
1971 FC Coppicewood Carla	C. Lawton-Evens and Capt. C. Qwens
1972 FC Robbie of Barnacre	Mrs. B. M. Jackson
1973 FC Harwes Silver	D. Bovill
1974 FC Crowhill Raffle	P. Stewart
1975 Nell of Bellever	R. J. Hill
1976 1976 FC Sport of Palgrave	D. F. Cock
1977 Kimble Kim	R. A. Longville
1978 FC Ashley Buster	C. R. Burgoyne
1979 FC Judy of Runwell	B. J. De'Ath
1980 FC Macsiccar Mint	R. S. Knight
1981 FC Inler Harryslin	J. Orr
1982 Sandvig Triumph	I. Bateson

All breed gun dog professional trainer Peter Moxon ready to work two interested "students" in the rabbit pen. British trainers utilized domestic rabbits in steadying Springers to flush and shot.

Readers desiring information on Springer activity in other countries are referred to the well-written *The Popular Springer Spaniel* by Dorothy Morland Hooper, published by Popular Dogs Publishing Company, London.

British trainers have used rabbits to start their young Springers hunting and retrieving for at least 100 years. Several years ago the government instituted a program to eliminate rabbits because of the destruction to crops and agriculture inflicted by literally millions of rabbits. This was a serious obstacle which required indominable British courage to overcome. They have successfully overcome this handicap, as one can see from the quality and quantity of Springers they export to the United States.

The Springer in America

The Springer Spaniel arrived in America at an early date according to G. Mourt's *"Journal of the Beginning of the English Plantation at Plymouth,"* circa 1622. He said one of the Pilgrims had a "Spanell" which chased deer. *The Sportsman's Companion,* published in New York, circa 1780, describes several varieties as fine shooting dogs when carefully trained. In the last half of the 19th century the sporting literature lists the names of more than fifty sportsmen who owned and used Spaniel gun dogs.

It was not, however, until 1910 that the first Springer was registered by the American Kennel Club—a bitch named Denne Lucy. In 1914, the

Canadian Kennel Club registered a dog named Longbranch Teal. But the real popularity of the breed in the United States did not occur until Eudore Chevrier of Winnipeg shot over a fine Springer gun dog in 1920 named Longbranch Teal. Chevrier was so impressed with Teal's hunting ability that he began to import English-bred Springers in great quantity for resale to American sportsmen.

Chevrier, along with G. T. Wolfe, Hayes L. Lloyd, E. T. Marsh, W. H. Gardner, and other Canadians, founded the English Springer Spaniel Club of Canada in July, 1922, and the first American trial for the breed was held two months later near Winnipeg. One of the winners was Alderbury Drake, son of the great British field champion Dalshangan Dandy Boy (a grandson of the first British field champion, Rivington Sam). The author's experience in shooting over Alderbury Drake in the 1930s inspired his interest in Spaniels.

The first Springer club in the United States, the English Springer Spaniel Field Trial Association, was organized about 1922 by Samuel G. Allen, William Hutchenson, and the three illustrious Ferguson brothers, Walton, Jr., Henry, and Alfred of Fisher's Island, New York. These five sportsmen had on-the-ground-advice and counsel from William Humphries, owner of the famous Horsford Kennels in England. The first trial was held at Fisher's Island in October, 1924, and was won by Aughrim

The Ferguson brothers organized the club that held the first U.S. field trial for Springers at Fishers Island, N.Y. in 1924. At left, Henry Ferguson with FTC Fleet of Falcon Hill. At right, Walton Ferguson, Jr., with Dual Ch. Tedwyn's Trex (imp.) and Trex of Chancefield. Walton Ferguson became the president of Westminster Kennel Club in 1934.

William Humphrey with FTC Aughrim Flashing and Horsford Hale, who placed first and second in the first U.S. field trial for the breed. Flashing later became the first U.S. field trial champion.

Arthur P. Moecher, organizer of the first two Springer clubs in the Midwest. Moecher, pictured here with FTC Busy Bruning and winner Benno Brunning of Ashaba, organized the first group training class for Springer owners in the United States in 1932. —*Stabler*.

George E. Watson, Sr., with Horsford Handcraft, a 1930 trial winner of ancient Springer bloodlines. Watson, grandfather of Forsyth Kineon and Betsy Watson, was an official of the parent association.

Flashing, owned by Humphries and later sold to Mrs. M. Walton Ferguson, Jr., to become the first United States Field Champion in 1929. In 1927, the American Kennel Club recognized this club as the "parent club" for the breed. Shortly thereafter "Standards and Regulations" for field trials and bench shows were established, modeled after their English counterpart.

The breed was advertised extensively in the 1930s and 1940s by such famous outdoor writers as Freeman Lloyd, Bob Becker, Will Judy, Maxwell Riddle, Gordon McQuary, and others. Their recognition of the breed's hunting talents did much to popularize it with United States hunters. Later on, such fine writers as William Brown, editor of *The American Field,* Henry Davis, Jack Baird, Joe Stetson, Mrs. Evelyn Monte, David Michael Duffy, and Arthur Swanson kept the sporting public well informed of the merits of the Springer, until his kind were found in American hunting fields and duck blinds by the thousands.

During the second quarter of the 20th century, the United States' pheasant population grew by leaps and bounds as a timely replacement of the ever-dwindling supply of native game birds. It was then that Springers found a real "home" on these shores. Some thirty field trial clubs were organized by upland game and waterfowl hunters and the breed was off and running. Stud Books maintained by the American Kennel Club and the American Field recorded the offspring of hundreds of top field dogs of imported and American-bred stock and these became readily available to hunters. Names of leading United States fanciers of field type Springers numbered in the hundreds, but it would be unfair not to particularly mention the names of those who contributed most substantially to the development of the breed in America.

In the East such early pioneers as the Fergusons, Dr. Sam Milbank, Harry I. Caesar, Buell Hollister, and Robert McLean were joined at a later date by such outstanding sportsmen as Dean Bedford, S. L. Hutcheson, A. M. Lewis, Richard Migel, Mrs. Evelyn Monte, Charles Greening, Joseph C. Quirk, Tom Gahagan, Edward Whitaker, Mrs. George Watson and daughters Betsy and Mrs. J. Kineon, B. B. Flick, R. L. Cook, George Brennan, Carl Shattuck, Dr. William Goodman, Bob Sommers, Hartwell Moore, Paul Thompson, Peter Garvan, Colonel Raymond Costabile, Harry Taylor, Joel Lovell, Mrs. Robert Shaw, and Albert Winslow. Men of the stature of Robert McLean and Sam Milbank merit especial recognition because of their leadership in the parent association and the National Clubs. Others, such as the Bedfords, the Watson sisters, the Hutchesons, and Joseph Quirk carried on extensive breeding programs with British and American stock.

The fine Eastern professionals of an early vintage include Will Sinclair, the Jr. and Sr. Jasper Briggs, Harry Cameron, William Witt, Alan Reid, and Adam Eccles. They were succeeded by the talented Larry and Stanley McQueen, Arthur Eakin, Luke Medlin, Julius Farkas, George Ladd, each of whom were experts at turning out smooth, polished field

The late Elmer Chick who handled winners of 4 National Championships (3 in succession) plus 10 Springers which placed. Pictured here with several champions, Elmer began hunting with Springers in the 1930s, entered field trials in the 1940s and won several before switching to professional status and achieving much success.

David Lorenz, Sr. and Jr. David Sr. is dean of the U.S. professional trainers. Beginning in 1952, he placed 15 Springers in National Trials, four of which were National Champions. He finished a dozen or more Field Champions and made many hunters happy with the estimated 1,000 gun dogs of several sporting breeds he trained. Son David Jr. can handle a Springer, too, and is a top U.S. wing shot. He is grandson of the late and great professional trainer, Martin J. Hogan, who achieved success in Great Britain, Africa, Canada and the U.S.

performers for the public. Lawrence McQueen handled three Springers to their National Championship.

Eastern U.S. sportsmen and women who have continued their long time association with one or more facets of Springer field activity include long-time Parent Club official Ed. Whitaker, B. B. Flick, Mrs. Peter Garvan, Mrs. Ruth Greening and Mrs. James Kineon. They were joined in the 1970s by Mr. and Mrs. Thomas Aunkst, Philip Benante, Edwin Gerger, George Cacchio, Done Cande and wife Cathy, Bernard Castellani, Robert Delaney, Edward Faraci, Larry Francovich, John Magine, and Mr. and Mrs. Joseph Ruff. Current Eastern professionals filling the ranks of those who have retired include Raymond Cacchio, Robert Daum, Gary Wilson and Mr. and Mrs. Robert Dengel, who perhaps have decided to become professionals too.

Middle Western sportsmen actively engaged in shooting over, breeding and competing in the trials include the pioneers, Arthur Moecher, who instituted the first training class for gun dog owners in America in 1932, B. F. Genty, John Harding, E. W. Wunderlich, Dr. Stuart Sowle, David Silberman, James Simpson, Jr., Ray Minette, George Sokup, Hugh Herdman, Fred Sehnert, Ted Mertes, Tom Vail, C. K. Hunter, E. J. Elting, Howard Messnard, Tom Stabbler, William Paschael, Julian Collins, and Lawrence Gillingham.

Those actively engaged with the promotion and use of Springers of a more recent vintage include Edward Porges, James Dodson, John Buoy, Mr. and Mrs. P. D. Armour, Jr., William Lane, Dan Langhans, Gordon Madsen, Donald and Betty Maher, Charles Mee, Dr. John Ripenhoff, Jim Ritchie, Keith Van Dusen, Mike Paracsi, Frank Zohrer, Steve Sebestyen, Roy French, John Olin, Joe Zbylski, Mrs. Barry Phelps, Leonard Aldrich, Wallace Crawford, John Braham, John Blanock, Ed. Abraham, Burton Bratburg, Mike Niklaus, Edward Luthman, Jack Redeman, Al Hric, Curtis Killaine, Tom Fussel, Arthur Mayer, John Pirie, and Jerry Baker.

Sportsmen and women in the Middle West who have long been associated with Springer field activity include John Buoy, Mr. and Mrs. W. Wunderlich, Frank Zohrer, George Sokup, Ray Minette, Steve Sabastian, Walter Retzlaff, Richard Csanda, and Marshal Lightfoot. Recent additions to the ranks of devoted Midwesterners include Albert Beedie, David Hopkins, Robert Casper, Dr. Warren Wunderlich, Dr. Francis Prock, Fred and Susan Neville, Tom Meyer, Drs. Mark and Eileen Schinderle, Fred Smalartz, Carl Smith, Bill Zipp. Professionals who continue currently to train good Springer field dogs include David Lorenz, Dan Langhans, Lou Craig, Don Brunn, and Al Hric. Professionals who have entered the field more recently include John Isaacs, Dean Brunn, Dan Phanz, Jerry Gregory, Ben Martin, Carl Strandjord and Barney Zeigler.

Far Western pioneer sportsmen who have been a constructive force in introducing Springers to the public include the names of Dr. Charles Sabin, Robert and Charles Bishop, Dr. Harry Shoot, Harry Leeding,

Lawrence MacQueen, a third generation professional trainer, with FTC Jonkit Joel. Two of MacQueen's cousins are professionals in England. All three have great talent as gun dog trainers.

U.S. National Field Champion Brackenbank Tangle demonstrates perfect carry of shot pheasant as he delivers to E. W. Wunderlich. Tangle's win record of 11 Opens and 16 additional Open placements is a near record. —*Shafer*.

FTC Elysian Eric and Dual Ch. King Lion, the first two field trial champions on the West Coast.

Donald Speer, George Higgs, Donald Montgomery, George Elliott, Dr. Jack Dodson, R. O. Bequette, Otto Lion, R. E. Allen, Clarence Pfaffenberger, Edward Roller, Lee Caya, Val Dervin, Dr. Rex Baldwin, Brian Ingoldsby, Sam Inkley, Glen Shay, and Ed Wright.

Westerners of more recent times include such fine sportsmen as W. T. Gibson, Bob Setron, Cecil Gipson, Albert Klein, Louis Sterling, Donald Shooter, M. A. Featherstone, Edward Cole, Edward Hanks, Joseph Crooks, James Driskell, Paul McClure, Kenny Williams, David Scott, Louis and Evelyn Bui, Dr. Marlowe Dittebrandt, Harold Jones, Leroy Johnson, Jack Redman, Ralph Newton, Joe Larrieu, J. H. Boyle, Art Perle, Dr. and Mrs. C. A. Christensen, Charles Johnson, Paul Diegel, R. S. Renick, Aidan Rourke, Dick Lane, Clark Hughes, Jack Feeney, J. P. Alvestad and Calvin James.

Texas sportsmen who believe that the Springer can serve a useful purpose as a gun dog in that spacious state have organized a field club under the leadership of Carl Tate, Fred Pontello, Joe Reese, and Ed. Pomykal.

Western professional trainers who specialized on Springers included: Roy Gonia, Roy Wallace, O. H. Kale, Bob Sanchez, Bob Croft, Paul Ruddick, Dave Brown, Harry Mitchell. Brown, Croft, and Wallace are still actively turning out fine gun dogs.

Interest in the Springer as a gun dog and field trial competitor is at an all time high as reported by the 49 U.S. clubs which hold recognized field trials for the breed. There are 39 clubs in Great Britain which hold Springer trials and nine in Canada.

Ron McKay with his good Springer, Tschantzen's Dogwood, chats with a group of Canadian sportsmen after handling his Springer in the 1982 Canadian National Field Trial. —*Peter Honcu.*

Canadian National Champion Marshfield Tagger, winner of 44 placements in Canadian and U.S. trials for his owner, outstanding sportsman Les Girling. Les was instrumental in helping to organize several of the 9 Canadian clubs that hold field trials for Springers annually.

Judith Nuss with Redwolf's Danforth Sergeant who she handled to 2nd place in a Canadian spring trial open stake. Judith, a 7-year veteran, is president of Edmonton Springer Spaniel Club.

Springer Spaniels in Canada

Early in the 1920s, Eudore Chevrier of Winnipeg, Canada revived an earlier American interest in English Springer Spaniels by importing large quantities of superior individual dogs from Great Britain. He joined with G. T. Wolfe, Hayes Lloyd, E. J. Marsh, W. H. Gardner and others to found the English Springer Spaniel Club of Canada in 1922. This club held the first American trial for the breed in the same year. In that same year, Herb Routley, an early sportsman interested in both field and bench dogs, founded his Trent Valley Kennel. His Springers placed in the first U.S. trials at Fisher Island in 1924 and many times thereafter, when he was not acting as a judge at Fisher Island and other U.S. clubs.

In 1950 there were only four Canadian clubs holding trials recognized by the Canadian Kennel Club. In 1960, George Webster and Ted Haggis, two Canadians who had each won a U.S. National Amateur, were leaders in organizing the first Canadian National field trial, which was held each year until 1964. In 1972, under the leadership of Jim Abbey, Les Girling and others, the Canadian National Trial was revived and has been held successfully ever since.

CANADIAN NATIONAL FIELD CHAMPIONS

	Dogs	Owner/Handler
1960	Apache Magic Clipper	Julian Collins
1961	Trent Valley Andrea of Athlorne	Thomas Atherton
1962	Apache Clipper's Gay Lady	Julian Collins
1963	Apache Clipper's Brown Ghost	Julian Collins
1964	Rogue O'Rock Acre	William Watt
1972	Cactus Of Camden	Millard Tewell
1973	Marshfield Tagger	Les Girling
1974	Tara 6th	Frank O'Grady
1975	Joysam's Solo Sam	Walter Retslaff
1976	Tara 6th	Frank O'Grady
1977	Marshfield's Gary	Jack Williams
1978	Schlitz Real Gusto	Craig G. Endsley
1979	Chevrier's Scarlet Quince	Bob Palmer
1980	Saighton's Scud	Janet Christensen
1981	Far Ridge Request	Carl Smith, Owner—Dean Brunn, Handler
1982	Sherwood's Best Chance	Denny Crick
1983	Canvasback Mike	Doug Day

The roll call of Canadian Springer fanciers must lead off with Lester Zimmerman, owner of Breezey Points Kennels, who ranks second only to Eudore Chevrier as a breeder of fine field dogs. He passed away recently but his wife Dorothy will continue to operate the kennels. Other devoted fanciers of the breed (mostly from Western Canada) include Jack Porter, Grant Cullum, Dr. Ross Campbell, Cecil Cramer, A. E. McMillan, Jonathon McGovern, Bob Palmer, William Savage, Darlene Savage, Blaine Mooney, Les Girling, Klaus Kyritz, John Eadie, Mel Wolfe, Jack Williams, Frank O'Grady, Dave McCurdie, Burt Butler, Judith Nuss and Cameron Tracey.

Dr. C. A. Christensen, M.D. and wife Janet, a graduate veterinarian, have to be the winningest gun dog field trial family in the world. As amateurs, they have jointly won 18 placements in U.S. and Canadian Open Nationals and U.S. Amateur Nationals (8 firsts, 4 seconds, 3 thirds and 3 fourths).

At left, Janet Christensen prepares to accept delivery of a shot but alive pheasant from quadruple National Champion Saighton's Scud. This great Springer with the desirable "soft mouth", has the other native talents of drive, nose, brains and trainability to accomplish 4 tough National wins in one year's time. And his ability as a super gun dog has now been equalled by his ability to pass on his excellence. One of his offspring won the National Open and National Amateur titles in 1983, and two others placed second and third in the 1983 National Open.

Below, Dr. Christensen sends Double National Open Champion Dewfield Bricksclose Flint off to hunt with a finger snap and hand motion.

Scene at the 2nd National Springer trial at Crab Orchard Wild Life Area near Herrin, Ill. in 1948. L. to r.: Judge Chuck Goodall; professional Roy Gonia with winner of the first National Championship, Russett of Middlefield; and official gun, the late Bun Genty. —*Shafer.*

"The Nationals"

Two events of the post World War II period greatly increased interest in Spanieling and also contributed a valuable by-product for the hunting man.

The first U.S. National Championship Field Trial was held in 1947 at the Crab Orchard Fish and Wild Life Federal Game Refuge at Carbondale-Marion, Illinois. Large entries in local trials resulted as sportsmen in 30 states attempted to qualify for "The National." Many fine dogs were imported as contestants and stud dogs as hundreds of sportsmen made their pitch to compete in this glamorous but highly practical event. This influx of new blood from England and Scotland created a reservoir of field dog Spaniels readily available for U.S. hunters. Sportsmen who joined the author in ten years of effort to secure approval for the first "National" were Bob Becker, Robert Bishop, William Kirkland, Dr. Charles Sabin, Conway Olmsted, James Simpson, Jr., and Harry Shoot. Factual proof of the field-bred Springer Spaniel's tractability and willingness to accept training kindly may be found in the fact that some 14 amateur handlers placed in the first 22 National Trials, with the 1960 event being won by a lady handler, Mrs. Julia Armour of Chicago. We doubt that any other breed has had so many successful amateurs appear in the winning circle in National field competition.

WINNERS OF THE NATIONAL OPEN
FIELD TRIAL CHAMPIONSHIPS FOR ENGLISH SPRINGER SPANIELS

Year:	The Springer:	The Handler:	The Owner:
1947	Russet of Middle Field	Roy Gonia, Wash.	Dr. Chas. Sabin
1948	Stoneybroke Sheer Bliss	Clifford H. Wallace, Ill.	Mr. & Mrs. P. D. Armour
1949	Davellis Wager	Martin J. Hogan, Ill.	David B. Silberman
1950	Whittlemoor George (Imported)	Steve Studnicki, Ill.	Mr. & Mrs. P. D. Armour
1951	Flier's Ginger of Shady Glen	Arthur Eakin, Pa.	C. M. Kline
1952	Stubbliefield Ace High	Stanley Head, Calif.	W. R. Gibson
1953	Micklewood Scud (Imported)	Steve Studnicki	Mr. & Mrs. P. D. Armour
1954	Ludlovian Bruce of Greenfair (Imported)	Larry McQueen, N.J.	Joseph C. Quirk
1955	Ludlovian Bruce of Greenfair (Imported)	Larry McQueen	Joseph C. Quirk
1956	Micklewood Scud (Imported)	Steve Studnicki	Mr. & Mrs. P. D. Armour
1957	Staindrop Breckonhill Chip	Elmer Chick, Ill.	Rux-Roy Kennels
1958	Staindrop Breckonhill Chip	Elmer Chick	Rux-Roy Kennels
1959	Brackenbank Tangle (Imported)	Elmer Chick	E. W. Wunderlich
1960	Carswell Contessa (Imported)	Mrs. Julia Armour, Ill.	Mr. & Mrs. P. D. Armour
1961	Armforth's Micklewood Dan	Steve Studnicki	Mr. & Mrs. P. D. Armour
1962	Kansan	Lem Scales, Kansas	Roy E. French
1963	Waveway's Wilderness Maeve	Clarence Wingate, Mich.	Mr. & Mrs. William Lane
1964	Gwibernaut Ganol (Imported)	David Lorenz, Ill.	John T. Pirie, Jr.
1965	Gwibernaut Ganol (Imported)	David Lorenz	John T. Pirie, Jr.
1966	Wivenwood Willie (Imported)	Larry McQueen	Dean Bedford
1967	Brackenbriar Snapshot	David Lorenz	Brackenbriar Kennels
1968	Tillan Ticket	Elmer Chick	Charles Mee
1969	Dansmirth's Gunshot	Daniel K. Langhans, Ill.	Daniel K. Langhans
1970	Saighton's Sizzler	Clifford H. Wallace, Ill.	John M. Olin
1971	Saighton's Sizzler	Clifford H. Wallace	John M. Olin
1972	Dot of Charel	David Lorenz	Charles T. Curdy
1973	Dewfield Brickclose Flint	Dr. C. A. Christensen, Ore.	Dr. C. A. Christensen
1974	Ty Gwyn Slicker	John W. Buoy, Ill.	John W. Buoy
1975	Dewfield Brickclose Flint	Dr. C. A. Christensen	Dr. C. A. Christensen
1976	Saighton's Ty Gwyn Slicker	John W. Buoy	John W. Buoy
1977	Joysam's Solo Sam	Walter Retzlaff, Wis.	Walter Retzlaff
1978	J-J Chelese Sara J	John Hiller	John Miller
1979	Burcliff's Brandi	Dean Brunn, Wis.	Dean Brunn
1980	Saighton's Scud	Dr. & Mrs. C. A. Christensen	Janet Christensen
1981	Far Ridge Request	Dean Brunn	Carl R. Smith
1982	Wind Riding Streak	Dr. Mark Schinderle, Mich.	Dr. Mark Schinderle

Mrs. P. D. (Julia) Armour accepts delivery of a pheasant from National Champion Carswell Contessa as the late Robert McLean, co-judge, looks on. Mrs. Armour's 1960 National win was the first for a woman in the U.S., Great Britain and Canada. It was twenty years before her great achievement was duplicated by Mrs. C. A. (Janet) Christensen. —*Shafer.*

The second event that was to have a stimulating effect on the breed and provide more and better shooting dogs for the hunting man was the National Amateur Shooting Dog Stake. The first event was held in 1954 due to the great effort of James R. Dodson. It was replaced after a few years by the National Amateur Championship, modeled along the same lines as

National Amateur Field Champion Sunray of Chrishall, winner of six consecutive first place awards including the National Amateur Championship in 1973, with owner-handler, Dr. Warren Wunderlich. Dr Wunderlich's Springers have placed in Trials 26 times, of which 5 were National placements.

The late Cliff Wallace, one of only two who have handled a Springer and a Retriever to National Open championships. In pre-National trial days, Wallace-handled Springers won seven out of eight Field and Stream trophies, emblematical then of the national championship. He handled the second National Champion, and closed his active career with back-to-back wins of the National Open in 1970 and 1971 with the late John Olin's FC Saighton's Sizzler. The two Springers with him in this photo are double Field and Stream Trophy winner FC Solo Event and FC Brecknohill Brigadier. — White.

the National Open Championship, when Dodson and other leaders recognized the superiority of this type of competitive test.

The first National Amateur trial was held in 1963 and was an immediate success, being well supported by amateurs from all sections of the United States. In 1967, Mrs. Janet Christensen of Portland, Oregon became the first handler to place in both the Open and Amateur Nationals in the same year. Dr. John Riepenhoff's back-to-back wins of the National Amateur in 1967 and 1968, and then Daniel K. Langhans' sensational winning of both the Open and the Amateur Nationals in 1969 established new records for these events.

Winners of the Amateur title have been:

	The Springer:	*The Owner-Handler:*
1963	Pam's Aphrodite of Camden	George Webster, Ontario, Can.
1964	Denalisunflo Sam	George Webster
1965	Saighton's Swank (imported)	Jack Redman, Mt. Gilead, Ohio
1966	Juliet Eb-Gar	Curtis Killiane, Clarkston, Mich.
1967	Gwibernant Gefni (imported)	Dr. John Riepenhoff, Columbus, Ohio
1968	Gwibernant Gefni (imported)	Dr. John Riepenhoff
1969	Dansmirth's Gunshot	Daniel K. Langhans, Morton Grove, Ill.
1970	Misty Muffet	Mrs. Janet Christensen, Cornelius, Oregon
1971	Saighton's Signal	Dr. C. S. Christensen
1972	Burtree Maverick	John Buoy, LaGrange, Ill.
1973	Sunray of Chrishell	Dr. Warren A. Wunderlich, Joliet, Ill.
1974	Sunray of Chrishell	Dr. Warren A. Wunderlich
1975	Joysam's Solo Sam	Walter Retzlaff, Milwaukee, Wis.
1976	Coginchaug Shine	John J. Mangine
1977	Sheila of Sherwood	Denny Crick, Sherwood, Oregon
1978	Cathy's Kris of Burnsget	Albert D. Beedie, Jr.
1979	Saighton's Scud	Mrs. Janet Christensen
1980	Saighton's Scud	Mrs. Janet Christensen
1981	Far Ridge Revere	Wayne Kilpatrick, San Ramon, Calif.
1982	Sherwood's Best Chance	Denny Crick

Registration figures at The American Kennel Club and The American Field continue to indicate that the Springer is much at home in America and that his kind, while never afflicted with the curse of extreme popularity that has been so detrimental to some breeds, will go on and on pleasing the hearts of the United States gunning fraternity for infinite years to come.

Pictured at a recent National Amateur Championship trial: Janet Christensen with quadruple National Champion Saighton's Scud alertly waiting to mark falling bird under eagle eyes of judges Paul Rupert and Jack Williams (hidden) as official guns (Dan Langhans and Chris Christensen) prepare to shoot released bird.

2

The English Springer
as a Gun Dog

ONE OF THE MOST EXCITING EXPERIENCES for a sportsman anywhere is to see a fine gun dog of any breed, well trained, well conditioned and with experience in the field, performing the things that he is capable of doing well. It's great and most satisfying, but the question frequently arises as to how the several types of gun dogs are supposed to perform.

The two great United States organizations which classify purebred dogs, The American Field and The American Kennel Club, have divided all purebred dogs into seven groups, which are:

1. Sporting Dogs No. I (Retrievers, Spaniels and Pointing Dogs)
2. Sporting Dogs No. II (Hounds)
3. Working Dogs (Boxers, Dobermans, Newfoundlands, etc.)
4. Terriers (Fox, Irish, Bull, Airedales, etc.)
5. Toys (Chihuahuas, Pugs, Pekingese, Pomeranians, etc.)
6. Non-Sporting Dogs (Poodle, Bulldogs, Dalmatians, etc.)
7. Herding Dogs (Collies, Shepherds, Old English, etc.).

There are more than 100 different recognized breeds in the seven groups, but the hunting dogs (of which there are more than 35 distinct breeds) all fall into Group I or II. These are classified under four distinct headings based on their manner of hunting and handling game—the Hounds, the Spaniels, the Pointing Breeds, and the Retrievers. Hounds are the oldest and fall into two types—those which hunt and seek game with their nose (trail hounds) and those which hunt with their eyes (coursing hounds).

Dr. John Phillips with a good Colorado Springer gun dog and field trial contender. Dr. Phillips is a successful breeder, trainer and handler of field-bred Springers. He has served as a National Amateur Club officer, and hunts his Springers with buddy Cliff Hankin in Colorado and Kansas on upland game and waterfowl.

At a National Amateur field trial, long time, dedicated Springer enthusiast Ed Whitaker, who headed up the Parent Association for many years, looks at his AFC Whyte Winter Drift while judge Len Ferrell makes notes and pretty Dominique Sekey, the dead bird shagger, watches.

Trail hounds such as Foxhounds, Bloodhounds, Beagles, et al, put their nose to the ground and search out game strictly with their nose. The sight or coursing hounds such as Greyhounds, Salukis, or Whippets search principally with their eyes and bring the game to the bag by their great speed.

The Spaniels such as English Springers and Cockers, called land or flushing Spaniels, search for game with their nose and flush (make it run or fly) when they come up on it. They are probably the second oldest hunting-breed type.

The Pointing dogs are of two main types: the older and more popular, the Pointer and the English Setter, and the so-called continental breeds, which are comprised among others of the Brittany, the German Short-haired Pointer, and the Wiemaraner. These dogs seek game with their nose and indicate it by freezing or "pointing" it when in close proximity.

The most popular Retriever breeds are typified by the Labrador Retriever, the Golden Retriever, and the Chesapeake Bay Retriever. They usually walk at heel or sit in a blind instead of searching in front of the gun, as do the several types of hunting dogs, and retrieve anything that is grassed or downed by the hunter. Each breed is a specialist and many sportsmen keep one or more of each type in his kennel. However, it is generally conceded by such noted authorities as Henry Davis, David Michael Duffy, and others who have had a world of experience with all types of gun dogs, that the English Springer Spaniel is a leading contender for the title of all around gun dog for the one-dog-sportsman who wants to hunt upland game and waterfowl. Having owned and shot over each of the several breeds for many years, we can only agree with the authorities—Spaniels are simply great.

The properly bred, well-trained and experienced Springer Spaniel, which has a 15 pound weight and strength advantage over his smaller cousin—the Cocker, is a joy to gun over. He should walk obediently at heel without leash, and when ordered to hunt will fairly explode, and always in the direction in which he is sent (right or left of the gunner). When he has cast 30-40 yards to the side, he will reverse his direction and whip back some 10-15 yards in front of his gunner at top speed. When he reaches the desired distance to either side of the hunter, he will again reverse direction and speed back in front of the hunter with great dash and hunting desire (almost as mechanically as the windshield wiper on an automobile). The Spaniel is a beater who covers all his ground to either side and in front of the handler, never leaving any game but always in gun range. When he strikes game (foot scent) he will drop his head and put his nose to the ground like a hound. He will persistently puzzle out the line (foot scent), increasing his speed as he approaches the bird or rabbit with his tail beating furiously and his animation quite visible. When his nose tells him that game is close, he will raise his head, take the body scent and drive in with a great rush that is guaranteed to drive it out from its hiding place.

FTC Busy Bruning of Ashaba, owned, trained and handled by A. P. Moecher. Busy was the second Springer to earn the title in the West.

John Buoy of Chicago with five good Springer gun dogs at heel. Buoy divides his time successfully between piloting United Airline jets, training Springers, and shooting over them in trials and in the field.

Occasionally a wise old Dakota or California cock pheasant will leg it down the field so fast that the Spaniel may get out of gun range in his eagerness to flush. The properly trained individual will then respond to his handler's voice or whistle command and stop instantly. His veteran hunter will then move up rapidly to his Spaniel and cast him off again. The Spaniel will pick up the line of scent and again move rapidly in the direction of the game. Sometimes it will be necessary to stop the dog several times before he is close enough to flush. When this happens, he will hup (sit down or stand) instantly at the point of flush, automatically or in response to a voice or whistle command, and await further orders. If the game is shot, the Spaniel will mark the fall and retrieve it on command; if it is missed, he will resume hunting on command. If the game was only crippled, he will put his nose to the ground at the fall and trail it out with eagerness and dispatch—10 yards, 50, or 200—sieze it in his mouth with a gentle grip and return it to his owner's hand. An experienced, trained, and suitably bred dog of this type will not only fill the game bag but will provide many thrills and excitement for the hunting party. A real sportsman who thinks the hunt is equally as important as the quantity of game brought home will never hunt without a trained gun dog. The Springer is the pheasant dog par excellence.

Spaniels, and we include them all, even though we suggest that the English Springer has an advantage over his several cousins, provide great recreation and pleasure for thousands of lucky owners in several areas of sporting activity. First and foremost, there is the combination house pet and hunting dog of which there are many thousands in America. He will play with the kids, hunt a few pheasant or waterfowl, sleep by the fire, and make "Mama" comfortable by barking at strange night noises. Then there are the bench show types which compete and are judged on physical conformation (see Section II). When they acquire some 15 points in open competition they are awarded the title of **Champion.** Next there are the Spaniels which are trained to compete in field trials (simulated hunting). When they win two All Age Open Stakes or two Amateur Open Stakes they acquire the title of **Field Champion** (or) **Amateur Field Champion.** Lastly there are the spaniels which compete in Obedience Trials. When they have acquired the proper score in competition they are awarded titles in ascending order of **Companion Dog, Companion Dog Excellent,** or **Utility Dog.** Each of the six titles indicates a distinct level of perfection, but there is no relationship between them. The Field Champions win on their ability to perform in the hunting field, the Champions are evaluated on their physical beauty and showmanship, and the Obedience winners receive an award for their ability to perform prescribed tests upon signal or command. The buyer should be aware of this in his selection of a puppy for a specific purpose. The several titles are awarded for excellence in strictly unrelated fields.

A great British field dog and sire. Eng. FTC Rivington Glensaugh Glean sired 12 English and American field champions, plus many winners and top shooting dogs. He won six British Open stakes and the British National Field Championship.

3

Selection of
a Prospective
Gun Dog Puppy

A SUBJECT worthy of the effort is the first requisite in training an English Springer Spaniel to work to the gun. This is a most difficult situation to control, because most people acquire their first dog for reasons based on sentiment rather than on cold, hard logic. The best advice that can be given to one interested in acquiring a high class prospective gun dog is to go to the nearest professional field trainer in the vicinity and ask for the names of individuals who breed field type Springer Spaniels.

If it is not feasible to follow this suggestion, one should spend a month or two talking with friends who hunt, and try to locate a breeder who specializes in hunting or field trial stock. Advice of this sort is much easier to give than to follow, because there are numerous titles and championship certificates that can be acquired by an English Springer Spaniel these days that have no bearing on its ability to find game and accept training of the type necessary to produce a good field dog.

At the risk of incurring the undying enmity of Springer breeders who specialize in producing show type dogs, the author in all sincerity is compelled to say that Springer dogs primarily of show bloodlines are usually poor risks if one wants to have a really high class gun dog. Also, the Obedience titles C.D. or C.D.X. or U.D. mean only that the dogs have been trained to perform certain routine acts such as walking at heel, remaining in one spot on command, or carrying a wooden dumbbell in its mouth while jumping over a hurdle, etc. There is nothing wrong with Obedience trials where dogs are tested on their ability to perform the above acts, and

Mrs. Evelyn Monte VanHorn, prominent writer, amateur handler, and judge of Springers and Pointing dogs, with George Webester, a successful Canadian Spaniel man.

Famous movie star Robert Montgomery was a top wing shot, and was frequently invited to shoot at field trials where he was not judging or handling his own Springer.

are graded according to their ability to do so. But there is no guarantee, however, or even suggestion, that a dog with these abilities (or its offspring) can scent a bird ten yards away, or exhibit an eagerness to crash into a duck pond on a chilly November day to retrieve a fat mallard drake that has fallen to the gun. The same facts hold true for puppies whelped from a mating of one or more show champions or from a bloodline of show champions.

The title of champion means only that the dog has near perfect body conformation and that its legs are straight, its coat the proper color and quality, its body formed in the manner prescribed by the breed Standard, and its ears the proper length, etc. It is basic logic to assume that Springers or their offspring which have been selected for these characteristics alone (this is true of most show strains), are not as well fitted to exhibit an overwhelming desire to hunt on a bitter cold day, or with the sun beating down in ninety-degree temperatures as occasionally happens during tte dove shooting season, the partridge season, or in a good duck marsh. And of equal importance is the fact that show strain bloodlines have not been selected for the ability to accept training and to respond kindly, as have the Springers which have descended from hunting strains that are pure and proven for many generations.

Again, it must be repeated and stressed that there is nothing wrong with the sport of showing dogs, or the dogs that are shown, or the people that show them on the bench or in Obedience trials. Both sports provide a valuable form of recreation which is greatly needed in our most complex and high pressure society. It is wrong, however, o expect the son or daughter of a show champion or Obedience winner to develop into a high class shooting dog—just as it is wrong to expect the offspring of the best field dogs to do well or win at bench shows. The two types are as far apart as if they were two different breeds. And the occasional bench-bred Springer that does well in the field is the exception which proves the rule.

It is true that practically any breed of dog (or even cat) will hunt. The same applies to almost any other carnivorous animal because they have descended from long-forgotten ancestors that had to hunt in order to live. There is an amusing and apparently authentic case of a hog that was taught to hunt and, according to the writer, to "point" birds. However, the manner of hunting and the animal's aptitude—both physical and mental—to perform the job are most important, too. If one desires to acquire a saddle horse, it would be most unlikely that the offspring of a Percheron draft horse would be acceptable as a pleasure horse.

An eminent German zoologist who kept a number of dogs and other pets and who gained world-wide recognition for his studies in animal behavior, felt most strongly on the subject. He said that breeding and using animals for work (hunting, herding, guarding, etc.) was the only way to maintain the good qualities necessary for the specific action required. He said further that when the whims of fashion were the principal factors in

The veteran sportsman Tom Fussell with FTC Tangles Pandora. Fussell trained and handled this excellent Springer bitch to both Open and Amateur Field Championships.

Mrs. Ruth Greening and Mrs. Jean Hutchenson, two excellent women handlers. The Springers are AFTCs that the ladies handled and trained to their titles.

determining a dog's appearance, the fate of the breed was sealed. Although the Herr doctor was not referring to hunting dogs in particular, it would seem that the general principle he laid down, of breeding for use rather than for appearance, would certainly be a case in point for selecting a gun dog puppy from hunting stock (bred for use) rather than from show stock (bred for appearance).

Mr. P. R. A. Moxon, a well-known English professional trainer and writer on gun dogs, sums up the subject of selecting a proper gun dog puppy prospect. He says: "Over here *(England—but it is equally true in the U.S., as most if not all U.S. amateur and professional trainers will agree)* there are two distinct types of Springers, and it seems that never the twain shall meet. I like the light-boned, fast, stylish type and have no time for the carthorse which our show people seem to love so much. The latter are far too big to deal with the sort of cover that Springers have to work in, and they lack working instinct and trainability."

Mr. Moxon has trained hundreds of dogs to the gun and his opinions are based on actual experience in the field with many, many individuals of both types. In the United States, professional trainers of the stature of C. H. Wallace and Martin J. Hogan arrived at the same conclusions. Likewise, such U.S. breeders as the late Colonel Joseph C. Quirk, of Connecticut, and C. K. Hunter, of Illinois, who produced winners in both bench and field, found that it required two distinct types to compete in the two phases of competition.

The chapter on the early history of the breed emphasizes that Springers and their ancestors had been used as hunting dogs for many, many centuries; also, that by the process of intelligent selection of stock having the talent or natural aptitude for field work, certain strains have been developed which could produce dogs with *extra* talent and ability for hunting.

The puppy selected as a potential gun dog should be from hunting stock. He should be the offspring of parents who have been owned and hunted by a man who takes his hunting seriously—or better still, from parents which have done well in field trials. This can be determined in part by a study of the five generation pedigree which most breeders are able to supply. High class gun dogs do not always appear, even from the proper breeding, but the percentage of success in producing high class hunting dogs is a great deal higher from field trial or hunting bred stock than from show stock. Perhaps as much as 100 to 1.

One should never forget that the gift puppy from the accidental breeding of some neighbor's Springer bitch, or the pet shop bargain at $25. may be a most expensive addition to the household. It costs just as much to feed and care for a poor specimen as it does for a good one, and it may cost a great deal more to train a poor one because it has not inherited the desirable qualities in enough intensity to enable it to accept its training kindly or to find birds easily. Then, too, the results may not be commensurate with the time, effort, and patience expended.

Clifford Wallace, of Wadsworth, Illinois, one of the really great trainers of Spaniels, Retrievers, and pointing dogs, stated on many occasions that it is cheaper and easier on the trainer's nervous system to dispose of a poor prospect at once if it is lacking in any of the important qualities of a gun dog than to try to overcome the shortcomings with extra training. Thus, if a puppy eight or ten months of age indicates little or no desire to hunt or to retrieve after being exposed repeatedly to the opportunity to do so, give him to a friend for a house pet and get another one that will hunt and/or retrieve.

When the new puppy is acquired, the eminent animal behaviorist, Dr. Michael Fox, suggests that he be moved to his new home at six weeks of age, or at nine weeks of age. Because eight-week-old puppies are at a critical stage of mental and physical development, even a short trip by automobile or plane might prove traumatic.

Once a new puppy is acquired, stop at a good veterinarian on the way home and have the puppy inoculated with such homologous serum as the veterinarian may recommend. Repeat this practice religiously every two weeks for as long as the veterinarian may suggest until the dog has received its permanent distemper shots. It is also good sense to have it inoculated for hepatitis. Both of these diseases are great scourges and have been responsible for the death of many, many thousands of dogs. The author can state frankly that before distemper vaccine came into common use, over fifty percent of his young dogs died before reaching eighteen months of age. Since the advent of vaccination for distemper, not a single dog has been lost from the disease.

The puppy, once it is home, should be established in the place previously prepared for its living quarters. An outside kennel, with concrete or hard surface runs, is, of course, ideal when it is equipped with a tight, draft-free dog house. It is well to remember that a puppy can stand cold weather and can stand a certain amount of wet weather. It cannot, however, withstand both cold and wet weather at the same time. As most puppies have not the sense of older dogs, they will frequently play in the rain until thoroughly wet and then spend the night sleeping wet. An almost sure result is mixed infection, which can lead to dire consequences if proper steps are not taken immediately.

If the puppy is to be a house dog, a bed in a draft-free and out of the way spot in the house should be provided in advance. Immediate steps should be taken to housebreak the puppy. And any small children in the household, as well as adults, should be indoctrinated with the knowledge that little puppies require much sleep to maintain good health and cannot be played with all the time.

54

Third generation Springer fancier Forsyth Kinson with FC Brackenbriar Boomerang delivering a cock pheasant. Brackenbriar Kennels was founded in 1929 by George Watson, Sr. and is being continued by George, Jr. and his two daughters, Forsyth Kineon and Betsy Watson, who are fine amateur handlers. —*Hargrave*.

Harold Jones, expert amateur trainer, accepts a retrieved pheasant from his fine FTC Sir Cricket. Cricket and two of his kennelmates were handled by Jones to their titles. —*Bui*.

Saighton Kennels' "brain trust", trainer John DeMott (left) with owner and breeding expert Talbot Radcliffe, starting a fat puppy in early retrieving a soft buck. DeMott departed his Ohio home in 1975 to join Saighton as kennel manager/gun dog trainer. Springers trained by DeMott have won 12 championships in the U.S. and Canada for an eight-year average of 1½ champions each year. A number of other Saighton Springers trained by DeMott have become fine shooting dogs in Western Europe and America.

4

Preliminary Training
of the
Springer Gun Dog

$\mathbf{T}$HE QUESTIONS most often asked about gun dog training are when and how to start, and what the various training routines are. The suggested time sequence must often be modified by the factors of aptitude and mental development of the individual dog, seasonal climatic conditions and the owner's available time. The sequence is based on practical experience and is basically accurate. If the new trainer-owner's motivation is strong, he will find the right dog, the necessary time and the correct, personalized training technique, with some trial and error perhaps, to get the job done.

Here is the general outline of the training schedule for a Spaniel:

Eight to Twelve Weeks of Age—Yard Work

1. Socialize the puppy with frequent play periods and short walks on the lead and collar. Teach the dog its name.
2. Begin early retrieving routine with knotted hand towel and hand claps.
3. Early lessons in HUP, COME, NO and STAY by voice and hand signals. Use no pressure.
4. Substitute the towel with the large canvas buck for retrieving. Use a cap pistol for first experience with gun shot.

Three to Six Months of Age

1. Continue yard work routines but require gradually more exacting response.
2. Substitute the hard buck for retrieving using a blank pistol.
3. Begin trips to the field and encourage puppy to find and chase game.

4. Teach the dog to KENNEL UP and remain in the car or the kennel.
5. Introduce to the water, if the air and water temperature is at least 50 degrees.
6. Introduce to planted pigeons—blank pistol fired as puppy chases them.
7. Steady puppy (no chase) to retrieving in the yard—retrieve only on command.
8. Continue routine for more response to hand, voice and whistle signals to HUP—STAY—COME—and turn while hunting.

Six to Nine Months of Age

1. Continue yard work twice weekly and require perfect response to all voice and whistle commands and hand signals.
2. Introduce to double land retrieves with soft and hard buck in the yard, then in the field. Always use come-in whistle and insist dog fetch only on command.
3. Begin retrieving dead, then live, clipped-wing pigeons after the discharge of blank pistol with dog steady at heel. Switch to shotgun if all goes well.
4. As he HUPS at heel, shoot live birds for the youngster to retrieve.
5. Begin double water retrieves with thrown birds after gun shot. Then finish off doubles with shot pigeons—dog required to be steady at heel.

Ten to Twelve Months of Age

1. Continue yard work twice a week in the field with both bucks and dead birds.
2. Begin steadying dog to flushed birds while hunting. Throw a few dead birds, then live pigeons over his head while hunting. If all goes well, shoot live, planted pigeons.
3. Introduce to trailing moving game.
4. Work dog in brace with another spaniel, if yours is now working well. Discourage at once any trailing, tagging-on (following the other dog) or playing. Handlers on parallel course 70 yards apart.

Twelve to Fifteen Months of Age

1. Weekly refresher of yard work or in field using all obedience and retrieving sequences with all commands.
2. Begin use of planted game birds (hen pheasants preferred). Spaniel to find, flush and retrieve with discipline and manner, showing ability to trail running birds and restraint to HUP when so ordered at long gun range.
3. Work dog dry (and with planted birds later) on crosswind and downwind course until acceptable pattern perfected.
4. Work occasionally on native game without shooting it—but discharge pistol!
5. Begin routine of working from blind, boat and through decoys, first with buck and then with shot pigeons.
6. Shoot some hand-thrown domestic mallards over water for the spaniel to retrieve.
7. Work the dog in the field in half-hour sessions with an occasional pigeon and game bird rolled in behind him. Expect him to be steady to wing and shot, much of the time automatically without command.
8. Concentrate on the dog learning the correct range of 35 to 40 yards to the side, and expect him to change direction much of the time without command.
9. Take the trained spaniel hunting on opening day and expect him to amaze his proud owner and shooting friend with his finish and polish. Pat yourself on the back for a job well done.

Before training is begun, it is essential that the puppy become well acquainted with the trainer and that there be a feeling of mutual respect, trust, and regard between the trainer and his prospective pupil. This may be brought about by the trainer's doing most, if not all, of the feeding and grooming, required in the everyday care of the dog. Further progress along these lines can be made by the trainer if he takes the dog for airings and short walks (around the block), and devotes a few minutes each day to

Successful trainers have long known the necessity of humanizing and socializing gun dog puppies, a fact that has been confirmed scientifically in behavior studies by Dr. Michael Fox, Clarence Pfaffenberger and many other authorities. John Isaacs demonstrates some methods for achieving this goal. At top, Isaacs interrupts a training session in which puppy is learning to walk on leash with a petting session which Junior obviously enjoys. Center, John displays affection for the puppy, which will be imprinted in the youngster's mind permanently. Below, But discipline is useless without some discipline. Here John demonstrates an effective but gentle method of applying mild force to a youngster when his mind wanders. —Photos by John Friend.

Finding and retrieving all the game shot is a most important function of any gun dog. At left, the first step—trainer John Isaacs teases a 6 to 8 week old youngster with a knotted handkerchief, which he slowly tosses out a few feet. At right, the puppy runs to the handkerchief, picks it up and returns it to the trainer and receives an enthusiastic petting reward.

After the puppy learns to enjoy the lesson on a hard surface, the trainer switches the lessons to short cover in the kennel yard, and repeats the throw and retrieve sequence. At left, the puppy completes and delivers the handkerchief to the handler. At right, trainer Isaacs now introduces the puppy to small canvas buck by first teasing the prospect a bit and then pushing it gently into his mouth, accompanied by much praise and friendly talk. Then the throw and retrieve sequence described above for the handkerchief is repeated.

60

playing and romping with the young hopeful until a thorough attachment for each other has been formed between man and dog. Ten days should suffice for this phase. If a mutual attachment for each other has not been formed by the end of this period, perhaps the trainer has the wrong dog or his "get-acquainted" methods are incorrect.

1. Retrieving

Even though a Springer has a natural desire to retrieve, it is well to fix the habit of retrieving firmly before the dog learns to hunt. Springer puppies enjoy hunting more than retrieving and, if their instinct to retrieve is not aroused at an early age, may become more interested in finding a second bird to flush and chase than in retrieving the first one.

The first lesson in retrieving may be started with a puppy as young as three months of age. It may be done as follows: A clothespin, or a handkerchief knotted three or four times, will serve as the object to be retrieved. The puppy should be taken to a sheltered spot in the kennel yard, the basement, or garage and allowed to sniff around until all the strange new scents have been investigated. He may then be called to heel and teased with the object until his interest is aroused thoroughly. While the puppy is still interested in the object, it should be held just out of reach and tossed slowly three or four feet away. Eight puppies out of ten (Springer puppies, that is) will run immediately to the object, seize it, and with a little coaxing return immediately to the trainer. The puppy should then be rewarded with plenty of petting and friendly words.

Be careful not to throw the object more than four or five feet and always with a slow motion, as very young puppies cannot see very well and quick motions may be just a blur to their eyes. Repeat this performance six or eight times and then stop while the dog is still enjoying the game. Always reward the puppy with petting each time he performs properly. Eight or ten throws each day for a week will work wonders.

After the first day or two, give the command "Fetch!" in a firm but subdued tone of voice each time the object is thrown. This will form an association in the dog's mind of the article to be retrieved with the command "Fetch!" Never fool the puppy by failing to throw the object, and never indulge in a tug of war to get the object from his mouth. If his grip on the object is too firm, which is most likely, a little gentle pressure exerted by squeezing the lower lip against the teeth (on the side of the jaw) will usually induce the dog to release his grip. The command "Give!" should be repeated as this is done, in order to teach the dog to release the object. Don't forget to make a fuss over the dog and pet him profusely.

After a week or so, the trainer should clap his hands together to produce a single sharp report each time the object is thrown. This is preparation for introduction to the gun and is most important. Within a few days, the puppy will come to expect the noise each time the object is thrown.

To test the progress, clap the hands together sharply without throwing the object. If the groundwork has been laid properly, the puppy will whirl immediately and look for something to retrieve when the sound is heard. Again, do not fool the young dog. Always be sure there is something to retrieve each time a throwing motion, or the noise of the hand clap, or the command "Fetch!" is given. A child's cap pistol should be substituted for the hand clap after a week or two, when in the trainer's opinion the young prospect will not be alarmed by the noise.

The little guy will probably retrieve beautifully for a few days or even a few weeks and then suddenly refuse to bring the object to hand. This is normal behavior and it is also normal when he attempts to bury the retrieving object in the ground or under some leaves in the hedge. Sometimes the trainer can nip this undesirable behavior in the bud by making an exaggerated show of appearing to run away from the puppy, and thus causing him to run after the trainer with the object still in his mouth. If this subterfuge does not produce the desired reaction, one may attach a ten foot fishing line to the puppy's collar and bring him gently to heel with very, very light pressure on the fishing line after he has picked up the retrieving object.

These lessons should be continued for several weeks until they have been well learned and have become a habit. Little else should be taught during this period, and if the dog is to be kept in the house, the retrieving should not be started until he is well housebroken.

Older dogs can be started on their retrieving in the same manner if desired, although the retrieving may prove a little more difficult. Teasing and coaxing and holding the object just out of the dog's reach may have to be repeated a number of times with a dog as old as one year in order to arouse his interest. His reactions will be similar to those of the puppy except that he will be less playful.

The trainer must always remember to show his pleasure when the dog performs properly. Petting and speaking kindly with a friendly attitude are highly recommended. A reward of food, or some tidbit is a poor practice for a field dog and belongs more in the realm of the theatre than the field. The trained seal performs because he will be fed. A good gun dog performs because he loves it and wants to work for his master.

When the dog has become well conditioned to retrieving, a suitable retrieving buck should be substituted for the handkerchief or glove. If the prospect is under four months of age, the new retrieving object should be a tightly rolled piece of burlap approximately eight inches long and about two or three inches in diameter. It may be rolled tightly and secured by thick rubber bands. This retrieving bundle can be used until the dog is five months old. At that time, a retrieving buck with feathers attached should be substituted for the rolled burlap.

The feathered buck is made by securing a 12- or 14-inch piece of 2 x 2, and rounding off the edges. It should then be taken to the local tinsmith, and a light metal sleeve attached which will entirely surround the wood. Eight or ten pigeon wings, or the wings of game, or even of domestic birds such as chickens, should then be attached by a number of strong, heavy rubber bands. The young dog is introduced to the feather buck as preparation for retrieving birds later on. Most puppies will take to the buck immediately, but if the dog displays any reluctance, his interest may be aroused by teasing him with the buck held just out of reach. This must be repeated until the dog's interest is aroused thoroughly.

Always remember to repeat the command "Fetch!" *every* time the buck is thrown and to fire the cap pistol at the same time.

If the prospect is at least six months old, it would be well to introduce him also to the hard canvas retrieving buck, which is a small boat bumper or fender stuffed with cork or kapok. It is well to get the dog acquainted with the new object, as it will be used in the water later. So the daily retrieving lessons should include the throwing of both feathered buck and the canvas buck.

One of the prime prerequisites of a good gun dog is that it retrieve with a soft and tender mouth. Starting young puppies to retrieve on a dead or shackled bird may sometimes result in the condition known as "hard mouth." This is a serious and objectionable fault and case-hardened offenders may ruin much of the game they retrieve by rendering it inedible. The method of teaching retrieving outlined above was first used in 1934 by A. P. Moecher. Using this method, a number of people have trained many, many dogs with good results.

After the dog has become well acclimated to the sound of the cap pistol, and has associated the sound with the act of retrieving, it is time to substitute a .22 caliber pistol for the cap gun. Blank cartridges should be used. It is most important to use the blank pistol with the act of retrieving. If the cap pistol has been used religiously, there will be no adverse reaction on the part of the dog the first time the .22 is substituted.

Take the dog to the training area in the field and work him on the feathered buck. Fire the .22 pistol the first time when the dog is some distance away on his journey to pick up the buck. If the noise appears to startle the dog, throw the buck even farther the next time, and be sure that the dog is 15 yards away before the pistol is fired. Two or three shots are enough the first time the transition is made from the cap gun to the .22 blank. If the dog appears to fear the noise, stop the shooting and go back to the cap gun for another week. The reason for this extreme caution will be explained in a later chapter.

If the noise appears not to bother the dog, the .22 may be used each time the dog retrieves until the sound has been heard at least 25 times. If no adverse reaction is observed, the trainer may gradually reduce the time interval between throwing the buck and firing the .22 until the shot is being fired while the dog is at heel. *Never discharge the pistol over or in front of the dog.* The gun should be held behind the trainer's back to eliminate muzzle blast in the dog's ears. Granted that a .22 does not make much noise, it is quite likely that no one has ever told the puppy this fact and his sensitive ears may find the sound objectionable if the piece is discharged in front of or directly over his head. This procedure is guaranteed to eliminate even the most remote chance of gun-shyness.

Considerable progress has now been made if the dog is responding properly to the various situations. If he is not responding, start all over with the early lessons and again follow the plan, step by step.

2. Introduction to Game

When the puppy has been retrieving to the sound of the .22 for at least two weeks, and is well adjusted to the noise, he should be taken to the field. One of the great advantages of owning a Springer is that he can be trained in a small area. The retrieving can be taught in a vacant lot and the dog's first introduction to game can be in a subdivision adjoining even our largest cities. Most areas of this sort in states where pheasants and rabbits are found will probably contain both varieties.

The puppy should be at least five or six months old when he makes his first trip afield. If he is much younger, he will have great difficulty negotiating the cover. The best time to work is early in the morning or twenty minutes before nightfall. Most species of game birds will be seeking the refuge of a weed patch in which to roost for the night and rabbits will just be starting to move about for their nightly forays in search of food and romance.

It is well to start the young dog out on rabbits because all dogs, regardless of breed, will invariably give chase to a fleeing rabbit, and Spaniels of all ages seem to have a particular fondness for them. The young hopeful who bumps into a rabbit or two and chases them by sight will no longer tag along at the trainer's heels but will be out in front hunting for more rabbits. When this time arrives, the young dog is making his first attempt to hunt.

Trips to the field should be scheduled as frequently as possible. If it is not possible to go daily, certainly Saturday and Sunday should be utilized fully. The early field sessions should not exceed 20 or 30 minutes time, but can be lengthened gradually as the dog's muscles develop and his wind and desire to run increase.

After he has chased a few rabbits, an effort should be made to bring the puppy into contact with pheasants or local game birds. Just before dark is an ideal time as the pheasants will sit tightly, and thus enable the dog to find and flush. If the first big cock that gets up startles him so that he does not chase, efforts should be made to encourage him to do so. The trainer should run after the bird for a few yards and exhibit great excitement. Most field-bred puppies will be off like a flash and chase the flying bird for at least a few yards—perhaps even as far as a few hundred yards. This experience on rabbits and pheasants or other game birds will speed up the puppy's hunting and increase his desire to find game.

It is more than likely that on future trips, the dog will dash away as soon as he is released at the edge of the cover and begin to use his nose as well as his eyes to find game. The position of the dog's head while hunting is a clue to the development of the hunting instinct. If his head is up and his neck is level with his body, the puppy is probably sight hunting. But if his head is down and his nose is to the ground, he is hunting by scent.

It should *always* be remembered, however, that the puppy must *always* be worked in the field with the wind blowing into the face of the trainer. There are two reasons for this:

1. It enables the puppy to scent game much better than when worked downwind (with the wind blowing on the back of the trainer's neck).
2. It will help, in most cases, to keep the puppy closer to the handler while he is working.

Once the puppy is hunting with enthusiasm and is beginning to appear bold and eager in the field, the early yard work can be commenced. It should be emphasized, however, that the retrieving lessons should be continued. Retrieving can be tried in the field but may result in the dog's ignoring the buck. Once the puppy learns to hunt, he may not be too interested in retrieving, except at home. This is normal and the retrieving should be given for five minutes at home before the trips afield.

If the trainer is unable to locate cover that contains rabbits and/or pheasants or other game birds, domestic pigeons will serve as a substitute. But better results will always be obtained by letting the young dog hunt wild game. Pigeons may be secured from farm boys or from the poultry market, and may be advertised occasionally in publications like the American Field. It is usually a good practice at first to place the pigeon (with flight feathers clipped) in cover and to let the young dog find it a few times. This will arouse the dog's interest and create much excitement on his part. He will catch the clipped-wing bird, and if the early retrieving work was done properly, will deliver it to hand. After two or three sessions with clipped-wing birds, the trainer can "plant" a few full-winged birds for the puppy to flush and chase.

Planting a pigeon is an easily learned skill. The method employed by many trainers is to grip the bird firmly over its wings with the right hand encircling the bird's body. Using lots of wrist action, the pigeon is then whirled rapidly for fifteen or twenty turns. The bird is then planted in the cover and will remain where it is placed. Best results are obtained by mashing down the cover into a nest approximately the size of the trainer's foot. This will permit the bird to flush without becoming entangled when the dog rushes in.

Some care must be taken in planting birds so the young dog will not learn to trail back to the bird by following the "bird planter's" footsteps. This may be prevented by walking in from the side of the area which the dog

Planting a pigeon. The bird has been whirled and made dizzy. It is being planted in a nest made by mashing down the cover.

Demonstration of planting a pheasant by placing bird's head under one wing and then swinging the bird in eight or ten large circles before placing in smashed cover, belly down. Another method is to squeeze bird's breast for 5-10 seconds, then place bird gently in cover, on its side. Either method when done properly will usually cause bird to remain where planted for several minutes.

will work. One can also carry pigeons in the pocket of a game coat and "dizzy" them (as explained above) while the dog is hunting. The bird can then be thrown with considerable force into a spot of cover on the right while the dog is working to the left. Never let the dog see the bird planted. A little practice will develop considerable skill in planting by both methods and little or no difficulty should be experienced. Pigeons may also be planted by tucking their heads under one wing, then placing them gently in the grass. Pheasants should be planted in this manner. The dizzying method is usually better, however, for piegons.

3. Basic Yard Work

The basic yard work consists of teaching the dog to "**hup**" (to sit), to "**stay**" (to remain sitting until ordered to move), and to "**come**" (to heel). The dog must respond to these three commands perfectly (both voice and whistle command) and continue these responses for the rest of his life. The importance of this early yard work, the ABC's of all types of training, cannot be overemphasized. The success of all future training hinges on the dog's learning to follow these basic commands. No hunting dog can be considered even second rate without this fundamental knowledge, and no gun dog can provide much pleasure, or function properly, until he has been so trained. These lessons must be learned well. They must be repeated at intervals during the lifetime of the dog and the better they are learned now, the fewer the problems that will arise in the future.

The old English trainers and some of the modern ones gave their gun dog puppies the early yard work before introducing them to game. Undoubtedly this sequence in the training procedure has great merit, especially in a country like England where there is greater concentration of game than in most sections of America. Teaching a young dog obedience usually curtails his enthusiasm to hunt, some more and some less. Because of the greater abundance of game, the English trainer can rekindle the enthusiasm to hunt after yard training much faster than most United States trainers. It is considered a better practice in America to have the young dog hunting and retrieving before he is given his early yard training. This is the reason for the sequence of training lessons suggested here.

Teaching a young dog to sit is an easy matter, but requires, on the part of the trainer, patience and a desire to succeed. In field work, it is customary for Spaniel owners now, as it was a hundred years ago, to use the command "**Hup!**" for the sitting act.

It is assumed that the young dog has acquired a good chain link "choke collar," and has made a good adjustment to wearing it. It is assumed, too, that the dog has learned from the early lessons to walk at heel on a loose leash, without tugging and pulling the trainer all over the countryside. If not, teach the dog to do so. Usually the dog will become accustomed to the collar if he spends a day in the house or kennel with the collar on his neck. A few strolls around the kennel yard or the block with a young dog held closely at heel on a short leash will teach him to walk quietly without pulling. The command **"Heel!"** should be repeated at regular intervals and be accompanied by a firm tug on the leash. If this mild restraint does not accomplish the desired results in five or six lessons, a small switch can be manipulated back and forth in front of the dog's nose on a line even with the trainer's leg in such a manner that the dog will receive a light tap on his nose if he attempts to forge ahead. This is a very easily learned lesson and one usually retained for life. In *all* his lessons it should be routine to reward the puppy by voice and by petting when he performs satisfactorily.

To teach the dog to sit, take him on a short leash to a quiet place in the garage or basement with no spectators or disturbing influences. Bring the dog to heel and give the command "Hup!" in a firm but quiet voice. At the same time, press down firmly but gently on the dog's rump, or hindquarters. Force him to sit, maintaining the pressure for five or six seconds. Then remove the pressure and at the command "Heel!," walk off a few steps with the dog still on the short leash. Then give the command "Hup!," stop, and press down on the dog's rump, again forcing him to assume the sitting position. Again maintain the pressure for five or six seconds, again repeat the command to "Heel!," and step off a few feet. Repeat this performance, but not more than ten or fifteen times at the first lesson. Gradually increase the length of time devoted at succeeding lessons until the dog is being worked for a period of ten or fifteen minutes daily. In a few days, the dog should begin to "hup," or sit, on command without the pressure of the trainer's hand. And within a week or ten days he should be letter perfect. The dog should be ordered to "hup!" every time he is fed, and should not be given the food until he responds. At other suitable occasions, the command should be given and the dog required to obey instantly. This command, followed by an immediate response by the dog, is extremely important. It should be learned well and obeyed without exception.

The next step in early yard work is to teach the dog to "stay." This is slightly more difficult and some young Springers do not learn it as fast as do others. It is relatively simple, however, if one is persistent and patient. The handler may start this training by taking the dog to a secluded training area in the yard or the basement and giving the command "Hup!." At the same time, the trainer should raise and extend the right arm upward with the palm outward and command in a stern voice "Stay . . . Stay . . . Stay," then take a step or two slowly backward while repeating the command. (In many cases, when he is commanded to "Hup" the dog will remain in position without being commanded to "Stay!". The trainer may then return to the dog while repeating the command "Stay!", and if the pupil has responded properly, he should be rewarded by petting and by voice. This procedure should be repeated ten or more times during the first lesson, with the trainer taking two or three slow steps backward from the dog.

In many cases, the puppy will learn what is required in a few lessons. He may not understand at first and if he attempts to follow the handler or

Instant Response to HUP. In this series, trainer Dan Langhans, working with Andy Shoaff's trial winner Brian Picolo, demonstrates a highly useful technique for developing instant response to the HUP command.

—*Photos by Andy Shoaff.*

As the trainer "Hups" the dog, he holds a concealed stick or fly rod tip behind his back.

As the dog walks at heel, the trainer gives the voice or whistle command "HUP", gently striking the dog at the same time. The dog is conditioned by surprise rather than by pain.

The trainer reassures and rewards the dog for the correct response.

Mrs. Peter Garvin with Denalisunflo Coffey, a favorite gun dog who she handled in trials and shot over in the field.

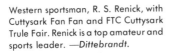

Western sportsman, R. S. Renick, with Cuttysark Fan Fan and FTC Cuttysark Trule Fair. Renick is a top amateur and sports leader. —*Dittebrandt.*

Bob Sanchez, California, widely known professional Springer trainer accepts delivery from a dog in training at the Cote de Casa gun club, of which he is manager. Sanchez is a recognized field trial judge and outstanding wing shot. He has annual attacks of White Wing and Mourning Dove fever, cured only by safaris to south of the Colorado River.

move from the spot, the puppy should be picked up bodily and returned to the original spot where the command "Hup!" was given.

The distances may be lengthened gradually until the trainer can walk the length of the garage without having the puppy move. If it is deemed necessary, the learning process may be speeded up with a very mild form of punishment such as a chuck under the chin or a mild shake to indicate disapproval. One should never strike the dog, and by all means *never* lose his temper. Assume an attitude of patience, kindness, and firmness. If the trainer loses his temper or patience, the training session must cease at once and not be resumed for the rest of the day. A blow struck in anger may do irreparable damage to the young dog's spirit.

When the puppy is responding properly indoors, the lessons may be continued in the yard, and then in the field each time before the puppy is cast off to hunt. At the end of two weeks, enough progress should have been made to enable the trainer to "hup" the puppy, give the command "Stay!", and then walk in a complete circle around the puppy at a distance of fifteen yards or more. A puppy eight months old or more should demonstrate enough progress to make this possible with two weeks of training, provided the trainer has established a routine of working with him almost daily.

If the puppy does not appear able to grasp what is desired, another method may be employed in teaching the "stay." In this method a light sash cord or a length of nylon cord may be attached to the puppy's collar. The line should then be passed through a hook in the garage wall, around a tree in the yard, or around a stake in the ground. Upon giving the command "Hup!", the trainer can soon convince the dog that it is essential to remain in the sitting position. The choke collar will help with the learning process. Proper response to the command must be demanded. And following the foregoing procedure for ten or fifteen minutes a day for a week will get the idea over to the dog. He can then be worked with the line slack, although still attached to his collar. When the dog responds properly, reward him by petting and proceed with the lessons with the line attached, but lying on the floor. If the dog remains at the "stay" several times, remove the line and proceed with the lessons with the dog free of all restraint. Gradually lengthen the distance and, if the response is good, move outdoors first, then into the field, and repeat the lessons. Any slack in response is the cue to resume training the dog in the secluded area with, and then without, the line. To "stay" must become a firmly fixed habit in the dog's mind, so the lesson *must* be learned thoroughly. There can be no deviation from perfection in this lesson, regardless of the time required for training at this stage. Accomplishing the desired results will be well rewarded later.

The trainer should remember always to raise his right arm above the head with the palm outward every time the commands "Hup!" and "Stay!" are given. Within two or three weeks, it will be possible to make the dog "hup" and "stay" by merely raising the hand above the head. This is a most valuable hand signal which will prove useful in the field throughout the dog's life.

The third and final act of obedience the young dog should learn in early yard training is to come to the handler when commanded to do so, regardless of what he may be doing. This can be taught easily after the dog has learned to "sit" and "stay." It is done by again attaching the light cord to the collar and commanding the dog to "Hup!" and "Stay!". The handler can then walk away five or six yards and give the command "Come!" or "Heel!" in a firm voice. A gentle tug on the line will indicate to the puppy that he is to come to the trainer. When he does so, he should be rewarded with petting. This routine should be repeated over and over again for fifteen minutes each day until the dog has become thoroughly conditioned to respond properly. Usually the dog is so overjoyed at being permitted to come in for a pat or two that the "come" response is soon learned. As with the other two basic responses, it is most important to ingrain firmly the act of coming *each* and *every* time the command is given. No dog is a trained dog if he won't come each and every time he is called.

A word of caution must be given here to the over-conscientious trainer: Guard against overtraining the dog. Too frequent use of the commands may destroy the puppy's initiative and might cause him to stop hunting. It is necessary to mix a little common sense with the training routine and ease a bit if the young dog appears to be bored or intimidated. The wise trainer will observe the action of the dog's tail because much can be told by its action and position. If the puppy enjoys the work, and he certainly should, the tail will be up and in motion much of the time. If the tail is tucked between the legs and the puppy goes about his work with much casting of his eyes toward the trainer and without a considerable show of enthusiasm, the trainer is employing methods which are too severe. In such cases it is well to stop all training for a week or ten days and permit the prospect to regain his confidence by daily play periods. The training can then be resumed with the trainer using a more gentle voice and applying more petting and fussing over the dog when he has performed properly. Giving the commands too often in the field can result in a lack of enthusiasm for the entire business. Be sure that the dog *likes* the training, because serious problems can arise later if the prospect is cowed, or shows evidence of boredom or lack of confidence.

When there is evidence of considerable pleasure in performing all three actions, both in the yard and in the field, it is then the proper time to teach the dog to respond to all three acts at the command of a whistle.

One of the most suitable whistles, the Acme, is made of plastic and is available at most good sporting goods stores. It comes in three sizes but the smallest size is the most suitable. It is wise to purchase two or three whistles so that if one of them is lost, another will be available. A lanyard or whistle cord should be attached to each so they will be ready for instant use. The plastic whistle is perferable to the metal type as it won't stick to the tongue in cold weather or chip a tooth if the trainer should fall.

The whistle commands are readily learned and most dogs experience little or no trouble with the three basic commands. Most trainers use one sharp blast of the whistle to teach the dog to "hup," two sharp staccato-like blasts given close together to turn or change direction, and a series of short chirping notes to bring the dog in to heel.

To teach the dog to "hup" on the whistle, return to the secluded spot in the yard or garage and put him on the short leash again. Walk the dog at heel and follow the same procedure as was suggested previously when the dog was taught to "hup" on the voice command. A few minutes each day for a week is usually sufficient. After the dog is responding in the basement or garage, repeat the performance in the yard and then in the field before, after, and while the dog is working. Anything short of perfection here must not be tolerated, so, if necessary, return the dog to the yard several times to insure perfection.

In *extremely stubborn cases* where the dog refuses to respond, another method devised by Steve Studnicki, one of the top American trainers and handlers of fine Spaniel gun dogs, may be employed. This method requires the exercise of great judgment and *should be employed only as a last resort.* The trainer carries a small switch in his hand but keeps it well hidden from the dog by pressing it tightly against his leg on the opposite side from which the dog is heeled. The trainer then walks ten or fifteen paces and blows one sharp blast on the whistle. At the exact instant that the whistle is blown, the dog is tapped firmly on the rump by the trainer, who manipulates the switch behind his back. After the blow, the switch must be returned rapidly to the trainer's side in such a manner that the dog does not see it. The dog is then heeled and walked another few paces where the performance is repeated. It is essential that light taps be struck and the whistle be blown at the same instant. The purpose here is to condition the dog's reflexes with this bit of very mild force so that he comes to associate the whistle with mild punishment.

It should be understood thoroughly that there is no place in dog training for the application of excessive force, and the light taps described above should never cause pain. The purpose, more than anything else, is to startle the dog and to condition his reflexes so that he will "sit" quickly. Five lessons in which the tap is struck not more than five times, with two or three day intervals between lessons, is a desirable course. Even this mild application of force should not be used if it is possible to get the dog to respond without it. It should be used only in severe cases with overly bold puppies that will not respond to the more conservative methods.

The greatest fault displayed by most trainers is their effort to rush the training beyond the dog's capacity to absorb it. A puppy six months old has a very short span of attention. He may not remember things very long and cannot concentrate on any one thing for very long. He gets bored easily and cannot stand much nagging or hacking. So the lessons must be brief and to the point and must *always* be discontinued while the dog is still enthusiastic about the work. It is easy to break a puppy's spirit or to make him hate the training sessions. If the trainer is in doubt, the lesson should be stopped at once.

If the schedule of lessons recommended in this chapter has been followed, the trainer now has a puppy at least ten or twelve months of age that will "hup," "stay," and "come" on command. He will hunt and find game and can retrieve the bucks nicely in the yard or field. He will "hup" and come to heel on either voice or whistle command, and will also "hup" when he sees the handler give a hand sign by raising his arm over his head. The dog will walk on a loose leash without tugging and pulling, and by now even the trainer can see the results of his work. The young dog is now said to be yard trained and is ready for the more advanced work in the field and in the yard.

U.S. Open and Amateur FC I Like Ike of Robert King's Breeze Point Kennel boldly flushes a training pigeon in the Maine woods.

5

Intermediate Field Work

THIS CHAPTER will be concerned with the intermediate field work, which, like the other phases of training, is of major importance. The main headings to be covered here will be:
1. Shooting Live Game
2. Quartering the Ground In the Proper Manner
3. Whistle Training
4. Steadiness To Shot and Wing

1. Shooting Live Game

Up to this point, little or nothing has been said about gun-shyness. There was a special reason for this, which can now be revealed. Many novice trainers do one of two things: (a) they either worry too much about introducing the young dog to the gun; or (b) they don't worry enough. It seems that there is no happy medium. It is the author's hope, therefore, that by avoiding the discussion of the problem prior to this point, his readers will consider the matter in its proper perspective.

Some of the early English books speak of gun-shyness, and certainly one who has had any association with dogs and hunting has seen many cases of this distressing reaction to gunshot. A pitiful sight indeed is the cringing, slinking, fear-ridden dog of any breed that has been *made* gun-shy by some unthinking or uninformed individual. The condition is produced entirely by man, for very few, if any, dogs are ever born gun-shy. Usually, if one takes the trouble to investigate each case that comes to attention, some bit of man's stupidity or ignorance will be found to be responsible for the condition.

One of the worst cases ever observed was that of a nice Springer bitch who would practically go into convulsions, not only at the sound of a gun, but also at the sight of a broom or any other object which bore even a faint resemblance to a gun. Several of her littermates were good gun dogs and perhaps this bitch would have been, too, if she had not been taken to a gun club at the tender age of three months. When she first heard the sound of a 12 gauge gun, she cringed and exhibited some evidence of fear. After two hours of the same medicine, the dog was in a blue funk and a most pitiful sight. Her inexperienced owners erroneously attributed her condition to car sickness. A day or two later, when a .22 rifle was discharged at a starling in her owner's yard, the puppy learned, then and there, to associate the sound of the gun with its appearance and from then on would almost collapse from fright at either the sound or the sight of anything even faintly resembling a gun.

A second common cause of gun-shyness is the Fourth of July firecracker thrown at the puppy's feet by some thoughtless youngster. The burning fuse usually attracts the puppy's attention and if he attempts to seize the firecracker or to paw it, the results are sure and positive. The noise and the flash burn will condition the puppy adversely and gun-shyness is the result.

Young dogs may also become gun-shy by being shot over without the proper preparation.

Gun-shyness can be cured but it is a long, slow process. Months of re-education may be required to overcome the phobia. It is so easy to avoid this condition by proper early conditioning, that one is inclined to think that no space should be devoted to the cure. However, a procedure for overcoming this most serious fault will be suggested in the chapter on correcting faults in Springer gun dogs. No normal hunting dog can *ever* be made gun-shy by following the procedure outlined in this book unless the dog is subjected to other outside influences.

The thoughtful reader will recall the suggestion that a sharp hand clap be associated with the early retrieving lessons. It was also suggested that a cap pistol, and later a .22 blank pistol, be introduced gradually into the retrieving routine. It should come as no surprise, then, to learn that any dog that was conditioned by this method is safely past the gun and the introduction to the sound of shot. Therefore, taking him into the field and actually shooting several planted pigeons with a shotgun for the dog to retrieve is rather an anticlimax.

That, however, is the next step and is a procedure that should be repeated subsequently on five or six occasions. If the trainer is not an expert shot, a friend who is a good wing shot may be invited to do the actual shooting, for it is most important that the first few birds be downed for the dog to retrieve. It is preferable to use a light 20 gauge gun the first time or two, and, of course, the birds should be shot while the dog is giving chase.

Continue these lessons for several weeks until the dog is thoroughly habituated to the sound of the shotgun and exhibits enthusiasm every time he sees the gun. It is well to remember never to shoot at close range directly over the head of a dog or a human, as muzzle blast is rather severe and has been known to rupture the eardrum or induce temporary deafness.

Gun shyness is a serious fault, and most difficult to correct. John Isaacs demonstrates a method of introducing a youngster to the gun which will practically guarantee that gun shyness will be avoided, and the dog will learn to love the sound because it signals that he will soon have the fun of retrieving.

Left, John Isaacs first revs up the dog by teasing with the canvas buck. When the dog's excitement peaks, the buck is thrown 20 to 30 yards distant and the dog is encouraged to chase it. When the dog is several yards away from the gun *(right),* a shot is fired. Long experience indicates that the dog will not even hear the shot, but if he does he will not be disturbed. Three more similar sessions, and a dozen shots later, and the youngster will be ready for a switch to feathers.

Left, After the prospect is first teased with a cold, dead pigeon, it is thrown for him and he is encouraged to fetch it, which he does promptly. But this time something new is required of the dog *(right).* He is commanded to HUP with a whistle blast when he brings in the bird, and verbally commanded to HOLD—HOLD—HOLD, which he does. In two or three sessions the trainer has expanded the youngster's learning to include introduction to the gun, exposure to retrieving feathers, and stylish delivery of dead game. —*Photos by John Friend.*

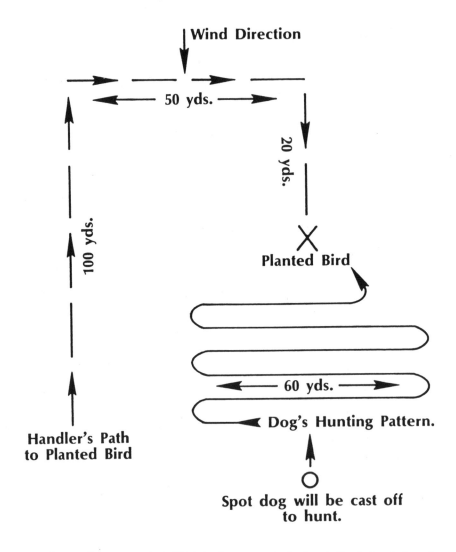

This diagram illustrates a method of bird planting to prevent a dog from trailing the handler's scent to the planted bird. It also illustrates the correct hunting pattern for a dog working into the wind.

2. Quartering the Ground

Not only must gun dogs of all breeds learn to hunt, but also they must learn to hunt in the places where game is most likely to be found. The big, wide-ranging, bird-wise Pointer or Setter will hunt the birdy places such as fence rows, where experience has taught that quail may be found. A Springer Spaniel will learn to work birdy places, too, but because he is a "flushing dog" and not a pointing dog, he must be trained to stay always within gun range. It is easy to see that the fast, keen, eager Springer will not stay within gun range unless taught to quarter back and forth in front of the handler. If the Springer is permitted to range out or punch out wide like a pointing dog, little or no game would be put up within gun range, because the Spaniel flushes birds instead of holding them by pointing. The trainer, then, must strive to make the young Spaniel quarter the ground in front of the gun in an almost mechanical manner. Later on, as the dog gains experience on game, he will break this rigid pattern occasionally, but he must be well grounded in the fundamentals of quartering first in order to produce the best results later.

An earlier chapter suggested that the young Springer always be worked into the wind. The reason for this procedure is to lay the groundwork for teaching the dog to quarter. In many young Springers of field breeding it appears to be an inherited characteristic to quarter almost automatically. When this is the case, the trainer's problem is relatively simple. All he need do is to widen the dog's hunting pattern some (encourage him to cast out as far as forty yards to either side of the trainer) and work the dog enough to make the quartering a habit. If the dog has not started to quarter naturally, he may need some guidance in the matter. This can be accomplished by setting the puppy down at heel and by then sending him out to the right side with a wave of the hand and the command "Hi-on". If the wind is in the trainer's face, the young dog will usually not hunt straight ahead, anyway, and by giving him a wave to the right, he will most likely respond as required. If not, the trainer can repeat the signal and walk in that direction.

When the young dog has gone out 35 or 40 yards, the trainer can give *two* sharp toots of the whistle to attract his attention, and walk to the left. When the dog reaches the extreme limit of 40 yards on the cast to the left, the trainer can again give two sharp toots on the whistle and head in the opposite direction. Three or four lessons should get the idea over that he is to hunt out to either *side* of the trainer rather than straight out in front. It cannot be emphasized too much that the trainer must *always* walk into the wind in early field work. The wind alone is almost enough to cause the dog to hunt the pattern that all Spaniel trainers desire, but if it is not, the trainer must encourage the dog to quarter.

Although no previous reference was made to the procedure, the trainer should have devoted some time to hand signals in the early retrieving lessons. The purpose of hand signals is to direct the dog to a

79

Janet (Mrs. C. A.) Christensen, highly successful amateur trainer and handler, demonstrates the correct procedure for teaching a Springer to quarter. The dog is Greenbriar Gamekeeper. At left, the trainer gets the dog's attention with whistle and hand signals. The dog is in the hupped position at this time. At right, the dog is sent to the handler's left with a positive arm signal and the command Hi-On.

The dog has completed his cast to the left, responded to the whistle command to reverse direction and receives a signal to cover the right side of his beat.

The dog now proceeds to quarter toward his right in response to the trainer's command.

retrieve he has failed to mark and also to indicate where he is to hunt. When young puppies fail to mark the fall of the buck, the trainer should utilize these occasions to teach the dog to take hand signals by indicating the location of the buck with a wave of the hand. A few such experiences are usually enough to accustom the dog to the fact that if he hunts in the direction indicated by the trainer's hand signal, he will find the bird or buck promptly. Another most effective manner of teaching a dog to respond to hand signals is to plant a few birds to the extreme right or left of the imaginary line on which the trainer walks as he works the dog. If the trainer will wave the dog into a half dozen or more live birds, it will speed up the learning process greatly.

3. Teaching the Dog to Turn on the Whistle

While the dog is learning to quarter his ground properly, the trainer should use the whistle as indicated previously. At first the dog will glance at the handler and probably follow directions as indicated by a wave of the hand. Eventually he will merely change his direction and when the two whistle toots are given, will hunt the other side of the handler, sometimes without looking for directions. If the dog is not responding to the whistle, the trainer can call out sternly, indicating that he means business. If this fails to produce the desired results, he should rush out rapidly and give the dog a brisk shake of the collar and sound two blasts of the whistle. A few such actions will make it clear that the dog must respond to the whistle signals. There are other methods, such as attaching a check cord to the dog's collar and forcing him to change directions when the whistle signal is given. Another method is to blow the "hup" whistle, which will cause the dog to stop (if the early training has been thorough), and, while the dog's attention is directed wholly to the trainer, then to indicate the direction in which the dog is to hunt. One, or a combination, of these techniques will produce the desired results.

It is the practice on the part of some trainers to use extreme force with stubborn cases, but such procedure is not recommended for the novice. Considerable judgment and skill are required if force is to be employed properly, and it is probable that more harm than good will result, even at the hands of an expert trainer. One can usually spot the force-trained dog, no matter whether he be retrieving, hunting, entering the water, etc. If, in learning to turn on the whistle, the dog does not respond to any of the foregoing methods, he can be stung by a marble discharged from a slingshot or by a pellet discharged from a BB gun in which the spring has been weakened. These methods are *not* recommended and are reported merely to indicate the steps that may be taken in extreme and severe cases. Years ago it was the custom of some trainers to fire a load of fine bird shot from a shotgun at a wilfully disobedient dog. Fortunately, this has been discontinued by the successful trainers.

Dogs that are *forced* to perform any of the acts required of good gun

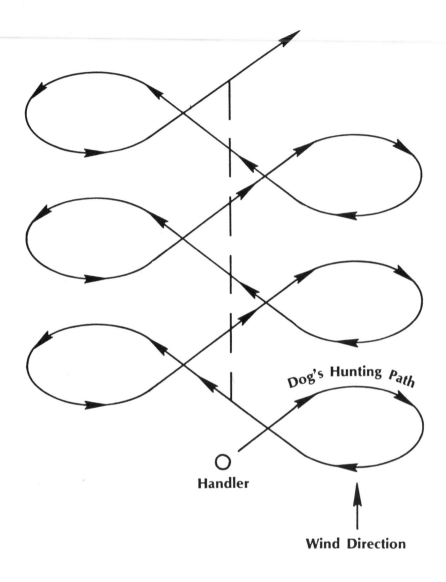

Dog's Hunting Path

Handler

Wind Direction

This diagram illustrates a normal, downwind hunting pattern for a flushing dog. A flushing dog's natural inclination to punch out downwind and then swing back upwind to the handler can be modified and controlled. This is done by casting him to the side and turning him with the whistle so that his downcourse distance becomes a modified figure-8 hunting pattern, always within normal gun range.

dogs never exhibit much spirit and animation, nor are they as dependable as those that are trained through constant repetition to perform the required acts. This statement is based on common sense, experience, and the findings of the animal behavior workers in the research departments of our leading universities. If by repetition a dog's reflexes become thoroughly conditioned to perform a certain act in a certain way, he often becomes a most dependable animal.

4. Steadying the Dog to Shot and Wing

One of the most important requirements of a good gun dog is that he be steady to shot and wing.

For those not familiar with the terminology, steadiness to shot and wing means that the dog will stop dead in his tracks and sit ("hup") at the instant that a bird is flushed or that a gun is discharged. The reasons for requiring a dog to react in this manner are both useful and practical. The following factual account of a South Dakota hunting trip illustrates the reason most vividly.

The hunting party in question was undertaken by three sportsmen who owned well-trained Spaniels and who were persuaded at the last minute to include the owner of an unsteady Spaniel in the party. When the group arrived in South Dakota and entered the first corn field, which was fairly alive with pheasants, the dogs were ordered to heel and the four hunters and their dogs proceeded down the corn rows about ten yards apart. About halfway through the field, one of the dogs dived through two rows of corn to flush a smart old cock that had squatted under some light cover, hoping that the hunters would pass him by. The bird flushed in front of the hunters and was dropped immediately by the center gun. The three steady dogs dropped to shot ("hupped") to await orders, while the unsteady Springer headed toward the "fall" to make the retrieve without command. He overran the "fall", proceeded down the field, and bumped into another pheasant which flushed immediately. He gave chase and within three minutes had flushed perhaps forty pheasants out of the corn, none of which came within gun range of the four hunters. No one had too much to say to the owner of the breaking dog, but a great deal of silent swearing took place.

Some of the birds that had been flushed were marked down in a slough about a half mile away. The four gunners headed in that direction with their dogs at heel. Upon entering the slough, which was a large one, all dogs were ordered to "Hi-on". As luck would have it, the unsteady dog flushed the first bird and took off on a wild chase. His actions again caused all the birds in the slough except one lone hen to flush out of gun range, and not one shot was fired, though a hundred or more birds had been in the vicinity of the hunters in the corn field and the slough.

A council of war was held immediately and, by vote of three to one, the unsteady dog was banished to the security of the automobile for the

Outdoor writer John Seyman's sharp Springer drops to flush and intently marks flight of bird. Seconds later he retrieved the shot bird on command, after marking the fall perfectly.

Reed, eager son of NFC Saighton's Sizzler, fetches a pheasant to owner Kathy Caude, wife of Donald Caude—president of the parent club. Caude reports that Reed is a super bird dog. His kennelmate FC Dungarvan Right On has earned a title, but Reed is apparently the No. 1 Springer at his Locust Valley, N.Y. domicile.

84

duration of the hunt. After this had transpired, the four hunters proceeded to work out some likely spots of cover and, with the help of three trained dogs, were able in a few hours to take their daily limit. The first hour of the hunt produced one bird for the bag, the next three hours produced twenty-seven which were flushed and retrieved by the three trained Spaniels.

A trained Springer steady to shot and wing and trained to work within gun range will *not* disturb new and unhunted territory ahead by chasing every hen pheasant that is flushed or every cock that is missed. It will be under perfect control and will be an *aid* to the gun rather than a hindrance.

The most common excuse given by the owner of an unsteady Springer which breaks shot and flush is that "he wants his dog to be there when the bird hits the ground in order not to lose the cripples". This is no argument at all and is really an excuse having no basis of fact. If permitted to acquire experience in hunting, any Spaniel gun dog with an average nose can learn to trail out and retrieve the crippled birds that fall before the gun, as well as those which try to avoid being flushed. The fact has been proved thousands of times in the hunting field and in field trials. It is the exception, rather than the rule, when an experienced Springer fails to produce a crippled running bird, even if he is held at the "hup" position for several minutes after the bird is downed.

To teach a dog to be steady, return to the yard and follow this procedure. First, stand in front of the dog and command him to "Hup!" and "Stay!". (Some trainers discontinue the use of the word "stay" at this stage of the training and rely on the word "hup" alone.) As the dog faces the trainer, the feathered retrieving buck should be tossed over the shoulder and the command "Stay!" or "Hup!" repeated several times. It may be necessary to make a quick grab for the dog to enforce the command "Stay!" because up to this time, he has been permitted to retrieve at will and may ignore the command to "Stay!". If the dog is restrained physically several times and scolded in a severe voice, he will usually revert to his earlier training and remain sitting as the buck is thrown over the trainer's shoulder. This lesson should be repeated several days in succession. If possible, the dog should never be permitted to retrieve if he leaves the sitting position without a command. Incidentally, the usual command for a retrieve is "Fetch!". At this stage the trainer usually couples the dog's name with the word "fetch", such as "Rover—fetch!". (Many trainers, especially those who follow field trials, gradually drop the word "fetch" and teach the dog to retrieve when only his name is called.)

After a day or two of standing in front of the dog to throw the buck, the trainer should then stand directly to one side of the dog, always being in such a position that he can provide the necessary restraint with his hands if the dog offers to make the retrieve without waiting for the command. This lesson should be repeated for several days until it is obvious that the dog has learned to wait for the command before retrieving. The trainer may then change position to a spot directly behind and throw the buck over the dog's head each time. In all likelihood, the dog will remain steady most of the time, but when he does offer to break, the trainer must stop him by commanding "Hup!" in a loud voice. If this fails, the trainer must endeavor to run and pick up the buck before the dog does. Men over 40 may figure out an easier method, but younger men will find that the above practice not only amuses their neighbors, but also is wonderful exercise to reduce the waistline and improve the wind. Patience and practice will assure results. And never fail to pet the dog when he has performed properly, but be sure to withhold petting and verbal praise when he has failed to respond as desired.

The next step is to "hup" the dog in front of the trainer some ten yards, and toss the buck in the near-vicinity of the dog. Insist that no move to retrieve be made until the command is given. Gradually increase the distance between man and dog until it is possible to drop the dog thirty yards away and toss the buck practically under his nose while he remains steady. It is a good idea to walk out occasionally and retrieve the buck by hand in order to teach the dog that he cannot retrieve every time. After all, some birds will be missed and the dog must learn very early that he cannot retrieve every bird that is flushed.

Once the Spaniel has learned that he must not retrieve until ordered to do so in the yard, it is time to return to the field. First, cast the dog off to hunt (into the wind) and as he approaches from the left, the buck should be thrown to the extreme right. The trainer should step in front of the moving dog and give the whistle or the voice command to "Hup!". In all likelihood, the response will be good and the dog will drop after a step or two.

Repeat this procedure five times or so, and then let the dog hunt for a while uninterrupted. There should be another session of shorter duration before the trip afield is finished. The trainer should then go home and "help" his wife paint the storm windows before she gets the idea that being a "Spaniel widow" is worse than being a "Golf widow"!

The lesson described above should be repeated five or six times and then a dead pigeon should be substituted for the feather buck. The puppy will exhibit much more interest in the bird than in the buck and may attempt to break the first time or two. If the buck is always thrown as the prospect approaches, the trainer will be in position to step out *between* the dog and the bird, and thus will be able to enforce the command physically. Of course, the command "Hup!" or the whistle command to "hup" should be given each and every time and repeated several times if necessary.

When the dog is responding to this situation *every* time the trainer may substitute a clipped-wing, live pigeon for the dead bird. The dog will be more interested in the live bird than in the dead one and may attempt to break a time or two. Firmness and patience are still the proper attitudes, and no slackness is to be permitted. As the dog learns that he must obey the command with the live bird, the blank pistol should be reintroduced. The

Superstake Jake flushes a pigeon during a training session as outdoor writer John J. Seynan ducks to take this photo, and owner/handler Doug Miller prepares to shoot the pigeon.

proper procedure is to fire the pistol, give the command "Hup!", and then toss the clipped-wing bird in a direction away from the dog. This may sound like something dreamed up by Rube Goldberg, but a little practice will soon enable the trainer to develop the proper coordination to perform all three actions simultaneously. It could be that the trainer will attempt to blow on the pigeon and throw the pistol on the first attempt. But such action will serve as a conversation piece at the office or as further evidence to the neighbors that Mr. Trainer is slightly "touched in the head".

One should be of firm resolve, however, for better days are coming. The freezer will be filled with fat cock pheasants and corn-fed mallards come November, and the trainer will receive twenty invitations to hunt with people with whom he had only a nodding acquaintance before he acquired the trained Springer Spaniel.

The next step is to kill some thrown flyers over the young dog as he sits at heel. It is wise to follow this procedure for 15 or 20 training sessions (50 to 100 pigeons) until the dog has become thoroughly conditioned to the fact that he must never retrieve until ordered to do so. It's a good idea to let him retrieve only four or five shot birds out of six. If the handler walks out and picks up an occasional bird while the dog remains sitting in his original position it will be helpful later on when two dogs are worked together while hunting or in a trial.

After the dog is responding well (perfectly) to the pistol and the thrown bird, the next and final step is to work on planted birds. The bird should be planted with its head facing down wind and the dog should be worked up to the bird on a cross wind (with the wind blowing against the right or the left side of his face instead of full into it). The trainer will have a better opportunity to step in front of the dog if he offers to break when the bird flushes. The whistle command to "hup" should be given at the exact instant the bird is flushed. If the dog has learned each step well, he will probably be steady on his first flushed pigeon. If he offers to break, the trainer (provided he has followed the plan outlined above) will be in a position to restrain the dog physically. It is well to have a friend along to do the actual shooting because the trainer will want to devote his full attention to the dog at this critical stage.

Enough progress has now been made so that one has only to repeat the foregoing procedure on every occasion possible. Most amateurs do their work in the field on the weekends. If the reader has any doubts about the success of weekend training, let him be assured that there are hundreds of sportsmen in the United States who do it successfully every year.

It is likely that there will be occasional lapses of memory on the dog's part as the training progresses. Low-flying birds or a bird shot too close may cause the pupil to break shot or flush. This is the time to "refresh" the dog's memory by running after him and carrying him back bodily to the point of flush. He should be placed firmly, and not too gently, on the ground in the sitting position, and chided in a rough tone of voice. A little repetition of the command "Hup, you so and so!" will usually do the trick.

There is one other method which may be used, but only as a last resort. This technique requires that a 40 or 50-foot nylon cord, called a check cord, be attached to the dog's collar and the command "Hup!" be enforced by a tight line as the bird is flushed. The check cord is believed by some to induce "pointing" in Spaniels if not properly used. The use of the check cord is not recommended to the hands of a novice trainer who might lack judgment as to its use. When all fails and it is decided, after mature reflection, that this is the only course left, the trainer must be as gentle with the dog as possible. Judicious use requires that all slack be taken up on the line immediately at the instant of flush, and that the dog be held steady rather than jerked to a standstill. He should never be checked up while running at full speed. Rough treatment here may cause the Springer to become confused and develop into a blinker or pointer—both of which are serious faults.

Pointing game might seem a desirable trait to the novice Spaniel owner, but there are several good reasons why a Springer can never become a really satisfactory pointing dog. In the first place, a Springer Spaniel dog does not have the range, nose, or the stamina to hunt like a Pointer or an English Setter.

It is undoubtedly true that the early ancestors of the Springer and the English Setter were one and the same dog. It is also undoubtedly true that Springers (or at least certain strains of Springers) carry the genes for the pointing instinct. However, during the last hundred years in America, the English Setter and the Pointer have been developed into wide ranging, big-going dogs that can really "carry the mail" as far as quail dogs are concerned. They have no equals in this type of hunting. The Springer (the field strains), on the other hand, has been selected for its ability to work to the gun and to accept training kindly. No Springer can range with a top bird dog and no experienced dog man wants one that points, because it could never be more than a fifth-rate pointing dog. Neither can good pointing dogs perform the functions of Spaniels.

A Springer cannot be developed into a satisfactory pointing dog for another reason, a reason which has to do with the Springer's nose. Through the last several hundred years, Spaniels have been bred for the type of nose that enables them to trail both fur and feathers and to locate game by body scent as well. Class pointing dogs rely strictly on body scent when it comes to finding game and have considerably less ability to trail moving game than do Spaniels. One cannot actually say that a Pointer or English Setter has a better nose than does a Spaniel, although they seem to be able to locate game by body scent from a greater distance than can a Spaniel. It is more accurate to say that the pointing dog's nose is better adapted to its specialized type of hunting, while the Spaniel's nose is better adapted to its specialized type of hunting, while the Spaniel's nose is more suitable for the work it is required to perform. It is the opinion of well-informed trainers, those who have had considerable experience with all three breeds, that each dog has a nose that is suited to its particular style of hunting and that even if it were possible to exchange the scenting apparatus, neither the pointing dogs nor the Spaniel could perform as well.

The last step in the intermediate training program for the Springer Spaniel is to make sure that "stopping to shot" is a firmly ingrained habit. During the earlier work it was suggested that every effort be made to have the dog in a sitting position when a pistol, and later a shotgun, was discharged. Some exceptionally bright Springer pupils are able to grasp the idea quickly from this early work and they become "steady to shot" after just a few training sessions. Even though this may occur, it is still sound training procedure, based on well-established principles of animal behavior, to devote some time to the specialized training which will make the dog letter-perfect in this department. One of the best places to give the special training for steadiness to shot is in the field with the blank pistol. To begin, cast the dog off with no planted birds and no wild birds, if possible. While the dog is quartering and responding to the whistle and to hand signals, fire the blank pistol. If the dog "hups"—wonderful. The only thing the trainer must do is to repeat the act eight or ten times and follow through with the same procedure for the next five or six trips to the field. If the dog does not stop and sit at the crack of the shot, the trainer immediately must give the verbal or whistle command to "hup".

During this phase of training, the blank pistol should be held high over the trainer's head. The act of firing the pistol, and giving the command "Hup!" by voice or whistle at the same time, will soon condition the dog to stop as he sees the trainer raise his arm overhead to discharge the pistol. This training procedure should be repeated at frequent intervals until the dog becomes thoroughly conditioned to "hupping" both to shot and to the trainer's upraised arm. On each occasion that the dog fails to respond, the trainer must rush ouh fast and scold the dog in a stern voice, accompanying the scolding with a shake of the collar if necessary. After the Spaniel's reflexes become thoroughly conditioned, he will be most dependable and reliable under normal circumstances.

The Springer puppy that was started in training some months ago is now an educated gun dog. He has finished "high school" and is ready for "college". Advanced training procedures will be described in the next chapter.

6

Advanced Field Training

THE PREVIOUS CHAPTERS on training have been concerned, primarily, with the man-made factors in the development of a fine gun dog. Up to this point, the emphasis has been on conditioning the dog to perform certain routine actions and to react in a desired manner to certain situations which give the trainer maximum control at all times. This portion of the education of a gun dog is most important because the dog's contribution to the function of filling the game bag is in direct proportion to the control which the handler can exercise in each and every situation which arises in the field.

Every experienced hunter knows that a wild, half-trained gun dog actually may be a hindrance in filling the game bag and providing a pleasant day afield, while a trained dog not only helps fill the bag, but is a joy to behold. Along with control, there are other attributes which a top gun dog must possess. These are natural ability and intense desire to hunt and find game, plus the experience to develop these instinctive traits. This chapter will be devoted to a discussion of these factors, which are of equal if not greater importance than control.

One of the more amusing aspects of the history of hunting which appears regularly in the works of authors both modern and ancient, is the frequent reference to the fact that game is in much shorter supply than it was in *their* father's day. In fact, one writer of the Middle Ages was so worked up over the fact, that he doubted that it was worthwhile to train or keep a hunting dog. If all the gloomy forecasts about the prevalance of upland game and waterfowl were true, all species of same would be as extinct as the mythical dodo bird and there would not be any purpose in this book or any of the others which appear each year on dogs, hunting, shooting, and related subjects.

The author does not want to break the pattern of gloom about the decreasing game supply which has been the hallmark of all writers on the subject for the past five hundred years. Therefore, the statement that it is difficult to give a gun dog the proper experience on game follows in the well-established pattern of those "who have trod these sacred halls before". The fact remains, however, that in these days of intensive cultivation of farm land and two automobiles in every farmer's garage, it is not always possible to put a young gun dog on wild game as frequently as one would like, because the fence corners are plowed and the marginal land is utilized for grazing and other agrarian endeavors. Therefore, the contemporary trainer of a gun dog will have to be alert to all possibilities for giving his dog the opportunity to develop the instinctive urge to hunt.

Every dog in general, and every Spaniel in particular, has some natural ability to hunt and to find game. It is up to the trainer to give the dog the experience necessary to develop fully whatever natural ability he may possess. The old adage that "practice makes perfect" is a truism when applied to a gun dog. The trainer, then, should take every opportunity to expose the dog to game and to do it as frequently as possible.

Students of the outdoors know that most species of game birds and animals usually follow a regular, clock-like pattern of action. An old hen pheasant will take her brood of chicks off the roost at about the same hour each day. They will feed and go to water and follow a most rigid schedule. The trainer of a gun dog will do well to work his dog in the field as early in the morning as possible or just before dark in the evening. The birds will sit more tightly at this time and the young dog will be able to find and flush them with greater ease.

A good routine to follow with a dog at this stage is to go to a field where game is known to abide. The dog should be "hupped" and then ordered to hunt (into the wind). When he strikes scent, the dog will usually indicate the freshness of the scent by his actions. On a day when scent lies well and the dog "makes game" strongly, he should be allowed to follow the line and come up with the bird or rabbit, if possible. The dog will usually trail faster than the handler can walk and may soon be out of normal gun range. When he gets to the limits, the handler should blow the stop whistle and insist that the dog respond by "hupping". The handler should walk up, pet the dog, and then order him to resume trailing. Young dogs will be momentarily confused and may experience some difficulty in again picking up the line of scent. If the handler remains perfectly still and lets the dog work it out, more often than not the dog will again pick up the line of scent and return to trailing.

The dog should be required to "hup" each time he gets out of normal gun range and never ordered to resume hunting until the handler arrives. Repeated efforts along these lines will increase the dog's ability to trail and will teach the handler much that he did not know before about both dog and game. If the dog is trailing a pheasant, he should be required to honor

Dan Langhans, outstanding professional, with National Open and National Amateur Champion Dansmirth's Gunshot (1969). This success and his friends convinced him to become a professional trainer. His record includes finishing several field champions, and winning or placing more than 60 times in Open competition between 1974 and 1981. He handled FC Chrishall Rover to Top Springer of the Year in 1980 with four first places, one second and two thirds. Rover's total record of 20 placements through 1981 included 8 firsts and a fourth in the 1981 National Open championship.

L. to r.: Candy Lorenz; her father, noted professional Dave Lorenz with FC Rivington Joe; Julia Armour, first woman to win a National Championship with NFC Carswell Contessa; and the late noted professional trainer, Elmer Chick, with FC Carswell Bedelia. —*Chicago Tribune photo.*

Mrs. Thomas (Iris) Vail with FC Findaway Luck of Burnsget, excellent Springer bitch producer and performer. Luck was high point winner in the U.S. trials in 1979, and her daughter Findaway Bon Chance was high point U.S. Springer in 1982, with littermate brother tied for runner-up in same year. Dave Lorenz handled all the Springers.

94

the flush and to remain seated for five or ten seconds. It is much better, of course, to shoot game over the dog every time he flushes. But this is not possible except during the open season or when using planted birds, so the next best thing is to let the dog learn to flush and hunt without shooting.

After the bird has flushed and the dog has honored the flush by sitting, he should be called in to heel, petted, and made over, and then cast off in the opposite direction from the flight of the bird. Young prospects will want to chase, but repetitive use of a firm "No!" and insistent whistle signals will serve to prevent a chase or bolt in the direction of the flushed bird. After the young dog has become proficient in following the lines of scent left by rabbits and bird, the trainer should occasionally cast the dog off the line and require him to hunt in another direction without flushing the bird or rabbit. The young pupil may be most reluctant to leave the line, but the handler must be firm and insistent, which will serve to increase the handler's control. This has a practical side, too, as no hunter wants his dog to follow game into a restricted area where hunting may not be permitted or to cross a highway in pursuit of game.

A word of caution is in order here in regard to the manner in which the dog is permitted to work, for the author recognizes fully the dangers of working up game which is not shot. If not properly controlled, a young dog may cease to mark or may develop into a low-headed rabbit dog with his nose glued to the ground and with little interest in anything else. These pitfalls may be avoided by never permitting the dog to potter or linger (smell around in one place) on stale scent. The novice trainer will soon be able to distinguish between stale scent and fresh scent, and so will the dog. If the young dog does not attempt to move out on the scent, he should be called off by whistle or voice, cast in another direction, and kept moving. A dog should *never* be allowed to potter. He should be kept moving and hunting; this will be no problem if the dog has been trained properly on the whistle. The trainer should, if necessary, enforce his command by a firm shake of the dog's collar or some well-chosen words suitable to the occasion. The dog must be kept moving and quartering in the desired pattern (similar to that of a windshield wiper on a car).

The answer to those who do not believe in permitting a young dog to work wild game which cannot be shot, lies in the fact that thousands upon thousands of hunting dogs have been trained this way down through the ages. Until the recent adoption by the pointing dog people of the use of planted game, nearly 100 percent of pointing dogs in the United States were trained almost entirely on wild game which was not shot for them. If one keeps the Spaniel moving and shoots a few pigeons over him each week, there will be little loss of marking ability and no encouragement to potter, *even if worked almost daily* on wild birds. This is no theory—it has been tested by actual experience on many thousands of dogs.

The trainer may have some difficulty in keeping the dog steady to flush on rabbits or other ground game at this period. If so, a little specialized yard work may be given. This is accomplished by taking the skin (or pelt) of a rabbit and fixing it to a croquet ball, with the hair on the outside. This simulated rabbit can then be concealed in the trainer's coat and rolled rapidly tn the ground in front of the Spaniel as he hunts. Much repetition will develop the dog's steadiness to rabbits. The basis of the training principle behind this trick is in keeping with well-established laws of animal behavior. If this act is repeated, and is accompanied each time by the stop or "hup" signal of the whistle or voice, the dog will have his reflexes conditioned so thoroughly that he will soon begin to drop to the simulated rabbit flush automatically.

It may be necessary to "refresh" the dog's memory by the use of stern words and a little shaking up at first, but once the idea is understood, the battle is practically won. When the dog has firmly fixed in mind the habit of stopping on the rolling ball with rabbit pelt, and is doing it automatically without a command of voice or whistle, it is a simple matter to substitute real rabbits for the ball and require the dog to stop at each flush.

In the early chapters on training, it was suggested that the command to "hup" be accompanied by the raising of the hand. During the advanced work in the field, further conditioning to this arm command should be given. At every working session, the dog should be required to stop and "hup" on the silent command of the upraised arm. It should be given, of course, when the dog is glancing at the handler. At first it may be necessary to accompany the hand signal with tne blast of the whistle. Later, as the pupil progresses, the whistle may be eliminated and the dog required to "hup" each time the hand is raised. This may serve a useful purpose if the dog is upwind from the handler on the windy day when the voice and whistle may not be heard. It will also prove most useful in the city if the dog attempts to cross from the opposite side of the street in front of an approaching automobile. It will serve a useful purpose on many occasions in the field, too, when the handler may observe game which he does not wish to disturb by a vocal command.

The dog should be encouraged to take directions while hunting or retrieving by being sent in a definite direction each time he is cast off to hunt. The handler should always point in the direction in which he wishes the dog to hunt. If the dog is slow to respond, a step or two taken in the desired direction will encourage the prospect to work toward that general area. Repeated efforts of this sort will produce the desired results. Many hunters who know the habits of game have trained their dogs to respond almost entirely to hand signals and have had excellent results. Certainly one in woodcock or grouse cover will not wish to arouse the entire countryside and disturb the game unduly by constant voice and whistle signals. The average Spaniel, and even those below average, have the ability to learn to take direction by hand.

Hand Signals to "Come In"

Another most useful response which all polished gun dogs should learn is to come to heel when a hand signal is given. There are several positions of the hands which may be used for this signal. But one which gun dogs seem to grasp readily is to hold the hands down to the side but slightly away from the body, with the palms out and the fingers spread. If a dog has been taught to respond to this silent command, it will enable the handler to bring the dog to heel in a strong wind when the voice or whistle signal might not be heard, or when two dogs are working and the handler wishes to call one in while the other hunts or retrieves.

Thirty minutes of yard work in which the dog is "hupped" and given the verbal or whistle command to come in simultaneously with the outspread hand signal is usually enough to get the idea over to the pupil. Additional work on this signal should be given in the field from time to time. For instance, when one has worked up a couple of pigeons and is returning to the automobile, the dog can be "hupped" as the trainer walks away. When the distance between man and dog is approximately 35 yards, the trainer may stop and give the voice and hand signal to come in to heel. After a few lessons, the voice command can be eliminated and only the hand signal given. The dog will soon learn to respond and if the response is not perfect, he can be encouraged by voice or whistle.

The trainer must always insist on immediate response to this command, as well as all other commands. The dog can be shaken up slightly if he fails to respond with alacrity and should be rewarded *every* time he obeys. The reward should be in the form of a kind word or a friendly pat.

It is never a good idea to call a dog to heel merely to pet him. This may establish a habit pattern in which the dog is constantly checking in to the handler. Most dogs soon learn to know when they have pleased their handler and most Springers, especially those of field breeding, have a strong desire to please. The dog should always be rewarded by voice.

The ideal gun dog is one that quarters his ground almost mechanically in training and learns to know his range. This means that he knows about how far on each side of the handler he is to cast and will turn automatically without a whistle or voice command. When a dog does this automatically, it is said that he "knows his range". This is a most valuable trait and the trainer who wants a really polished dog should make concerted efforts toward this goal. It has a practical purpose, too, in that constant whistling and yelling will disturb game in the field and is most annoying to friends who may be hunting with the dog's owner. Overhandling indicates that the Springer is only half trained.

The trainer should, first of all, know his dog and how he works. Second, he must learn to develop confidence in his dog. If a handler sees that his dog is at the limits of his range (to the side) and there is a likely spot of cover 15 feet beyond the spot at which the dog would normally turn, it is well for the handler to refrain from blowing the turn whistle because the dog probably should work the small spot of cover. The wise handler will let the dog go another few feet to check the likely looking spot and will take a few steps in that direction, in the event the dog pushes a bird or rabbit from the spot. A good, experienced dog should demonstrate some "game sense", and working out a spot of likely looking cover or continuing down a fence line for a few yards is one indication that game sense is developing.

It is well to trust a dog in these circumstances, or many others of a similar nature, because most dogs can find more game accidentally than any human can find on purpose. One should always trust the dog's nose. If he indicates game, no matter how sparse the cover may be or how unlikely it appears as a logical place for game, the wise hunter will always trust the dog. Occasionally the dog will be wrong, but he will be right more times than he is wrong if he has an average nose and has learned to use it.

There are many occasions when it appears that a Springer is wrong and that he has become completely befuddled about a bird, especially a crippled running pheasant. At one of the National championship field trials for Springers a few years ago, a cock pheasant was shot over one of the dogs. In full view of the handler, the judges, and the gallery, it appeared to run rapidly in the same direction it was flying when shot. The handler sent his dog to make the retrieve, which is always very sporting. The dog went to the "fall" (spot where the bird struck the ground) and trailed it in the direction in which everyone thought the bird had gone. After a few seconds, the dog (apparently still trailing) turned and headed back toward the handler, who attempted to stop the dog and send him in the opposite direction. He responded as ordered but would hunt out for a few yards, then reverse his direction and head back toward the handler. After the third time, the handler gave up and let the dog have his head. Imagine this man's surprise when the dog picked up and retrieved the cock which had attempted to hide virtually at the judge's feet. Unfortunately, this sort of thing happens to everyone who trains dogs, and will continue to happen in the future. Put as much trust in the dog as possible and always remember that the dog's nose, while not infallible, is more likely to be right than wrong.

There are a good many times during the shooting year when a situation arises where game is very abundant and the anxious hunter will have a fast and furious few minutes of shooting, with several birds down. If this occurs in a duck blind, or a hot mourning-dove stand, the dog should be kept at heel during the few minutes of fast shooting and not sent to retrieve until several birds are on the ground.

According to Clifford H. Wallace, one of the leading Spaniel and Retriever professional trainers, it is improbable that most dogs can mark and *remember* accurately the fall of more than three birds. Even this feat of marking and remembering requires considerable experience. It would seem, therefore, that teaching a gun dog to accept help in situations of this

98

sort would be almost a "must" for serious hunters. There are also numerous occasions when a lightly shot bird will fly over a hill or beyond some trees and then change direction when out of the dog's line of vision. All retrieves of this sort can be handled much faster and with little or no wasted time if the trainer is willing to spend a little time teaching the dog to take directions.

A young Spaniel can be started on this phase of his education by the use of two retrieving bucks (double retrieves). A very young dog has a short span of attention, and even though one throws two bucks for a five-months-old puppy, he will probably forget about the second by the time he has brought in the first. Nevertheless, the puppy should be started on double retrieves at a very young age. It will be necessary for the trainer to walk out a few times to the second one while repeating the command "Get back!" and making, at the same time, a throwing motion with the arm. After several sessions of ten minutes duration, the young prospect will soon catch on that there is something for him to retrieve when he hears the "Get back!" command and observes the throwing motion of the trainer's arm.

As the dog learns to handle double retrieves, both of which are in about the same location, the handler can begin to toss the bucks farther and farther apart, until after two or three weeks, the throws are made in exactly opposite directions. To make the work a little more difficult, one of the bucks can be thrown while the dog is retrieving the first one. When this is done, the handler should always give the dog the direction of the second fall by pointing his arm on a plane level with the dog's head in the direction of the fall which the dog did not see. The command "Fetch!" or "Get back!" should be given at the same time. If this practice is repeated at regular intervals, the young dog soon learns to attempt a retrieve even though he has not seen any object fall. When he will do this, he is well on his way to becoming a good blind retriever.

As the dog attempts these blind retrieves, he will not always be able to find the buck immediately because of wind direction and faulty memory. A dog may be within three feet of a buck, or even a live bird, and not be able to scent it if the wind is blowing from the dog to the buck or bird. This is the reason experienced dogs will sometimes cast out in circles when searching for a shot bird. They are using the wind and have learned by trial and error that the bird may be found if they circle around and take the wind just right. This is the time to get the idea over to the dog that he can get help from the handler. The dog should be allowed to search for the unmarked buck and then his attention should be attracted by voice or whistle; the handler should then wave his arm in the direction of the fall. Repeated practice will teach the dog that he can look to the handler for help.

As the dog gets older and more experienced, it is best to give him the stop whistle, and after he has "hupped", to indicate the location of the bird with a wave of the hand. When the dog is taking directions nicely, the job is completed. Brushing up will be required from time to time and the trainer should devote five minutes to blind retrieves in the field at the conclusion of each session of bird work and shooting.

It has been proven repeatedly in the animal behavior clinics that a dog's vision is more acute on moving objects than on stationary ones. If the dog marks the fall short, the command "Get back!" should be given and a throwing motion with the arm repeated simultaneously. Persistent effort will teach the dog to respond by hunting out farther, or to the right or left, as the case may be. When the dog is going out willingly to make cold, blind retrieves (looking for a bird he did not see and without a shot from the gun), he is approaching that degree of perfection that entitles him to be described as a good blind retriever. This is a most useful attribute in hunting and one that a really polished dog should have.

One word of caution is necessary, however. All work on blind retrieving should be done in moderation and intermixed with practice in "marked" retrieving. If too much work is given on blind retrieving, it may cause some dogs to lose interest in marking and depend too much on the trainer's help in locating the bird. When this condition develops, it is said that the dog is "overtrained". A good gun dog will always show initiative and persistence at the fall of a shot bird. He should work until the handler stops him to give directions. If the dog searches for a minute or two, and then stops of his own volition and looks to the handler for help, the blind retrieving work should be discontinued for a month or two and the dog permitted to retrieve only marked falls. No help should be given to a dog while he is acting in this manner.

One way to start a dog on blind retrieves, if he was not given the work on doubles in the early stages, is to drop a dead bird behind the handler in full view of the dog (which is walking at heel). When the handler is a few yards away and down wind from the bird, the dog may be commanded to fetch, and throwing motions may be made with the arm in the direction of the bird. As the dog learns to go back a few yards and pick up the dead bird, the distance may be increased a few yards until the dog is going back as far as 50 yards for a bird which he did not see the trainer drop. Some dogs will learn to follow directly to the fall, the line of scent left by the trainer. When this occurs, the trainer should take pains to toss the bird a considerable distance to the right or left of his foot scent so the dog will have to search for it and not just follow the handler's foot scent back to the fall.

Placing dead birds or the buck in cover while the dog is concealed or otherwise unable to watch, is another way to start blind retrieving. One can also secure the help of a friend to plant dead birds or the buck in this phase of the training routine.

By the time he has learned all, or nearly all, of the actions described in the various chapters on education of the gun dog, the average Springer Spaniel will be approaching two years of age. If these various lessons have been well learned, the owner has a beautifully trained, polished, experienced gun dog which will provide many hours of pleasant recreation in the field. Both man and dog will be healthier and happier for the time spent in the outdoors and can look forward to eight or more years of good hunting together. If the trainer has devoted the time required to teach the dog everything suggested, it is quite likely that he will have joined a field trial club so that he will have an additional motive for spending more time afield with his dog. Most field trial enthusiasts shoot over their Spaniels for forty or more weeks each year, and it is debatable whether they derive more pleasure from field trials and hunting, or in the weekly training sessions with their friends. Real dyed-in-the-wool fans say it is the greatest sport in the world and will back this statement with money or action. The author is quite prone to admit that, after 50 years of such activity, he has found no reason to disagree with the above opinion.

In conclusion, it should be said that no two dogs ever respond to training in exactly the same way. It is, therefore, impossible to prescribe a training method that will fit each dog perfectly. The language barrier, which prevails among all humans, makes it impossible to explain in exact detail every individual act which the trainer must perform. It is assumed that the person interested enough to follow the routines and suggestions reported here will understand this fact. Any training routine should be mixed with an equal part of common sense, and the trainer must *always* be sure that the dog enjoys the work.

The major requirement of a good trainer is the ability to teach the dog to *respect* the trainer rather than to fear him. The various training exercises suggested are designed to promote this condition. By applying extreme force, anyone can force any dog to "hup" in five minutes. It takes much longer to *train* a dog to "hup" or to perform any other action. But the end results are much better by training than by forcing.

One should never lose sight of the fact that for every unit of force applied to a dog, there will be an equal unit of reaction. If, for example, a dog is beaten and forced to retrieve, the reaction may show up in the manner of flushing game. Dogs beaten to force steadiness may become blinkers. Dogs beaten or forced to turn on the whistle may become bolters. Thus, training, and not forcing, is the desirable method.

Some trainers who use extreme force do produce an occasional good dog, but for every good specimen they turn out, they ruin ten.

There is never an occasion when a dog should be beaten or abused. The trainer who thinks so is 50 years behind the times. One should keep this fact in mind at all times and never, never abuse a gun dog. It is wrong from the standpoint of the well-established natural laws of animal behavior and from the standpoint of acceptable human behavior. This principle was learned by actual experience and has had a good deal of thoughtful consideration and study. It is hoped that this suggestion, above all others, will be followed. It is the single greatest training aid in this book.

It is important to introduce prospective Springer gun dogs to water at an early age. The first prerequisite is to NEVER throw him in from boat or shore. The second is to start on a day when water and air are near 60 degrees or higher.

There are several ways to start. We begin by wading in shallow water and encouraging the puppy to follow us a few times until he is swimming on his own. Janet Christensen, for example, takes several dogs, puppies and children to the beach and encourages the puppies to get into the act and join the fun.

In this series of three photos, John Isaacs demonstrates a unique method. He begins by having his pretty daughter, Roselinde Isaacs Krahbutz, carry a youngster out to a bird in shallow water—a bird he has already learned to retrieve on land. When Junior grabs the bird, trainer John whistles him in to shore.

When Junior plods through the muck, he is encouraged to deliver the bird to hand without shaking, with voice and/or whistle commands. —*Photos by John Friend.*

7

Water Work

_____

ONE OF the most useful functions a Springer Spaniel can perform is to retrieve dead and wounded game from water. The dog's expert performance of this function will pay for his keep many times over, so the wise sportsman will make every effort to provide the necessary training and experience which make for good water retrieving.

If one wishes a really top duck dog, one of the Retriever breeds, particularly the Labrador Retriever, is the specialist at this work. The Retrievers have the required coat (two of them, in fact) and can stand the tough, grueling conditions that prevail in retrieving ducks and other waterfowl from icy water in freezing temperatures. However, the average United States sportsman, who can get in only a half-dozen days of duck shooting each year, will find the properly trained Springer an excellent water retriever as well as a top upland game dog.

The prospect's initial introduction to water is all important. Here is a good procedure to follow:

After the puppy is six or eight months old and is retrieving nicely from land, he should be taken for his introduction to water to a nearby pond or lake with gently sloping banks. The trainer should be equipped with waders or a bathing suit, for it will probably be necessary for him to enter the water. A nice warm sunny day in the late spring or early summer should be chosen for the comfort of both dog and man.

A boat bumper or canvas retrieving buck should be taken along, and a blank pistol, too; water work should not be started until the dog has been shot over in the field.

At first, let the puppy ramble about the banks of the lake for a short period of time, say five minutes, until he feels at home and has investigated all the strange new scents.

After the puppy has become acclimated and adjusted to this new terrain, the trainer should call him and walk out a few feet into the water.

There is a good possibility that the dog will follow and frisk around playfully in the water. If he does, he should be allowed to play and dash in and out of the water to his heart's content. If the trainer remains in water up to a depth of about six or eight inches, the dog will, too, although he may dash in and out in a playful mood.

If the dog attempts to swim, so much the better. If he makes no effort to swim, the trainer should walk out a few feet until he is in water approximately up to his knees. If the dog does not follow, he should be coaxed (not forced) to venture out this far. If he swims and wades to the trainer, he should be petted and made over as a reward for the effort.

Many young Spaniels have an instinctive liking for water and will start to swim immediately. Their first efforts are usually quite clumsy and they will splash a good deal with their front feet, which they attempt to lift out of the water with each stroke. Some encouragement by voice and petting will help build confidence and many of them enjoy the swimming from the very first experience.

If, however, the young dog exhibits any fear of water, it will be necessary to build up his confidence by making repeated trips to the pond and by letting the dog become adjusted by repeatedly coaxing him to enter as the trainer wades close to the shore. If the trainer is patient, even the most backward pupil will respond eventually to kind treatment and encouragement.

Once the dog appears to have overcome his first mild fear or uncertainty, a short retrieve should be tried in the shallow water where it is not necessary for the dog to swim. This may be on the first trip, or the fifth, depending on the pupil's response to the new experience.

When first sent to retrieve from water, the puppy should be started from the position at heel and very close to the water's edge on a gently sloping shoreline. The buck should be thrown only three or four feet and never into deep water. Because the puppy has been retrieving the buck at home in the yard, he will know immediately what is expected. It is entirely possible that the dog will dash into the water, seize the buck and deliver it to hand. If he does so, he should be praised and rewarded by voice or petting.

The retrieve should be repeated five or six times in very shallow water. Then the distance should be increased gradually, so that the puppy will have to swim a few strokes to reach the buck. After three or four successful retrieves at this distance, the lesson should be stopped for the day. It is always important to quit while the dog is still enthusiastic and enjoying the work. The trainer should then put on his walking shoes and take the dog for a brisk run in cover for some ten minutes to dry off. And it is always a good idea to check the dog's ears to insure that they are dry, for it is possible that the excess splashing resulting from dashing about in shallow water and from clumsy attempts to swim may have caused considerable water to enter the ears. Ears that are damp inside make ideal breeding places for fungus and infection which can cause trouble later. A towel or handkerchief may be used to dry out the inside of the ears if they appear wet. Do not rub—blot up the water.

The trips to the pond should be repeated at frequent intervals and the length of the retrieves gradually extended until the puppy is swimming out 30 or 40 yards. The young dog should, of course, be required to sit at heel and await the command to retrieve each time the buck is thrown. After the first two or three lessons, the dog's swimming will improve and there will be considerably less splashing with the front feet.

After the dog has learned to like the water, the blank pistol should also be used each time the dog retrieves, until an association between the sound of the shot and the thrown buck is well established. The proper sequence of action is to fire the pistol and *then* throw the buck. It is assumed, of course, that the dog has been shot over, or at least has heard the pistol discharged on land a number of times before he has taken to water.

As the dog gains confidence and is completing 40 yard retrieves with ease, the trainer should enlist the aid of a friend as he proceeds to the next phase of the training. The next step is to have the friend place himself on a point of land, or on a boat, raft, or island, 40 or 50 yards away but in full view of the dog. The friend should then fire the pistol and throw the buck high in the air, at a distance not greater than 40 yards from the dog. At the command to retrieve, the young prospect should enter the water briskly, swim out, retrieve the buck, and deliver it carefully to the trainer's hand. If the dog attempts to do anything other than to return to the trainer, a few calls on the whistle should lead him to do as he should. The distance of the retrieves can gradually be increased until the young dog is swimming 100 yards or more each time.

No lesson, however, should be extended so long that the dog appears to be getting bored or tired. It is always wise to stop while he is still keen and fresh, and never work the prospect until he tires. If trips are made repeatedly during the summer, the young dog will become an expert swimmer and will learn to love the water.

In the early water work, the trainer should stand close to the water's edge in order to take the buck from the young Spaniel, before he has a chance to put it down. Most young dogs will drop the buck immediately after they are clear of the water in order to shake the water from their coats. If the trainer stands close to the shoreline during the early lessons and accepts delivery of the buck before the dog is entirely clear of the water, it will be helpful. The distance which the trainer stands from the water's edge can be increased gradually until he is back some 10 or 15 feet.

By repeated urging and coaxing, the dog eventually can be taught to hold the buck until it is safely delivered to the trainer's hands. All dogs instinctively want to shake to remove water from their coats. With patience and plenty of encouragement, they can be trained to delay the shaking action *until after* they deliver. When the dog attempts to drop the buck to shake, the trainer can help eliminate the fault if he will run back from the water a few yards, as if he were going to leave the area. At the same time, he

In this series of six photos, professional trainer John Isaacs demonstrates techniques he employs for teaching Springers to enter water boldly and with gusto. —*Photos by John Friend.*

The prospect is teased and revved up with a live clipped wing pigeon, which is then sailed out 50 yards into the water.

Dog is released to retrieve simultaneously with thrown pigeon, with both splashing down as Springer jumps in.

Springer returns to Isaacs with live bird gently held in mouth.

The trainer has moved back several yards from water to teach dog he must deliver live bird to hand without stopping to shake. This is important to teach because a live but crippled game bird might fly or swim away if the dog stops to shake at water line.

—Continued.

The early training was successful. The Springer learned to love water retrieving and will now enter with gusto from high point of land or pier several feet above water line.

He now jumps in from flat shore line.

should warn the dog repeatedly to "Hold it!". This will help overcome the vice and will speed up the return. Every effort should be made to instill the idea in the dog's mind that he *must* deliver before shaking. If the habit of shaking before delivering the object becomes fixed, it is difficult to overcome.

There is a good practical reason for insisting on immediate delivery of the buck. If a hunting dog is sent to retrieve a crippled duck or goose, the cripple may run if it is placed on the ground while the dog stops to shake. In such cases, the cripple may take cover in the nearest patch of cattails. A keen Spaniel will, of course, go after the bird and, if it is a strong runner, there may be a time lapse of 10 or 15 minutes as the dog relocates and retrieves the bird. This is wasted time, for while the dog is chasing a cripple up and down the bank or in the water, no ducks or geese will come in to work the blocks.

A good water retriever must be taught to work through blocks or decoys without becoming tangled in the anchor lines. This phase of the Spaniel's education is accomplished by starting the dog (after he is well adjusted to the water) to retrieve a dead pigeon, pheasant, or duck.

After the Springer is handling the dead bird properly and appears to like the work, one decoy should be planted on *the shore* and the dog permitted to investigate it thoroughly. After he has sniffed and checked it over, the dog should be called to heel and sent to retrieve a thrown dead bird, so that it is necessary to pass to one side of the decoy. After a few retrieves near the land-locked decoy, it should be moved a few feet into the water, and the dead bird thrown in such a way that the dog has to pass the decoy to reach the bird. If the dog attempts to molest or retrieve the decoy, he should be scolded and told in no uncertain manner (with stern use of the word "No!"), that he is to leave it strictly alone.

A few retrieves to one side of the floating decoy are usually enough to get the idea over to the dog that he is to ignore the wooden duck and retrieve only the dead one. The trainer can then gradually increase the number of decoys to two, three, four, five, etc., but they should be placed in very shallow water and the dog always sent to retrieve to one side of the setup. The direction of the retrieves should be changed gradually until the bird or buck is thrown directly over the decoys. If the dog attempts to swim through them to reach the thrown bird, he can be warned away, by sternly repeating the word "No!".

If he persists in swimming through the middle of the decoys (they should be bunched in a small area at first), he eventually will become fouled in the anchor lines, and probably will complete a few retrieves with one or more decoys dragging behind. The stern use of the word "No!" will eventually teach the dog to give the setup a wide berth, especially after he has become fouled a few times. Getting the idea over is just a matter of patience and persistence on the part of the trainer. The application of good common sense, and the gradual introduction of each new step, will work wonders and produce excellent results with any normal Springer.

When this lesson has been mastered, the decoys can be moved further out in the lake and spread to simulate a regular setup in a duck marsh. The dead pigeon or bird can then be thrown from the island or boat and the dog sent to retrieve from the mainland with a big spread of decoys between the dog and the thrown bird. If given lots of water work, the dog will learn eventually to handle the situation. And when he does, this phase of the training is completed.

All that remains is to teach the dog to work from a blind and a boat, and to pick up a live duck. This can be done by building a small brush blind with a small hole on one side, adjacent to the spot where the dog is *always* required to sit. A few birds thrown after the blank pistol has been discharged, or a few live pigeons shot from a boat or island, soon will condition the dog to sit in the blind in the proper position to observe the proceedings and to mark the fall of the birds. He should be required to sit in one place from 10 to 15 minutes at a time, and the trainer's assistant instructed to throw the bird and fire the pistol after such a length of time has elapsed. The dog soon will learn to watch for the falling bird every time he hears the shot and eventually will be a good marker from a blind.

Training a dog to work from a boat is a relatively simple matter if it is not attempted until he has learned to retrieve from water. He should be taken for a short boat ride and required to sit in one spot in the boat. After the young prospect has been in a boat two or three times and is no longer nervous (he may be, the first time or two) a clipped-wing pigeon should be thrown from the boat while the boat is beached. The dog should then be urged to retrieve from the land-locked craft.

When he returns with the bird, the dog should be urged to enter the boat to make the delivery. Naturally, one should use a flat bottom craft with as little free board as possible. One should not attempt to work the dog from a canoe, unless he is an expert seaman and the canoe is a very beamy, stable craft. It is assumed that if this type of training is given to the dog, all duck shooting will be done from a very stable craft, one that a wet, 50-pound Springer could not capsize.

When the dog has acquired the knack of retrieving in and out of the beached or land-locked craft, it should be moved out into shallow water and the performance repeated. If the water is just deep enough to float the craft, the dog will be able to climb in after his retrieve and deliver to hand.

After the dog is working well from the boat in shallow water, the boat can be moved out to a depth of three or four feet and the performance repeated. When the dog returns to the boat with the bird, it should be taken from him while he is still in the water, and then he should be encouraged to climb into the boat. It will be necessary to coax him a good deal at first, and perhaps to render some aid by a pull on his back or the ruff of the neck. He should be rewarded by voice and petting every time he gets in the boat either with, or without, the help of the trainer. Many Springers can develop the knack of climbing into a boat with low free board by hooking their front feet over the gunwale and pumping their back feet. Some never

109

acquire the knack and will always require some human aid to perform the act. In any event, it is a great help to have a dog that will enter the water from a boat to retrieve, even if he does require some help to get back in.

It is most important and cannot be overemphasized that one should never force or throw a dog into the water from a boat. (Any dog of any breed can be taught to swim and love water if the trainer is patient and makes the lessons easy and short.) Also, a new lesson should never be attempted until the previous one has been learned carefully. One must *never* forget that a dog must not be forced to do anything. He should be trained, and he should be rewarded with a pat or a kind word for all of his successful actions *every time* he performs them. Experienced trainers develop this habit until it becomes an unconscious action on their part every time. Developing the habit will pay many dividends.

Most dogs want to please their masters. If one makes a game of all the lessons, especially in the early stages, the Springer soon will learn to look forward to the training sessions. Once an action becomes a habit, the dog can be depended upon to perform as desired. This applies to both land and water work and the wise trainer will never forget it.

Some dogs that have had a bad fright at the water never recover from it. In such cases, force training is the answer, but only as a last resort. It should *never* be attempted by the novice, and is properly employed only by a good professional or experienced amateur. Results of force training in the water or on the land are not always uniformly good. It is a risky business and should be employed only as a last resort.

Regardless of the breed, every good duck dog that is worthy of the name must learn to take directions and to complete blind retrieves on land and in the water. The reason is obvious to any duck hunter and will not be discussed here. But the technique for teaching a gun dog this most worthwhile and useful function should be started in the early training, as suggested elsewhere in the chapters on training.

If the dog has learned to perform on land as suggested previously, it is relatively simple to teach him to do the same thing in water. Most dogs that will take hand signals on land, will do so in water if given a little work. In this case, the trainer should always precede any hand signals given in the water by the "hup", or stop, whistle command. Naturally a Spaniel cannot "hup" or sit in deep water and the "hup" whistle command, in this case, is given merely to get the dog's attention. Once he looks back at the handler, the proper signal may be given to send the dog to the right or to the left or farther out. This latter command should always be accompanied by the voice command "Get back!".

If the dog does not catch on to the hand signals in water, the handler may speed up the learning process by tossing a small stone in the desired direction as he waves the dog to the right or left or orders him to go farther out. This practice is usually not necessary, except in extreme cases, and should be discontinued after a few sessions in order that the dog will not grow to expect the stone-tossing act each time he is sent for a blind retrieve in the water.

Blind retrieves and other difficult types of retrieves are taught in great detail to all of the Retriever breeds. They perform to perfection and all laymen and gun dog people are constantly amazed at the skill they demonstrate both in land and water work. Spaniels can learn to perform equally well, and do so every day, but usually not with the finish and polish that is required of a high class Retriever gun dog.

If each step has been followed as suggested, and the young dog has not been started on a new lesson before the earlier one was mastered from water, blind, or boat, through decoys and in open or marshy water, he should now be a good retriever. It only remains now to try out the dog's new skills and to develop them fully by shooting lots of fat mallards over him. One should keep one eye on the dog on the first few hunting trips, and correct at once any slackness which deviates—even slightly—from the routine learned in the summer training. From much hunting experience with wild birds, the dog will learn to hunt for cripples on the banks of rivers and streams, and to work out the cattails and wild rice beds when a strong cripple attempts to hide. He will also learn to pursue, and eventually capture, a diving cripple. And when he has successfully done so, there won't be enough money in America to buy him.

As a final step in the water training procedure, a few domestic mallards should be procured from a farmer or a poultry market. The dog should first retrieve a dead duck from land a few times and then try it from water. If the results are good, the dog may go on to the next phase of the procedure. The legs and the wings of one of the ducks should be shackled with a light cord. The duck should then be tossed into the water and the dog permitted to retrieve it alive a few times. He will need this experience to enable him to handle cripples during the shooting season. If the trainer was fortunate enough to get a diving duck, it will teach the dog much about this type of behavior which wing tipped mallards sometimes exhibit.

In any event, if the dog handles the live ducks in good fashion, the one remaining requirement is a blustery, windy day when the duck season opens. Such a day will guarantee that both trainer and the dog will have themselves a ball.

If the shooting is good, two or three trips to the trainer's favorite duck marsh will finish out the dog's education to this type of shooting. If the ducks are not working, the trainer can call a few crows to test his shooting eye and the dog's retrieving ability. In any event, he now has a trained duck dog.

A Springer clearing a fence as he retrieves a live pheasant. Note the firm but soft grip by which this dog executes a perfect carry.

NFC Micklewood Scud, a truly great, stylish performer. Owned by Armforth Kennels and handled by Steve Studnicki to double National titles and one 3rd. He was a producer as well as a classy winner and sired several winners.

112

8

Training Procedures
To Correct Faults

THERE are any number of faults which Springer gun dogs may display. A few of the more common ones will be discussed in this chapter. But before considering them, keep foremost in mind that it is much simpler to train a dog properly in the first place than it is to correct a fault. The evidence to support this fact was revealed several years ago by the animal research people at Cornell University. In their studies, they learned that the old adage, "You can't teach an old dog new tricks", was not true. You *can* teach an old dog new tricks (correct a learned or acquired fault), but it requires ten times as much effort or units of energy to reeducate the dog as was expended in learning the trick (improper act or fault) in the first place. This most valuable contribution to the knowledge of animal behavior must be utilized fully by the trainer who desires to correct a fault in a gun dog.

The most common faults of Springer gun dogs fall into two broad categories. They are (1) those faults or characteristics which are inherited, and (2) those faults or characteristics which are acquired.

Four of the most common inherited faults are: lack of desire to hunt; unwillingness to accept training kindly; poor nose; and, perhaps, the tendency towards hard mouth. Five of the most common acquired faults are gun-shyness; blinking; hunting out of control; breaking shot and flush.

It is possible for a dog to acquire other bad habits which render him unsuitable as a reliable gun dog. But limits of space preclude a discussion of other than the most important ones.

1. Inherited Faults

The worst possible fault that a prospective gun dog can have is the lack of desire to hunt. This condition is to be found in all breeds, and all strains within the breeds, but fortunately it is the exception rather than the rule in Springers (at least in the working strains). The owner of a new puppy should not expect him to start hunting immediately after he is put down in cover. The desire to hunt is an instinct, and it develops slowly in some bloodlines—faster in others. It must be given a chance to manifest itself in the dog, however, by repeated contacts with game. As a rule, no puppy will hunt the first time he is taken into the field, but a dog of almost any breed will learn to hunt if given full opportunity to develop his instincts to do so.

If a young dog between the ages of six months and a year is put on suitable game (birds and rabbits) 15 or 20 times, he will, if normal, eventually put his nose to the ground and start to search for more game to find and chase. If he does not do so, the owner had best consult a professional or good amateur trainer and ask for advice. If an older dog between the ages of one and two years exhibits no interest in hunting after he has been in close proximity to a number of game birds, rabbits, or planted pigeons (say 30 or 40), it would be wise to consult an experienced dog man for advice. If it is determined that the dog has little or not interest in hunting, he should be disposed of promptly to someone looking for a house pet, and be replaced with a dog from a proven hunting strain.

One of the worst things that can happen to any sportsman is to have a gun dog with a poor nose. Fortunately, this does not occur too frequently, but there is little that can be done about it when it does occur. All experienced dog people know that a puppy or Spaniel of any age must first learn to use his nose before a decision can be made as to whether he has a good one or a poor one. According to David Lorenz, of Barrington, Illinois, who has trained gun dogs of all breeds, about half of a dog's scenting ability is in his head. In other words, a dog not only must be born with a good nose, but also must learn to use it.

A young puppy, when he first strikes the scent of game, will often make several stabbing motions in different directions. This is perfectly normal conduct in a green puppy and the trainer should not be discouraged if the dog fails to locate positively the first five or ten times he comes in contact with game. After considerable experience, the dog will be more positive and will go directly to the bird once he takes the scent.

Young dogs are usually not able to follow the trail or scent line of birds, or rabbits either, until some experience has been acquired. They will leave the trail after following it for a few feet or yards, and fail to produce. This is not a fault, for much experience is required for a Spaniel to learn to trail and "catch up" with a running pheasant or rabbit. Most can and do learn it, if given the experience.

It should be remembered that in the late spring and summer, when cover is green, a dog's scenting ability will decrease as much as fifty percent.

114

The same is true even in the autumn, if there has been a long dry spell.

If other dogs appear to scent and find game, but the prospect being trained cannot do so after long and often repeated attempts, the dog should be disposed of and a new prospect acquired. Lack of ability to scent may be inherited or can be the result of a disease such as distemper. Regardless of the reason, it is likely that no improvement will be made, and the dog will be better off as a pet in the home of some friend or neighbor.

One of the most controversial subjects among Spaniel field people is the question of hard mouth. It goes without saying, however, that the Spaniel has a hard mouth if he picks up a dead bird and mangles the carcass to the point that it is not fit for the table. The question which disturbs field trial fans is the dog (and it is not a rare occurrence) which catches a live pheasant or pigeon, and kills the bird while carrying it in to the handler. It is argued by some that this should not be held against the dog because it could never happen in actual hunting. There are others who feel that even though the bird is not damaged enough to ruin it for the table, the dog should still be penalized. Most judges follow a middle ground and assess no penalty unless the bird shows considerable evidence of crushed ribs or a crushed backbone—always the true mark of a real hard-mouthed dog. Mr. Charles Alington wrote a most interesting chapter on hard mouth in his very excellent book, which should be read by all trainers.

There is some evidence to indicate that the *tendency* toward hard mouth is an inherited trait. This is by no means a certainty, but it has been observed that certain Spaniel strains have produced several dogs through as many as five generations which exhibit a tendency toward the fault. For this reason, it would appear that the fault might have some genealogical background. Be that as it may, the best and only positive cure for a genuine case of hard mouth is to prevent it before it develops. This may be done by thoroughly conditioning carrying reflexes until a firmly established habit pattern of quick pickup and fast delivery becomes second nature to the dog. A. P. Moecher, one of the pioneer Springer fanciers in the Middle West, worked out a system for conditioning a dog's retrieving reflexes to the desired degree. His system is described in the chapter in "Preliminary Training of the Gun Dog".

Once a dog acquires the fault of crushing the backbone or rib structure of birds while retrieving, it is most difficult to overcome the habit. Corrective measures may be instituted by preparing a canvas jacket, to which carpet tacks are attached, and requiring the dog to retrieve a dead bird which has been wrapped in the jacket. The results are never positive, although this may work in some cases. Occasionally, a Spaniel that has developed the fault will gradually improve his carry if he has lots of game killed for him. This is not always true, though, and cannot be relied upon 100 percent. Sometimes working the dog in the yard with a clipped-wing pigeon will produce results if the trainer follows the procedure of offering the bird to the dog and taking stern action if the bird is mangled.

Requiring the dog to hold first a dead pigeon, and later a live pigeon, in his mouth in the yard for five or ten minutes at a time will sometimes produce results. If a month or two are devoted to the training, a trainer with patience and understanding may be able to "talk" the dog into holding the bird tenderly and retrieving the same way.

Force breaking to retrieve will also produce results in some cases, but is a procedure best handled by the professional or experienced amateur trainer rather than the novice. The author is not aware of any sure-fire system except that of properly conditioning the dog's reflexes in the beginning.

It is most interesting to note that early writers refer to hard mouth, and it would appear that the fault has been prevalent for many, many years. It is entirely possible that it may have been a desirable trait when Spaniels were used extensively for hawking. Early writers mention that it was the function of the dog to flush the game for the hawk and then be on hand when the hawk dropped to the ground with its prey, in order to hold it until the hunter arrived on the scene. When large birds were the victims of the hawk, it stands to reason that one service a Spaniel could render would be to attack and kill if the hawk had not previously done so.

Fortunately, hard mouth does not appear too often in modern Springers, and most trainers will not be involved in corrective measures.

2. Acquired Faults in Gun Dogs

Perhaps one of the greatest faults that a gun dog can have is the acquired fault of blinking, which is usually man made. Blinking is the disgusting action of a dog that refuses to acknowledge game by flushing or by eagerly questing it. An exhibition of blinking may consist of anything from a slight bit of bird-shyness to an outright refusal to go near a bird. Some blinkers will circle a bird repeatedly, while old, confirmed cases will even avoid a bird they scent, and actually hunt in the opposite direction.

In a human, an act similar to blinking might be called a perversion. It comes under this same classification in gun dogs. It is the worst fault that a gun dog can have outside of downright refusal to hunt.

If a young gun dog exhibits *any* tendency toward bird-shyness (such as a reluctance to flush, or circling a bird repeatedly) the danger signals are flying, and it is time to institute corrective measures. This usually consists of putting the dog in the kennel for a month or two and eliminating all training. At the end of the rest period, training may be resumed with clipped-wing pigeons. The dog should be encouraged to catch the pigeons and to chase rabbits to his heart's desire. When he retrieves the birds or chases a rabbit, he should be made over and petted profusely. If he refuses to give chase, the trainer can set an example by running after the game and exhibiting great animation and excitement.

The clipped-wing birds can be thrown for retrieving in the yard and when the bird flutters and attempts to escape, most young blinkers will overcome their perversion enough to give chase and to show some interest. Such action must be encouraged and every aid given to the dog to restore his confidence. Sometimes blinking occurs in a very young puppy which is introduced to game too early. The sound of the pheasant or pigeon beating its wings as it flushes may frighten a shy young dog. One solution here is to keep the dog away from game until he is older. Good results are usually obtained with clipped-wing birds in the yard if the prospect is six or more months old. Younger dogs should be allowed to mature before they are exposed to game again if they show fright the first time or two they are in contact with a flushing bird. Exposing the young blinker to birds gradually and giving him much praise will serve to build up his confidence. Also, working him with another dog may prove beneficial. Blinking that results from training methods which are too severe or too advanced may be cured if corrective measures are started before the fault becomes fixed as a habit.

The terrible fault of gun-shyness is usually considered a man-made one, although some animal research people came up with the theory a few years ago that it might be inherited. Very few experienced trainers will agree with this theory, however. A dog becomes gun-shy when confused and thus fails to comprehend why the gun is fired. If one follows the suggestion outlined in Section I of the chapter on preliminary training, the chances are 100 to 1 that gun-shyness will never be a problem.

When the condition is observed, the first thing to do is to stop all work and to return the dog to the kennel for a few days' rest. The trainer should think back and try to recall the events that may have caused the confusion in the dog's mind. Naturally, repetition of the events that frightened and confused the dog should be avoided at all cost. If the subject is only six or eight months old, the hand clapping procedure outlined in the chapter on preliminary training should be started, and mixed with kind treatment. If the trainer is persistent, this will probably help overcome the dog's fear of the noise. This statement is based not only on practical experience, but also on sound psychological fact. The simultaneous application of two stimuli will serve to condition the dog to accept the lesser, which in this case will be the hand clap. If the dog really loves to retrieve, the trainer can then progress by easy stages to the use of the cap pistol (at feeding time or when the dog is retrieving).

If enough time is taken, and the lessons are carefully and widely spaced, the dog will respond as desired and in a month or two may be introduced gradually to the 20 gauge shotgun again. If the prospect is older and exhibits fear or nervousness when the shotgun stage has been reached, he should be taken back to the yard, started over with the hand clapping, and worked up progressively through the cap pistol, the .22 blanks, and the shotgun.

If the gun-shy dog is older and represents an extreme case of gun-shyness, the condition may be corrected by the old and often used method of discharging a cap pistol or .22 blank at feeding time. The theory behind this method is the well-established psychological principle of associating

117

two stimuli (one good and one bad) simultaneously. The bad becomes associated with the good in the dog's mind and the fault is thus corrected or overcome.

To introduce this procedure, food is offered to the dog and a cap pistol is fired immediately when he starts to eat. If he leaves the feed pan and cowers in his kennel, the trainer should speak a few encouraging words and urge the dog to eat. When he again starts to eat, the pistol should again be fired. This is usually enough to drive the dog away from the food for good, and the trainer should then remove the pan and offer the animal no more food until the next day. At this time the above procedure should be repeated and the same action followed. If the dog refuses to eat after the cap pistol has been fired a time or two, the trainer must harden his heart and again remove the food.

Usually, after three or four days the dog's hunger will overcome his fear of the gun and he will gulp his food rapidly even if the cap pistol is fired several times. The lesson should be repeated each time the dog is fed until he has learned to eat without flinching. This may require several weeks or months, but the system is sure and will work if the trainer is persistent.

As a salve to the trainer's conscience, it may be said that while this method is severe, it will rehabilitate the dog to a normal life. Gun-shy dogs go through life flinching from automobile backfires or other common noises, and their existence is one of abject fear and anguish. Realizing that he is helping to rehabilitate the dog to live a normal fear-free life may help the trainer harden his heart in the early stages. It is a cinch that the dog will eventually become hungry enough to eat no matter how often the gun is fired. And that is the secret of the cure.

The ability to mark accurately the "fall" of a bird and to retrieve it with dispatch is a most valuable attribute of any gun dog. Springer Spaniels that refuse to retrieve are only performing half of the job. Their refusal to perform this function is usually due to the fact that they have not been trained to retrieve or because they associate some unpleasant experience with the act. The first cause is relatively simple to overcome, but the latter is more difficult.

If a young puppy refuses to retrieve, the trainer should first make sure that some member of the household is not throwing sticks or other objects and failing to follow through by accepting the object when the dog returns with it. After this possibility has been eliminated, the puppy should be started on the routine suggested in the chapter on preliminary training. If the dog shows no interest in running after a thrown object, such as an old glove or the buck, it will be necessary for the trainer to spend considerable time in an attempt to arouse interest. A towel can be dragged along the ground and the puppy allowed to pounce on it. When he becomes interested, the towel should be knotted once or twice, then tossed for the dog while he is in full pursuit. The trainer should never engage in a tug of war with the puppy but should tease him just enough to arouse his interest and then throw the object slowly. The procedure outlined in the chapter on preliminary training can then be followed.

If the Springer has not been started on retrieving until he is two or three years of age, he may exhibit little or no interest at first. His interest may be aroused by having another dog retrieve in very close proximity to the backward pupil.

A number of years ago, a friend brought a Springer bitch about seven years old to the author's home. Patty was a good hunter but would not retrieve. She would run to the bird and stand over it until her owner came to pick it up. On the day in question, repeated attempts were made to get Patty to retrieve a dead pigeon. She refused point-blank. Several other Springers were then brought out and permitted to retrieve in the presence of Patty. After fifteen minutes of this work, the bird was thrown and Patty retrieved it promptly. Six weeks later she was a good retriever.

It is a well-established fact that dogs can learn certain acts by observation. It is also a well-established fact that dogs are subject to jealousy. They can learn to hunt, to retrieve, and to react in certain desired (also undesired) ways by imitating the actions of another dog. Experienced trainers take full advantage of this fact in working with their dogs.

If a Springer suddenly stops retrieving after he has been performing the act for some time, the trouble may usually be diagnosed as resulting from some bad experience which the dog has associated with the act. In such cases, it is probably well to permit the dog to rest for a period of several weeks. He can then be started on the basic or pre-retrieving routine outlined in the chapter on preliminary training. Plenty of patience and copious use of kind words and petting will usually bring him around in time. The trainer should be cautioned against giving up too early. Any dog can be taught to retrieve if the trainer is persistent and kind. However, the dog with his tail between his legs and a hangdog expression is an indication that the trainer has used too much force—unconscious force, perhaps, but still too much. The trainer must relax and make the training a game. Since every dog can be taught to retrieve, it is the trainer's fault in most cases if the dog fails to respond.

Hunting out of control, which means working well out of gunshot range, is usually the result or lack of early training. When a Springer prospect works in such a manner, two simple corrective measures are required: (1) he should be worked only into the wind for a month or two; and (2) he should be taught to turn on the whistle. The training technique to teach both are outlined in detail in the chapter on intermediate field work. If a dog will turn on the whistle *every* time and has learned the simple hand signals, it is an easy matter to get him to hunt within range in the desired pattern. The use of the whistle and the work into the wind alone will usually produce the required pattern of work. The trainer must be sure, however, that the dog knows and understands the whistle signal perfectly, and then must insist that he respond.

The veteran sportsman Tom Mofield and his father with limit of Illinois geese retrieved by a Springer gun dog that loved its work. — *Curtis.*

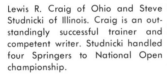

Lewis R. Craig of Ohio and Steve Studnicki of Illinois. Craig is an outstandingly successful trainer and competent writer. Studnicki handled four Springers to National Open championship.

The Springer's ancestors were hunting dogs 500 years before field trials were introduced in England, and John Isaacs hunted upland game with Springers before he became a noted professional field trialer. Here John and Springer Lady Bird of Stoke exhibit a bag of Spanish hare taken while John was a GI stationed in Spain.

Breaking to shot and/or wing is a serious fault and a clear indication that the dog's early training in the yard has not been learned thoroughly. Even though the culprit may be of mature age, the best solution to the problem is to return to the early yard training and to progress along the lines previously suggested in the several chapters on training. If they have little or no work between the annual shooting seasons, many hunting Springers develop the habit of breaking to shot or wing after having been steady. This may be due to the fact that the owner relaxed his efforts and permitted the dog to retrieve a few times without the command. If such is the case, a refresher course is in order, with a new start being made on the early yard work. Usually the desired results can be obtained by a day or two devoted to each step, if the trainer is firm and does not permit the dog to complete any retrieve in the yard or field until ordered to do so.

There are several electronic devices on the market consisting of a special dog collar by which the trainer can deliver by remote control a light electrical shock to a dog that is some distance away. Undoubtedly such devices have merit in special cases, but their use is NOT recommended for the novice trainer. They should be used sparingly, and only by a professional or experienced amateur who understands principles of animal psychology and the temperament of the individual dog.

There are other faults that a dog may acquire. Most of them can be corrected by going back to the fundamentals and treating the dog just as if he were to be started on his early training again. Not as much time need be spent on each step as with a brand new prospect, but each lesson should be repeated until the dog is exhibiting the desired qualities of obedience, control, and enthusiasm. The absence of any one is fatal to a top gun dog.

Mr. and Mrs. Harold Jones with FTC Sir Cricket after completing a series at a National Trial under judge Jim Dodson, who looks on from the left rear.

Big, bold FC Saighton's Superspeed, noted sire as well as fine performer. Imported from England by Dr. John Riepenhoft, who handled him to U.S. title. Noted professional John Isaacs recognized Superspeed's prepotent ability as a sire and acquired him. He sired 374 puppies—some became U.S. and Canadian champions and trial winners, and a number of others became fine hunting dogs. —*John Friend*.

Mrs. Evelyn Monte VanHorn, well-known writer and sportswoman, chats with Aidan Roark as FTC Rex On The Rocks listens intently. Roark was a top U.S. polo player before he became interested in Springer gun dogs.

9

Training Aids
By Successful Trainers

TRAINING ENGLISH SPRINGER SPANIELS to become smooth, polished, effective gun dogs is both a skill and an art. And while practical experience in the field is the principal way to acquire the skill and develop the art, exposure to the opinions of several trainers can broaden one's perspective by suggesting other methods and techniques for achieving desired results. We have therefore asked a number of successful professional and amateur sportsmen and sportswomen who train Springers as a vocation or as a hobby—all but one of whom are personally known to us—to contribute a few basic ideas on training gun dogs. We will outline their qualifications briefly.

MRS. C. A. (Janet) CHRISTENSEN:

Janet Christensen, a graduate veterinarian and the wife of an Oregon ophthalmologist, who is also a successful amateur trainer, has handled 16 Springers to their championships, one of which won four National titles during a twelve-month period. They were a National Open in the U.S. and in Canada, and in two U.S. successive National Amateur titles. We list the substance of some of her training philosophy and procedures.

1. "It is more desirable to show a dog how to perform correctly repeatedly than to trick or force him into making the correct response."
2. "Minimal force should be applied only as a last resort and only if the dog knows why he is being punished."
3. "The use of a blind hallway is excellent for starting a seven week old puppy on retrieving as he can travel in only one direction, back to the trainer."

Dr. C. A. Christensen with double National Open Champion Dewfield Bricksclose Flint. The Doctor is the other half of that winning Christensen husband-and-wife team with two National Open Championships, a National Amateur Championship, and another amateur placement in Open. The team record is not complete, but *The Springer Bark* reported in 1973 that the Christensen team had placed Springers more than 100 times in AKC-recognized field trials. —*Andy Shoaff.*

E. W. (Ernie) Wunderlich with fine FC Chrishall Rover, who earned high point field Springer of the Year in 1980 with 4 firsts, 1 second and 2 third placements. Wunderlich, dean of the U.S. amateurs, was shooting over his Springers in the late 1920s. He was a charter member of the first two Illinois Springer clubs, co-organizer of the first U.S. training class for Springer owners, owner of 8 field champions (two of which were National champions), co-judge of several dozen field trials including two Nationals and holder of a British shooting record for 20 consecutive grouse kills.

4. "The next step in teaching retrieving is to take the puppy for walks in shorter cover where he is only required to fetch a canvas buck and come when called. When this lesson is mastered, substitute live clipped wing pigeons for the canvas buck. Slackness at any level is corrected by rushing out to the prospect and applying a shake or two of the collar and a few harsh words."

5. "The trainer will find it easier to control the youngster for any work in the field, including retrieving, if he is always worked into the wind."

6. "Puppies are steadied to wing and shot after chasing only a dozen or so birds. No mechanical devices are used since they have learned to respond correctly from early yard training."

7. "Quartering is taught by handler zigging with the dog which is always worked into the wind."

8. "Young dogs are started on released pheasant in the early fall and are expected to be steady to wing and shot and to retrieve only on command as a result of previous training in the yard and field."

E. W. ("Ernie") WUNDERLICH:

Ernie Wunderlich is an outstanding amateur trainer, successful hunter, and world class wing shot. He hunted his Springers on upland game and waterfowl in Illinois, Wisconsin, and Canada several years before becoming a charter member, founder of the English Springer Spaniel F.T. club of Illinois in 1934. He has owned eight field champion Springers, two of which were National champions, broken a 100 year old British shooting record and established a new one for cleanly shooting 20 consecutive driven grouse in Scotland, judged several dozen field trials including two nationals, "invented" a system of teaching spaniels obedience retrieving and achieved recognition as an outstanding authority on Springer gun dogs.

1. "The necessity to frequently correct a Springer gun dog in the field is positive evidence the dog has not been properly schooled in the yard."

2. "To obtain proper response and avoid confusion a trainer should always use the exact same commands to direct and control his dog. This will speed up learning and increase memory span."

3. "It is desirable training technique to arrange a playtime for a gun dog a few minutes each day or at least a couple times each week when the dog is on his own and not subject to commands or direction of any kind."

4. "No one can learn how to train a dog by reading a book because no two dogs will respond or progress exactly alike. However, seeking other opinions as outlined in several books can be helpful in defining goals and suggesting various ways to reach them."

5. "Though yard work is the basis for discipline and immediate response to all commands, it is the ABCs of dog training."

6. "When a Springer stops while hunting to command, flush or shot it is better procedure to walk out on him before sending him on to hunt then to call into heel before doing so."

Jess and Dominique Sekey with 1983 National Open and National Amateur Champion Saighton's Scout (second from left), a double win only achieved on three previous occasions, one of which was by Scout's sire, Saighton's Scud. Jess and his wife Dominique are both outstanding amateur handlers and trainers.

Colorado Springers and their owners at end of a training session. L. to r.: Jim Sullivan with Raider and Gualt; Hugh Eggert with Crown; Dominique Sekey with Streak, Snow, Chef; Rich Kloss with Bell and Scrapper. Colorado hunters can work their Springers on pheasant, partridge and waterfowl in the grain country east of Denver, or on ruffed grouse in the mountains to the West. These fine Springers can fill a game bag as well as continue to win trials.

126

WILLIAM F. ("Bill") BROWN:

Bill Brown is the long time editor of the American Field, member of Trial Hall of Fame and recognized authority on the several breeds of gun dogs.

1. Bill Brown's remark that the fine pointing dogs of America, because of their fine selective breeding, need no encouragement to hunt and only mild training restraint, and that this demonstrates their great ability as gun dogs, might also be said about field bred Springers.

W. T. ("Cotton") PERSHALL:

Cotton Pershall, long time trainer and kennel manager for the late John Olin, trained Retrievers which won eight National Championships, five of which he handled himself. Three of the Retrievers he trained were schooled so thoroughly that their owners were able to handle them to a national title.

1. When a reporter asked Cotton for his magic formula for training and handling, he replied, "There is no magic formula; it is mostly blood, sweat and tears. Patience is the main thing and repetition. You show them the stuff you have already shown them over and over again. There are no shortcuts."

JOHN KENT—legendary British trainer:

John Kent handled and won with a Clumber Spaniel on his first trial in 1905. By 1914 he had scored 55 placements in British trials with several breeds. Before his death in 1976, he advised he had trained 1,000 dogs including sheep and herd dogs. Several of the Springers bred in his kennels came to America and won trials here.

1. John Kent said: "It is easier to preserve a canine saint than to reform a canine sinner."
2. "It requires dedication and hard work to produce good dogs. Gimmicks never work."
3. "Even with the proper amount of work and training, you can't be sure your dog will be a winner, but without it you can be sure he won't."
4. "Luck in a field trial is a bonus."
5. "You can beat a lot out of a dog, but you can't beat anything into him."

A. P. ("Art") MOECHER

Art Moecher was a founder and first secretary of the first two Springer clubs in the U.S., west of the Hudson River (in Illinois). He organized and operated the first training class for Springer owners in the U.S. He trained and handled the second Springer Field Champion in the West. He bred good Springers, sending his best bitches to Henry Ferguson's studs at Fishers Island. He sold the offspring for a very modest sum to hunters and field trialers only.

127

1. Art Moecher believed that the most important characteristic of a good Springer gun dog was good mental balance. Without it he felt no Spaniel could qualify as a good gun dog, regardless of nose, hunting desire and bottom.

JOHN ISAACS

John Isaacs is a successful Ohio professional all breed gun dog trainer who specializes in Springers. He handled Springers which scored 180 wins in Open and other stakes between 1971 and 1983. In his eagerness to learn, he traveled from Army duty in Spain to England, and at every opportunity studied British dogs and training and breeding methods. He probably breeds more good field Springers than anyone in America. He found time to do some historical research for us on the Spanish origin of Springers. He has trained several hundred gun dogs for hunters and field trialers in his Ohio kennels.

1. John has said, in substance, that it is necessary to get the dog's confidence, attention and response with the least amount of applied force. "Never hassle a dog to where he is weary."

2. "A good nose is the number one attribute of a Springer gun dog."

3. "Superior intelligence is of equal importance as it requires brains for a nose to be used to the best advantage."

4. "Intense hunting desire comes next. A good dog must burn with desire and love of hunting."

5. "Class and speed are of great importance. A Springer gun dog which has the ability to perform at top speed and unusual accuracy is a class individual and far superior to the individual which performs routinely at half speed."

6. "Other important and desirable attributes include good temperament, willing response to command, and the ability to accept training kindly. The Springer gun dog which responds willingly, naturally, and boldly with manners is far superior to the individual which sulks and/or performs mechanically."

DOROTHY MOORLAND HOOPER

Ms. Hooper is the author of the fine British book "The Popular Springer Spaniel." She writes that the Springer in England is the handyman of the gun dog breeds because of their versatility in handling all types of upland game and waterfowl. Her well-written book outlines the activity of Springers in Africa, Italy, France, Sweden, Spain, Holland, Australia, New Zealand, and of course the British Isles. She reports that the breed is used for all types of game in Australia and New Zealand, where they shoot rabbits all summer and quail and ducks all winter over their Springers. Ms. Hooper shoots over her Springers, handles them in trials and shows them on the bench.

CLARENCE J. PFAFFENBERGER

We first learned of Clarence Pfaffenberger's interest in canine behavior from conversations with him when we judged his Cocker Spaniels during field trials in California and Oregon in the 1930s and 1940s. Later when on duty with the Navy in San Francisco, we helped him collect prospective war dogs donated to Dogs For Defense and continued our discussions on canine behavior. After the war, Pfaffenberger's association with a California organization which trained dogs for the blind motivated him to travel 4,000 miles to Bar Harbor, Maine for advanced research and study in behavior at Jackson Memorial Institute. The quotes here are from his book, "The New Knowledge of Dog Behavior", which is must reading for anyone who trains dogs for any purpose.

1. "Less than four out of ten dogs, not specifically bred, selected, and tested as prospective guide dogs failed to make the grade after training. However, puppies which scored high on tests for desirable characteristics as did their parents, developed into successful guide dogs at a high 94% success level."

2. "Puppies are unable to learn anything before they are 21 days old. After this date their brain has developed and they are able to see, smell, hear, walk and learn."

3. "A dog which has 'learned to learn' at the most productive age for learning (3 weeks of age to 7 weeks of age) can continue to learn at a later age. In other words, you can teach an old dog new tricks if he was trained to learn at the most productive age."

4. "Training during the ages of 5 weeks of age and 12 weeks of age will be learned faster and retained longer."

5. "Puppies must be socialized and humanized between ages of 21 days and 7 weeks to achieve normal relationships with other dogs and with humans."

6. "Seven weeks of age is the best time to wean puppies and send them off to a new owner."

The 7-year-old really fine hunting Springer, Duke of Blenheim, delivers a released hen pheasant to sportsman-owner John Friend, as he is tuned up for the coming Ohio pheasant season. Friend, a member of the Ohio State University staff, is an excellent photographer.

Two fine West Coast pheasant dogs owned by Sam Inkley. One is an old line field bred Cocker and the other a Springer—top hunting dogs that could win at trials, too. The spaniels flushed and retrieved the several limits of birds for several hunters.

10

How To Hunt Game
and Waterfowl with
a Springer Spaniel

T HE Springer Spaniel gun dog is equally at home on land or water, and on fur or feathers. He is, however, the pheasant dog *par excellence,* and has no peers (nor has he had for the past several hundred years) in this hunting. His greatest usefulness on upland game is as a beater who will sweep back and forth on a 50 to 80 yard front, five to ten yards in front of the gun or guns. A well-trained Springer will drop (sit) to flush and/or, shot and retrieve only on command. He is equally at home on native game or when used on released game at a shooting preserve.

The Springer Spaniel is, in our opinion based on considerable experience with the several hunting breeds, the top pheasant dog in the United States. When hunted on native pheasant during the best shooting hours (the hour after sunrise or the three hours before sunset) when birds are feeding, he should always be worked into the wind when possible. This will keep him closer to the hunter and require less handling by whistle or voice. Stubble fields or picked corn fields are natural feeding places for pheasant, but difficult for the quartering dog to handle since birds can see the hunter for 100 yards or more and are likely to run rather than hide. Under such conditions one or two hunting companions should be stationed at the far end of the field to "block". Running birds or those which the dog and gun flush wild can be taken by the blockers. There will always be a bird or two which skulks along the fence or ditch at the end of the field and a good Springer will use his nose and push them out fast as well as those which attempt to hide or duck back.

Bill Brauer and noted outdoor writer David Michael Duffy with bag of 12 Canadian sharptail grouse, flushed and retrieved by Duffy's favorite Springer, Flirt. Duffy's book, *Hunting Dog Know-How*, has no equal.

Joe Crooks and Virginia Diegel with 12 Oregon ducks proudly retrieved by the still wet Sunny of Silvercreek. Springers are fine water dogs.

In light cover, running birds will require some handling to keep the eager Springer within gun range. He will have a nose full of feathers and want to go. Spaniels should quarter under such conditions, but if the temptation is great, because of good scenting, let him get out to medium gun range (30 yards), then sit him down with one blast of the whistle and hurry to him. Then cast him out to resume his trailing of the hot scent. Sometimes it will require several stops and fast walking before the Spaniel can flush in gun range.

After the first day of the pheasant season the birds become wary and often take to heavy wet sloughs where movement is difficult for Spaniel and man. In such conditions give the dog his head and don't insist on quartering. The rough ground will usually enable the hunter to keep up as the dog zigzags after the hopping birds, who may circle, duck back, or use numerous tricks to avoid flying. An experienced dog will eventually put the bird up for a shot.

Soil bank or uncut hay fields are ideal spots to work a Springer. Pheasant roost in such places and rest in them during the middle of the day. However, an hour or two after sunrise and before sunset are the most productive hours to hunt.

When working pheasants in standing corn, it is usually the wise procedure to make the dog heel as the several members of the shooting party spread out and drive down the field. When within 50 yards of the end, cast the Spaniel to the right or left and keep him quartering. Often he will raise a bird or two in the fence row at the end, but if game is exceptionally wary and wild, a blocker stationed at the end will usually get a shot.

Hunting doves with a Spaniel conserves game, because the dog will find most, if not all, of the birds that are dropped, whereas 50% is par for the dogless dove shooter. An ideal spot is the edge of a feed patch, (stubble field, picked corn, etc.) adjacent to a water hole. Pre-season cruising will enable the smart hunter to locate several such spots that doves are using. When the flight pattern is determined, the gunner should conceal himself in a fence row or against a tree, with the Springer sitting at heel. When the morning or evening flight begins it will be fast and furious, and it's well to keep the dog at heel until there are several birds on the ground before sending him to retrieve. He will learn to remember the last one or two downed but may need direction on others. Doves will seldom flair from a moving dog, so don't worry if Rover is too excited to wait until several are downed. When doves want to come in to feed, or to a water hole, nothing can really keep them out—early in the season. The experienced Springer will learn to search the skies, and when he sees incoming flights or pairs his furious tail action and eyes will reveal the fact.

Spaniels have a special love for rabbits which are found in fence rows, briar patches adjacent to cover and feed, brush piles, hay, grain, or stubble fields. When hunting open fields, keep the dog quartering and work into the wind. Let the dog work the brush piles but stay on the opposite side. When hunting fence rows, let the dog work the fence line for 10-20 yards,

Oregon sportsman Paul Diegel prepares to give FTC Mahogany Kit and trial winner Sunny Weather of Silver Creek a workout in water retrieving. This is an excellent way to keep gun dogs in condition during hot summer weather. —*Dittebrandt.*

FTC Timpanagos Papaya retrieving a mallard duck to James R. Dobson.

then swing him out with hand or whistle to the right or left. He may pick up a rabbit away from the fence. Such tactics will help keep him in gun range. It's wise to keep the dog moving, rather than let him potter with a low head on last night's stale scent. An experienced Spaniel will let the hunter know soon enough when he strikes hot ground scent. When working a Springer on any type of game, keep him MOVING. When he strikes hot scent of either fur or feathers, his head will go down and he'll be off like a shot. When close enough to take the body scent, his head will come up as he dives in to flush. If permitted to potter on old scent much trouble can result.

Shooting game birds in timber with a Spaniel is great sport. We will describe the Springers work on woodcock and ruffed grouse as if they were the same bird, even though their habits are slightly different. In early autumn shooting of either bird, they are likely to be found in medium to heavy timber and underbrush. Since it is difficult to keep track of an eager Spaniel in timber, some hunters "bell" their dogs. Spaniels achieved great renown as woodcock dogs in Britain in the Middle Ages and with experience can still fill the game bag.

The dog should beat the cover in timber as he does in more open terrain, except his casts to the side should be reduced to 15-20 yards by handling. In exceptionally heavy early fall cover he will squirm under and through most productively and move out birds which might never be flushed otherwise. Later in the autumn as the leaves and ground foliage die, the experienced Springer will automatically increase the distance of his side casts and cover more ground. When game is shot and the dog sent to retrieve, often a dog will refuse his first woodcock. But a five minute retrieving lesson in which the shot bird is thrown a half dozen times, and the dog encouraged to retrieve, will overcome this difficulty in short order.

Years ago, in the Wisconsin woods, one of our Spaniels flushed a woodcock which towered, fell, and lodged in a spruce tree unknown to us. We ordered the dog to the vicinity repeatedly, and when our shooting partner located the dead cock in the tree we learned a valuable lesson about trusting the dog. Keep the Spaniel moving from side to side in timber and listen for the bell when he is out of sight. The tempo of its sound will often tell you exactly what the dog is doing. Use hand signals to direct him in all hunting when possible. The human voice disturbs game. Use the whistle when he can't see you, but use is sparingly. Too much whistle disturbs game, and may make the dog immune to its command.

There are four types of waterfowl shooting in which a Spaniel may be used most effectively:

1. Shooting from a blind over decoys
2. Pass shooting
3. Jump shooting
4. Shooting from a boat.

Shooting from a blind is the most common method in each of the four great fly-ways. We expect our Spaniels to sit quietly without whining or moving and with his head in the special "dog-door" at one end of the blind. A young dog may need to be leashed his first year to prevent bolting when game is downed, but if thoroughly trained and firmly handled the leash can be eliminated after a few trips to the blind. When a flight comes in, never send the dog to retrieve until things slow down a bit, since ducks usually won't work the blocks with a dog splashing around near them. Obviously with several ducks down for a half hour or longer the Spaniel will have to be directed to some of them, but he'll improve his area of search with experience and will find the cripple which came to life and tried to dive or sneak down the shore.

Pass shooting with a Spaniel is much like dove shooting, except the dog should *always* be well hidden from sight. Between flights, he can be allowed to retrieve the dead and cripples, which he will trail out with dispatch. Occasionally "Rover" will need a little "refresher" course in manners if the action is fast, but do it thoroughly, and don't nag him all day because it will ruin the shoot for you and your shooting companions. A well-conditioned Spaniel can work in temperatures down to 10-20 above zero. We usually have an old piece of "tarp" to cover our dogs on cold, blustery days.

Jump shooting with a Spaniel on any species of waterfowl is great fun. When working large marsh areas it is well to keep the Spaniel at heel because even a well-conditioned one may run out of gas as he half swims, walks, and jumps through much heavy, aquatic vegetation. When a duck or snipe or lone goose is jumped, "Rover" will soon learn to stand on his back legs at the crack of the gun to mark the fall. At the command to "Fetch!" he will slither off through the marsh grass in the direction of the fall. If he fails to mark for any reason, direct him to the fall with hand signals as described in the chapters on training.

Working a Spaniel from a boat can be tricky. Small duck boats are out, of course, but he can be used satisfactorily in a beamy craft which won't capsize when he leaves or enters after a retrieve. The dog should never be chained to the boat because he can drown both of you if he should fall or jump in while on the leash. Instead, he must be taught to sit quietly in one spot and to remain there at all times. There can be no exceptions to this rule. Frankly, we only use Spaniels from a boat on rare occasions, and it is not really a recommended procedure.

There have been shooting preserves in America for many, many years but the quantities have increased tremendously since World War II. Most of these establishments, regardless of whether private, semi-private, or public, release pen-raised pheasant, quail, or chucker partridge at frequent intervals for the members. Almost all have strict rules about the dogs which are used, because an untrained dog of any breed can ruin the shooting for everyone in the area. Working a Spaniel on a walk-up type shoot is much like hunting him on wild birds. He should quarter the ground in front of the guns like a windshield wiper, and not bore out down the field. Working into the wind will help prevent "punching ouh", since all dogs—both domestic and wild—naturally swing out further down wind than upwind when hunting. It is most important to keep the Spaniel under control to preserve shooting since there is usually much more game and more people present. Loud shouting and whistling are most undesirable. Keep the dog under control, and don't take him along unless he is under excellent control. It's bad etiquette, and may be embarrassing if you are asked to take him out of the field.

Many preserves have pass duck shooting in which duck are released. This may be a combination of pass and blind shooting with the former more prevalent. Again keep the Spaniel at heel and under control. Send him to retrieve during lulls in the shooting and never—repeat, *never*—let him run wild and steal shot birds from a nearby station or blind.

Cover at some preserves is grown and/or cut in narrow strips. Since experienced Spaniels seldom like to leave the strips of cover, the wise, courteous handler will keep his Spaniel at heel, and if it is necessary to fight him to cross to the adjacent strip on each cast, use him strictly for retrieving. Working a normal 30-50 yard front in row-stripped areas requires training and experience. Condition your dog to such conditions when you are alone and won't disturb the countryside, and all the game and people therein.

Cecil Gipson and FTC Shooters Lucky Headliner after a successful Western pheasant hunt.

137

Drs. Mark and Aileen Schinderle with NFC Wind Riding Streak, who Dr. Mark handled to the National Open Championship in 1982.

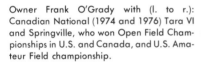

Owner Frank O'Grady with (l. to r.): Canadian National (1974 and 1976) Tara VI and Springville, who won Open Field Championships in U.S. and Canada, and U.S. Amateur Field championship.

Albert D. Beedie, Jr. with National Amateur Field Champion Cathy's Kris of Burnaget (1980). Beedie handled his fine Springer to five National placements, as well as a number of other placements in championship trials.

11

Why Field Trials
for Springer Spaniel
Gun Dogs?

FIELD TRIALS for Spaniels are competitive hunting contests, in which released game is substituted for native game in order to provide each dog with equal opportunity. The dogs are worked in braces on parallel courses, but do not cooperate with each other. The handler of each dog is accompanied by an official gunner and a judge. All dogs that perform creditably in the first series are called back for further testing in a second series (under the other judge), and in Championship All Age stakes, may be called back for a third series with both judges observing one dog simultaneously.

The Spaniels (and not their handlers) are under judgment, and are scored on: their ability and desire to hunt and to find game; the width of their hunting pattern, and the way they cover the ground; the degree in which they work to the gun and their response to hand, voice, or whistle command; their ability to flush and mark the fall of shot game; their steadiness to flush and shot; and their ability to find and retrieve with a soft mouth all game shot for them.

The events normally scheduled by any of the thirty Spaniel clubs in the United States are a Puppy Stake, followed perhaps by a Shooting Dog Stake (handler does own shooting), an Amateur All Age Stake and an Open All Age Stake. Both of the All Age Stakes carry championship points, and the winner of two in each category acquires the title of either Amateur Field Champion or Open Field Champion. Trophies and ribbons

Edward Pomykal, Carl Tate and Fred Pontello, who organized a Springer club in Texas in order to prove to fellow sportsmen that Springers are at home in any climate or any type of cover.

The late Ed Pomykal with Springer at starting line of a Colorado field trial, with judges Ernie Wunderlich and Chuck Goodall (seated).

are awarded winning and placing dogs, plus qualifying certificates for each of the National Championship events. The titles A.F.C. or F.C. in any pedigree are highly meaningful and the *only* titles the prospective owner of a Spaniel gun dog should look for or accept.

To answer the novice who asks, "Why Field Trials?", we can detail 100 reasons, but the broad appeal is the sport of breeding and/or training a high class gun dog with which the owner can compete against other sportsmen with similar ideas. We have hundreds of friends in trials in all sections of the country who will say they want a better hunting dog, that they enjoy the outdoor recreation, that it improves their shooting and hunting lore, or that it's thrilling and exciting to train and handle a hunting dog. All are good sound, acceptable reasons. However, the sport of shooting game over dogs is a basic motivation. Moreover, the field trial fancier stretches the shooting season for a few weeks to many months, since he can usually find an excuse for working his dog on planted game several times each week or month, depending on the degree of his addiction. Many of our friends belong to Spaniel Clubs at which one can find a kindred soul in the training areas 52 Saturdays and Sundays each year. Obviously, such individuals become top wing shots (a dozen dogs will be worked on 50-75 birds each session and the birds have to be shot). There are, of course, "golf widows", "fishing widows", and "spectator sport widows", but there are few "Spaniel widows" because Mama often joins the head of the family when he takes "Rover" to the field for training. Some of the gals get so attached to the family gun dog Spaniel that they get in the act, too. Many have done exceptionally well, and Mrs. Joe Crooks in California is an outstanding example. She and Joe have two Field Champions and Doris put the first win on each of them, with Joe handling both dogs to their second (easier?) win.

Owners and their Cocker Spaniels who participated in the first field trial for the breed held since 1965. Most are members of the North East Spaniel Club. Leadership and promotion by Vance Van Lanon and Patrick Fischer were an important step in returning the field bred hunting Cocker to the U.S. scene.

The late Peter Garvan (left) and Bucky Moore, two dedicated expert Spaniel men who divided their time between superior type American Cocker Spaniels (as shown here) and Springers. Garvan's wife Billy continues to breed fine field bred Cockers from the old bloodlines originated by Peter's father.

12

Other Spaniel
Flushing Breeds

THE TECHNIQUES and training procedures outlined in
this book for English Springer Spaniel gun dogs may also be utilized with
confidence to train any flushing dog including all other Spaniel breeds (or
Retriever breeds) used primarily to find and flush game before the gun.
However, the Springer Spaniels' popularity with hunters and field trailers
as revealed by experience in hunting and field training in 16 states, plus
critical analysis of breed registration figures, leave no doubt that the
Springer is without peer as the No. 1 flushing dog.

The Springer's early ancestors rank as one of the oldest breeds of
hunting dogs which probably rank in second place only behind the hounds.
The ancient spaniel families are mentioned in two early books, the first of
which—*"Livre De Chase",* published in 1387, is reputed to be the first book
devoted exclusively to sporting dogs and hunting. The second, entitled *"Of
Englishe Dogges",* circa 1576, describes several types of spaniels. The one
which is described as *"spryngeth the byrds and bewrayth flight by pursuite"*
is obviously an ancestor of the modern Springer Spaniel. A water dog
mentioned was probably the ancestor of the ancient Irish Water Spaniel
and perhaps some of the more recent Retriever breeds. A third, described
as a "croucher", was probably an ancestor of the several breeds of pointing
dogs. And finally one spaniel type described as a "belly warmer" and used
to warm the laps and beds of women in the Middle Ages in their fireplace-
heated castles, were ancestors of some of the small Toy and pet type
Spaniels one sees today.

Spaniels arrived in Colonial America at an early date. One G. Mort
reported one at Plymouth in 1622. By the 1800s a sporting magazine

reported names of 50 United States citizens who hunted with them on Long Island, N.Y. However, game was so plentiful in many sections of America that hunters did not really need dogs to bring home game bags of 100 or more upland game birds or waterfowl.

In 1926, the American Kennel Club only registered 1,034 Springers. However, 57 years later, in 1983, the number swelled to 22,626. The 20-fold increase demonstrates dramatically that the Springer, which ranked 15th on a list of 128 purebred breeds, is a superb gun dog and a popular show dog, too, with special talents in each area and a fine disposition that also qualifies him as an acceptable family pet. Hopefully, his rank will never increase to a higher level than 15th, and thus discourage their adoption by puppy factory operators with their detrimental effect on the breed.

The Cocker Spaniel (American type)

The great little Cocker Spaniel, descendants of the ancient 14th century fine cocking spaniel hunting dog was probably the No. 1 flushing dog in late 18th and 19th century America. But a breed popularity explosion in the 20th century proved detrimental to large numbers of the U.S. Cocker bloodlines; thousands of Cockers were bred with total disregard for temperament and acceptable hunting characteristics. Numerous cross-road breeders with no knowledge of genetics, and motivated only by a desire to sell puppies, produced dogs that were not suitable as hunters and/or bench show prospects, or even pets. A few knowledgeable ethical breeders like the Roland Harrimans, the Peter Garvans, Albert Winslows, Charles Greenings, Henry Barols, Jack Dodsons, Hartwell Moores, Joe Stipes, Clarence Pfaffenberger, Paul Bishop, Dr. Start Sowle and several dozen others, continued to breed hunting Cockers with good temperaments, but when their ranks were thinned by retirement, the super little U.S. hunting Cockers virtually disappeared. Mrs. Peter (Billie) Garvan, almost the only remaining one of the old line breeders who is still operating, reports that the demand exceeds the supply.

The last Cocker National Field Championship was held in 1962 and the last stake carrying championship points were held in 1965. However, there is a bright spot on the horizon for U.S. Cocker Spaniels. Patrick Fischer, of Northeast Wisconsin Spaniel Club, reports that they held a field trial for Cocker Spaniels in August, 1983, which attracted an entry of ten pretty good gun dogs. He also reported that club president, Vance Van Lanen, has imported a number of English Cocker Spaniels from Great Britain, of top field breeding and will attempt to introduce well-bred hunting Cockers to the American scene.

Cocker Spaniels of the American variety have ranked near the top in purebred dogs population for many years, and in 1983 supplanted Poodles as No. 1 with 92.836 registrations for the year. Hopefully, American sportsmen will help bring Cockers back as hunting dogs by acquiring an American Cocker type from Mrs. Peter Garvan, or some of her friends, or investing in an English Cocker from Wisconsin or directly from the old sod.

The American Water Spaniel

The American Water Spaniel, formerly known as the American Brown Water Spaniel, is slightly smaller than the Springer, and bears a close resemblance to the Irish Water Spaniel in coat and color. However, the American Water Spaniel does not possess a rat tail like the Irish dog. There were 339 registered with the AKC in 1983. Their popularity with hunters declined in the last 50 years when the larger, stronger, Labradors and Golden Retrievers replaced them as gun dogs.

The Clumber Spaniel

The Clumber Spaniel is a stocky, heavy, white dog with lightly ticked body and noted as a slow methodical worker. Tradition has it that Clumbers have a superior nose. However, the two we shot over, seldom hunted faster than at a trot and could not have possibly passed or missed game at that pace. It is alleged that they originated in France, and at least one writer has intimated they were related to the ancient Alpine Spaniel and/or the Saint Bernard which they do resemble, if one forgets their shorter legs. The American Kennel Club listed only 126 Clumbers in their new dog registrations for 1983. Perhaps most of them, if not all, were bred and used for show purposes.

The Boykin Spaniel

The Boykin Spaniel, a chocolate brown, wavy-coated often yellow eyed, docked tailed dog, is the newest member of the ancient family of spaniel type dogs. The Boykin is alleged to have originated about the turn of the century, when Alexander White found a spaniel type dog wandering near a church in Spartenburg, S.C. He took the dog home as a pet, but when it demonstrated a desire to hunt, he sent it to his friend, Whitaker Boykin, in Boykin community near Camden, S.C. He trained the dog and according to legend it was a sensational turkey, duck, and dove dog. By methods not made clear by writers and supporters of the breed, that first dog was bred to a number of other dogs of unspecified breeds and apparently had such dominant genes that a new breed which bred true to type offspring was started. Their fame in the Southland as turkey, duck, and dove dogs, grew by word of mouth to such an extent that a number of owners organized the Boykin Spaniel Society in 1977. According to society secretary Ms. Kitty Beard, who supplied photos of the breed, a registry and study book was started in 1979. By the end of the following year the society had 300 members/owners. By August, 1983, 2,154 individual dogs and 459 litters had been registered.

The rather mysterious Boykin Spaniel, with Cocker-type head and dark brown color, has been lauded throughout the Southland as a superior turkey, duck and dove gun dog. A number of outdoor writers have praised his ability as a gun dog (including Harry Reynolds, of the *Memphis Commercial Appeal*—a writer who really knows a good gun dog when he sees one). We suggest that if the breed is to attract the interest of more hunters, it needs competitive exposure in field trials for Springers and/or Retrievers, or both. Perhaps this will come, as it has been rumored that the Boykin Spaniel Society is considering seeking recognition by the American Kennel Club and/or the American Field. —*photo, Boykin Spaniel Society.*

Welsh Springer Spaniel, Am. & Can. Ch. Fracas Little Caesar, owned by D. L. Carswell, Amityville, NY.

The breed is not officially recognized by the American Kennel Club.

In our search for someone who we believed had the experience with Spaniels to be entitled to an opinion, we found three good Spaniel people. The first was the well-known, successful professional trainer, John Isaacs. He reported that a client sent him two Boykins for training. After several weeks of work, Isaccs decided that both dogs were hyper-active and poor risks as gun dogs. The other two we consulted were Cliff Hankin and his son, Rex Hankin. Cliff is an experienced amateur who has trained some winners, shot much native game over Springers in several states. Rex reported that if a good Springer could be rated at 10, his Boykin deserved a rating of 9. His father concurred in this. Cliff added that he bought the Boykin for his son because the Boykin he kept and worked for a friend impressed him as a potentially good hunting dog.

Welsh Springer Spaniel

This attractive, white/red coated dog resembles a Springer but is perhaps slightly smaller. His ancient ancestors were probably the same dogs as those from which the modern Springer, Cocker and all other Spaniels except the Clumber descended. For many years the Welsh was a popular gun dog in many sections of the British Isles. However, in recent years their number in Britain expanded from 150 to approximately 500 in 1975. In the U.S. there were only 227 registered with the American Kennel Club in 1983. None have appeared in U.S. field trials, nor have they been observed by the author in pheasant or duck country. Some have appeared in U.S. and British bench shows.

The English Cocker Spaniel

The English Cocker Spaniel, which is somewhat larger than the American Cocker, continues to attract owners in the U.S. In 1983, 1,393 were registered here. Some of the bloodlines of the English Cocker, especially those more recently imported from Great Britain, are programmed with hunting characteristics. The sportsmen who are members of the North East Spaniel Club at Green Bay, Wisconsin, are using English Cocker Spaniel imports which they hope will rejuvenate Cockers as gun dogs in the United States.

. The other breeds of the ancient spaniel family, the Sussex and the Field Spaniel, have retained only a resemblance of their former popularity in the U.S. as gun dogs. We suggest their decline is due in part to faddish and extremely impractical breeding objectives. The short legged Sussex could never handle typical U.S. pheasant cover. The Field Spaniel has a better body conformation for a gun dog but in appearance is just a slightly larger black Cocker Spaniel. There were only 53 Field Spaniels and 27 Sussex Spaniels registered in the U.S. during the calendar year of 1983.

The late Freeman Lloyd, pioneer Springer advocate and writer in America.

Maxwell Riddle, famous author and widely respected all-breed judge. Honored by the Dog Writers' Association of America as "Dog Writer of the Year" for the time in 1984.

Dedicated Evelyn Bui, who contributed a giant effort in publishing The Springer Bark. Her excellent professional promotion of the breed came to an end when the magazine had to be discontinued.

William F. Brown, editor of The American Field magazine. Brown is an authority on the several breeds of gun dogs and the author of numerous books and articles on gun dogs.

Selected Reading

Publications of value for the trainer and shooting man.

United States Periodicals of Value to Sportsmen:

THE AMERICAN FIELD, a weekly which reports field trial results of several breeds as well as factual information of interest to the sportsman. (William Brown, *Editor,* 222 W. Adams St., Chicago, Ill. 60606.)

GUN DOG, a new publication covering all the hunting breeds with feature stories by well-known authors. (David G. Meisner, *Publisher,* P.O. Box 68, Adel, Iowa 50003.)

Books on Gun Dog Training (Published in the United States):

THE INTERNATIONAL ENCYCLOPEDIA OF DOGS. *Edited by Stanley Dangerfield and Elsworth S. Howell.* A modern up-to-date compilation of facts about many breeds in many countries, told in a comprehensible manner.

THE MODERN DOG ENCYCLOPEDIA *by Henry Davis.* An outstanding, comprehensive work covering history, breeding and training of all breeds in all phases of their activity.

HUNTING DOG KNOW-HOW *by David Michael Duffy.* A first class work on the several gun dog breeds by a practical hunter who knows what to say and how to say it.

THE SPRINGER SPANIEL *by Maxwell Riddle.* A well-organized book covering bench, field, and obedience tests for Spaniels. Bloodline charts of leading Springer sires.

ANIMAL BEHAVIOR *by John Paul Scott.* A psychological explanation of animal behavior.

GENETICS AND THE SOCIAL BEHAVIOR OF THE DOG *by John Paul Scott* and *John L. Fuller.*

SHOOTING PRESERVE MANAGEMENT—THE NILO SYSTEM *by Edward L. Kozicky* and *John Madson.* A comprehensive discussion of preserve management containing much information of value to the preserve shooter.

HOW TO TRAIN YOUR OWN GUN DOG *by Charles S. Goodall.* The carefully detailed, step-by-step training routines described in this book are designed to help novice and experienced dog owners avoid the pitfalls and disappointments of hunting with what might be called "spot trained" dogs.

British Books of Value to the Spaniel Trainer:

SPANIELS FOR SPORT *by Talbot Radcliffe.* One of the best training manuals in existence, in which Radcliffe—a highly successful British Springer breeder—up-dates the classic work of H. W. Carlton, *Spaniels:* Their Breaking for Sport and Field Trials.

FIELD TRIALS AND JUDGING *by Charles Alington.* Will broaden the knowledge of any shooting man who works with dogs.

TRAINING AND FIELD TRIALS *by P. R. A. Moxon.* A fine training manual by a professional gun dog trainer.

DOG TRAINING BY AMATEURS *by R. Sharpe.* One of the classic works on how to train a Spaniel gun dog.

SECTION II

Show and Obedience Springers

by

Julia Gasow

JULIA (MRS. FRED H.) GASOW

Julia Gasow has twice been voted "Dog Woman of the Year" (1971 and 1980)—regarded by many as the highest accolade in the sport.

Mrs. Gasow has bred show English Springer Spaniels since the early 1930s, and her Salilyn Kennels has accounted for more than 300 champions and more than two dozen all-breed Best in Show winners. In 1970 and again in 1975, she was named the "Dog Breeder of the Year" by *Kennel Review* magazine, and dogs she has owned or co-owned have won the Ken-L Ration Award (honoring the dog in each Group that wins the most Group Firsts for the year) a record number of times.

—Photo by Booth

To my husband,
Fred
to whose unselfish love, continual encour-
agement and ever-dependable help I owe
whatever success I've enjoyed in the sport of
dogs—and who, more than anyone else, has
helped keep it fun for me.

An historic photo—the first English Springer Spaniel Specialty at Englewood, New Jersey in 1922. W. J. Hutchinson, a pioneer of American interest in the breed, is third from the right, and the famous writer and breed advocate, Freeman Lloyd, is at far right. —*Photo by the late Rudolph W. Tauskey, and presented by him to Mrs. Gasow.*

Introduction to the
Show Springer Section

WHEN the 1974 edition of *The New English Springer Spaniel* was being planned, I was pleased and flattered to be asked to provide a section on the show Springer to complement Charles Goodall's classic section on the field Springer. Modernly, the field and conformation Springers are of two different "worlds", and the recognition of this by including a separate show section, to my mind made the book more complete and more serviceable.

Now, a decade later, it is time for a new updated edition, and I am again happy to be a partner in its creation.

As before, the widened scope of the book limits the depth with which we can treat the history of the show Springer. I have mainly confined myself to the current scene—limiting consideration of past dogs to those who have been most influential in producing today's greats. And while I've tried to give due notice to outstanding winning, I believe their contributions as sires and dams are more important and more lasting.

In this regard it was gratifying to note that the ten top winners at the time of the 1974 edition all stemmed from the ten dogs that I had selected as being most significant in the period from 1945 until then.

Now a decade of new statistics prompts a reevaluation and updating of this list of ten most significant producers. Some of the more recent dogs have supplanted earlier greats in the importance of their influence upon today's competitors.

Along with this new evaluation, based upon statistics, I have offered a few frank observations, based upon close to fifty years of experience with the breed. For those who see it differently, I can only say that these are the judgments that have worked best for us at Salilyn.

Ch. Salilyn's Aristocrat, following upon his win of Best of Breed at the 1968 national ESSFTA Specialty, is pictured winning the Stud Dog Class at the same show under judge Peter Knoop. Risto, at left, is followed by his son, Salilyn's Colonel's Overlord (winner of the Puppy Dog 6-9 months class) and his daughter, Salilyn's Sophistication (winner of the Puppy Bitch 6-9 months class). These littermates became outstanding champions.

Again I have tried to make the presentation as pictorial as possible. Almost every dog mentioned is pictured, and in many cases pedigrees are also included.

I'm sure readers will find the all-new section on Grooming very helpful. Also helpful, I hope, is the question-and-answer chapter on care of the English Springer—these are the questions most frequently asked by those who purchased dogs from our kennels over the years.

In the Introduction to the 1974 edition, I expressed some appreciations that merit repeating: to Fred Hunt and George Pugh, for their help; to our dear friend, Mary Valentine, who typed the manuscript as a labor of love; and to the many fellow Springer enthusiasts who cooperated so wholeheartedly in sending me pictures and pedigrees of their notable dogs.

Now, for this 1984 update, Springer breeders and fanciers have again shown their interest in our breed by sending me pictures and valuable information on their dogs. They all have my sincere appreciation.

Nellie Fitzgerald was a constant help and supported me in every way, particularly by collecting statistics and by contributing important grooming instructions. My thanks to Carol Crane for her typing of the new material, and for her help beyond the call of duty.

Nyleen LaShier has my deep gratitude for her complete article on Obedience, just as Jim Eadie has for his highly knowledgeable and valuable section on Tracking.

—JULIA GASOW

Three generations: (l. to r.) Ch. Salilyn's Citation II, grandsire; Ch. Inchidony Prince Charming, sire; and two of Prince Charming's sons—Ch. Charlyle's Fair Warning and Ch. Salilyn's Aristocrat.

157

Left, Eng., Am. & Can. Ch. Springbok of Ware. *Right,* Dual Ch. Flint of Avondale, whelped 1921. Springbok an Flint were the most prominent of the many Springers imported to America by Eudore Chevrier of Canada.

Eng. & Am. Ch. Nuthill Dignity, 1930 Best in Show winner. Imported from England by E. de K. Leffingwell.

Ch. Woodelf of Breeze, Dignity's daughter, behind many of our top-winning Springers of today.

Am. & Can. Ch. Norman of Hamsey, the first English Springer to win the Sporting Group at Westminster (in 1933). Owned by the Blue Leader Kennels of Santa Barbara, California.

13

Bench Springers in America

THE FIRST SPECIALTY SHOW for English Springer Spaniels in the United States was held at Englewood, New Jersey in 1922. The exhibits were field trial dogs—their owners great sportsmen, to be remembered for their contribution to both bench and field.

These gentlemen ran their dogs in a field trial one day, combed out the burrs, and then the following day showed them for conformation. However, this first Specialty touched off a spark of enthusiasm for the joy of winning on Springer beauty as well as field ability.

Fanciers continued to run and show their dogs successfully as late as the early 1930s. But more and more they became critical of the overall appearance of the "non-conformist" field trial Springer, whose owner was interested in only that one phase of the sport. They became aware of the importance of coat and feather in the ring, and a show-minded individual no longer cared to subject his prospective winner to the general hazards of field work.

This was the beginning of a division in Springer type, represented by two distinct sports within the breed. Over the years, these groups have grown farther apart, with some resulting friction along the way.

Many felt that this division would be the ruination of the breed, but results have proved quite the contrary. Each of the two phases has become so highly specialized that we now have English Springer Spanisl superiority on two fronts, as it were: ability unsurpassed by any other breed in field trials, and a bench record unmatched by any other breed since 1967.

Today field trial enthusiasts and bench enthusiasts are pretty much agreed that each dog does best within its own sphere, and that neither does well the work of the other. It is also agreed that the field trial dog is too high strung to make a good house dog.

Eng., Am. & Can. Ch. Showman of Shotton, imported from England in 1939 by Paul Quay.

Ch. Clarion Rufton Tandy (at 9 months of age). This bitch is said to have been the model for the 1932 standard revision.

Ch. Runor's Agent, owned by Norman Morrow, pictured after winning the Group at Trenton.

From personal experience I can advise against crossing these two strains if your aim is to produce a show-winning Springer that can compete creditably in field trials. From the first breeding of such a cross it would take at least four generations back to bench breeding to have a show dog. By this time, naturally, the speed and field ability gained would be lost. It is easy to produce an excellent hunting dog from bench breeding, but almost impossible to breed a show Springer from field trial stock.

Significant Bench Springers of the 1920s and Early 1930s

Most active in the importation of many English Springer Spaniels that began in the early 1920s was Eudore Chevrier of Canada. Mr. Chevrier bought extensively, and did well with the breed in Canada under the banner of "Avandale". Most notable of the many he imported were Dual Ch. Flint of Avandale, bred by the Duke of Hamilton, and Eng. Am. & Can. Ch. Springbok of Ware. But in sum, Mr. Chevrier's dogs were a heterogeneous lot. He was basically an importer—not a breeder—and established no set line.

In 1928, E. de K. Leffingwell, a Californian, imported Ch. Nuthill Dignity from England. Dignity became a tri-international champion. He had an outstandingly beautiful head—good enough to outweigh the fact that he was, reportedly, somewhat spindly, with weak pasterns and a curly coat. He was a fine showman, and did top winning on both coasts through the early 1930s, including Best of Breed at Westminster in 1930.

Dignity was an important sire as well. Mrs. Betty Buchanan, Breeze Kennels, Denver, Colorado, bred her Dilkusha Darkie to him to produce the ever-remembered bitch. Ch. Woodelf of Breeze, behind so many winning Springers of today.

Robert Elliot also used Nuthill Dignity to advantage at his Elysian Kennels. Dignity is the grandsire of the famous Elysian quintuplets, one of which—King Lion—became the first dual champion in America.

Tragically, Nuthill Dignity got loose one day and ran to the mountains and was never seen again.

One of the important English imports, although a somewhat controversial one, was English, American and Canadian Champion Showman of Shotton, brought over in 1939 by Paul Quay of Chagrin Falls, Ohio.

Showman's winning career started immediately upon his arrival. He was shown exclusively by one of the leading handlers in the country, Billy Lang, who later became a licensed all-breed judge, and then an American Kennel Club field representative. Billy campaigned Showman extensively, piloting him to many Best in Show wins in an era before the Springer's great popularity as a Group dog.

Though outstanding in the show ring, Showman's influence on the breed remains questionable. The West Coast profited from him by

Ch. Adonis of Avondale — a representative winner of the earlier show Springers.

Ch. Elysian Emissary, 1934 Best in Show winner.

Ch. Timpanogos Melinda, winner of the Sporting Group at Westminster 1942. Owned by R. E. Allen and handled by Harry Sangster.

establishing his powerful rear movement in their bloodlines. In the East, Norman Morrow's best winner, Ch. Runor's Agent, a great moving dog, was sired by him. But Norman himself said of his dog, "Agent was short in foreface and neck and had a somewhat harsh expression."

Billy Lang wrote, well after Showman's retirement, "Showman of Shotton was a mean-eyed rascal and contributed nothing in the way of soft expressive eyes to the breed." Edward Dana Knight, well-known breeder-judge, wrote: "Let's face it—Showman is the greatest disaster that's ever happened to American Springers. There were many things to like about him, but he sired a high percentage of shy dogs and an astonishing number with bad feet."

Mr. Charles Toy, whose Clarion Kennels was named for the country in which he lived—about sixty miles from Pittsburgh, was doing much to improve the breed with his English imports during this whole period. Such Springers as Clarion Rufton Trumpet and Clarion Rufton Tandy were great then, and I think would look good today. As a matter of fact, the latter was used as a "model" for the revision of the English Springer standard in 1932.

Mr. Toy's close friend, R. E. Allen of Provo, Utah, a highly respected breeder of champions, did well for the Springer cause with his Timpanogos dogs. Possibly his best were Ch. Melinda, Group winner at Westminster in 1942, and Ch. Timpanogos Radar.

And I must certainly mention George Higgs, whose Boghurst Springers were winning then and are still in the rings today.

There were many other winners at the time, but they have left little, if any, imprint on the breed. The dogs, generally, were longer in body than our present Springer. They were short on legs with poor fronts. Most were heavily ticked.

Salilyn's Taurus (at 3½ months), a cross of bench and field breeding.

ENG. & AM. CH. RUFTON RECORDER
(Boss of Glasnevin ex Rufton Flirt)
Whelped May 11, 1926

14

The Recorder Influence

ENGLISH and AMERICAN CHAMPION RUFTON RECORDER had the greatest impact of any single dog on our show Springer of today. He was purchased by Fred M. Hunt directly from his English breeder, R. Cornthwaite, and imported to this country in 1933.

Mr. Hunt was well known to the dog world long before this date. He had established his Green Valley Kennels in the beautiful farm lands of Devon, Pennsylvania, had produced several show champions, and for years had taken an active and enthusiastic part in field trials.

Mr. Hunt had purchased Recorder strictly for breeding purposes. The dog was seven years old at the time and therefore an unlikely show prospect. But Recorder was an English show champion, and his sire—Boss of Glasnevin—had been a field trial winner, at one time considered the top prospect in England. Thus Recorder had everything to offer Fred's breeding program.

Very shortly after this great dog's arrival in America it became evident that he was not too old for the show ring, after all. He was active, gay, in good physical condition—in fact, Fred felt that he was the best Springer he had ever seen.

Accordingly, he entered him in several shows and Recorder immediately created a sensation. Many exhibitors were highly critical of him—not suprising, really, for he was very different from the dogs they were producing. He represented change—a "new model" Springer that some refused to accept. But the more serious breeders recognized in him quality and style not to be surpassed during the era.

He was taller than his competitors and far more compact, standing on well-boned, perfectly straight forelegs that offered great breed

Dual Ch. Green Valley Punch. Punch is pictured below retrieving a pheasant for his owner, Fred Hunt.

Ch. Green Valley Oak, an important producer.

improvement. And his feet were excellent. Though plain in head, his appearance was enhanced by a collar and markings of pure, sparkling white' making him stand out against the heavily ticked dogs of the day.

I am grateful to have seen him shown in 1934 at the English Springer Spaniel Club of Michigan's first Specialty Show, where he was Best of Breed from the limit class (now extinct) over 104 entries. The judge was Freeman Lloyd. Recorder finished his championship in record time.

Since names of Rufton Recorder's direct descendants appear many times in the pedigrees of our current winners, it is interesting to know how they came about, remembering, of course, that we can only touch the high spots in the space allowed us here.

Mr. Hunt leased Woodelf of Breeze, a Nuthill Dignity daughter for two breedings to Recorder. The first produced the most famous litter in Springer history, consisting of six bench show champions. One was Green Valley Punch, who also achieved a Field Trial Championship in 1938. We have not had another dual champion Springer in America since. The other five bench champions were all important winners and all good producers.

One bitch in the litter was never shown. Her bone was fine, and her head unattractive. Her eyes, small and slanting, suggested the name given her—"Orienta". But although not herself show material, Orientia is significant because of her progeny.

In 1935, Mr. Hunt bought Dunoon Donald Dhu from Andy Dunn in Canada, and did well with him in the States. He was a short well-balanced dog, though large and lacking in angulation.

While resting on his laurels at Green Valley Kennels, his championship certificate hanging on the wall, Donald Dhu took a fancy to our ugly duckling Orientia and, when no one was looking, jumped the fence and bred her. A black male puppy from this litter was sold to William Belleville of Langhorne, Pennsylvania, and was registered "Roderique of Sandblown Acre". As we shall soon see, Rodrique was to be the first of a line of top winning and producing dogs for this well-known kennel.

Ch. Tranquility of Melilotus, outstanding bitch, owned by Mrs. R. Gilman Smith (Mrs. Frederick Brown).

Ch. Dunoon Donald Dhu, Best of Breed at Westminster 1938. Owned by Janet Henneberry.

Dunoon Donald Dhu was soon sold to Janet Henneberry of Golf, Illinois, who loved him so dearly that she named her kennel for him: "Donnie Dhu."

Fred Hunt brought over another bitch from Mr. Cornthwaite in England named Rufton Rosita, and bred her to Recorder to produce Ch. Green Valley Hercules. Hercules, bred to his half-sister Orientia, produced Tranquillity of Well Sweep, who became the dam of Ch. Tranquillity of Melilotus, Mrs. R. Gilman Smith's outstanding bitch.

Recorder was bred to his granddaughter, Ch. Green Valley Dinah, to produce Ch. Green Valley Oak. Oak, bred to his half-sister, Ch. Green Valley Judy, a Recorder daughter, produced Ch. Green Valley The Feudist.

Recorder was the sire of Ch. Field Marshall, the foundation of Bob Morrow's Audley Farm Kennel, and when linebred through Green Valley Oak, gave Norman Morrow the foundation for his Runor Kennel, Ch. Audley Farm Judy.

Recorder and his offspring are back of Walpride Springers, Rumack, Charlyle, Kaintuck, Wakefield, Inchidony, Frejax, Salilyn and others.

Fred Hunt personally handled Recorder to his championship, as he did most of his Springers. He also ran Green Valley Punch, exclusively, for his Field Trial Championship. Mr. Hunt seldom entered a dog in the Specials class, having little interest in campaigning a dog for Group winning.

In 1941 he was transferred to Detroit, Michigan, so closed Green Valley Kennels. But in a span of ten years, he had finished 56 champions!

Important Sires Following Recorder

In the wake of Recorder, two sires—above all others—can be credited with leaving their imprint on top-winning Springers of today. They are Am. & Can. Ch. Rodrique of Sandblown Acre and Ch. Inchidony Prince Charming.

Bred at the Green Valley Kennels of Fred Hunt, Rodrique was sold to William Belleville as a puppy. For Mr. Belleville, Rodrique represented an exciting new interest—the dog game. He became the foundation of Sandblown Acre Kennels, named for the Bellevilles' sandy acre of land in Pennsylvania. He was the sire of 28 champions, most of them outstanding producers, including Ch. Co-Pilot of Sandblown Acre with 28 champion get.

Mr. Belleville was the head tomato grower for Campbell Soup Company at the time, and although fairly well along in years and completely inexperienced in dog breeding, bred a good number of winners—all descendants of Rodrique. Unfortunately, this success was short-lived. He found that his theories for breeding bigger, better tomatoes were not applicable to breeding dogs.

A lineup of Ch. Inchidony Prince Charming's get. At extreme left, Ch. Salilyn's Aristocrat. At far right, Ch. Charlyle's Fair Warning.

Am. & Can. Ch. Rodrique of Sandblown Acre
(Ch. Dunoon Donald Dhu ex Green Valley Orientia)
Whelped March 12, 1937

Just as Rufton Recorder was the link connecting Mr. Goodall's early history in this book to our modern Springers, (with Rodrique of Sandblown Acres as the stepping stone in between) Ch. Inchidony Prince Charming stands as the solid beginning of today's winners.

Life moves at such a fast pace around us that it is natural to expect to find many changes in our breed during the past twelve year period. Some of the "Modern Greats" of yesterday are no longer found prominently in pedigrees today.

We all want to know the Springers that are in the winning circle today—those making Parent Club records by achieving recognized awards and that are generally in the public eye. Most interesting of all, we want to find the dogs that have produced them and continue to remain prominent in current pedigrees.

One statistic remains unbroken: Ch. Green Valley Punch, bred and owned by Fred M. Hunt, in 1938, is still the last English Springer Spaniel Dual Champion.

Some Memorable Springers of the Past

Am. & Can. Ch. Frejax Royal Salute
Whelped 1945
By Ch. Sir Lancelot of Salilyn
ex Ch. Frejax Lilac Time
Breeder-Owner: Fred Jackson,
Frejax Kennels.

Ch. Melilotus Royal Oak — Whelped 1949.
By Am./Can. Ch. Frejax Royal Salute
ex Ch. Tranquility of Melilotus
Breeder-Owner: Mrs. R. Gilman Smith (Mrs. Frederick Brown).

172

Ch. King Peter of Salilyn — Whelped 1949.
By Firebrand of Sandblown Acre, CDX ex Salutation of Salilyn
Breeder-Owner: Mrs. F. H. Gasow.

Am. & Can. Ch. Walpride Flaming Rocket — Whelped 1950.
By Ch. Chaltha's The Gainer ex Walpride's Sensation
Breeder-Owner: Robert J. Walgate, Walpride Kennels.

Am. & Can. Ch. Salilyn's Macduff
Whelped 1954
By Ch. King William of Salilyn
ex Shercliff's Lady Debby
Breeders: Robert E. Gibson
and James Mitchell
Owner: Mrs. F. H. Gasow — later
sold to William and Elaine P. Randall.

Am. & Can. Ch. Waiterock Elmer Brown
Whelped 1956
By Ch. Waiterock Whistle
ex Tahquitz Merry Mischief
Breeder-Owner: Juanita Waite Howard.

174

Ch. Wakefield's Black Knight
("Danny")
Whelped 1959
By Ch. Kaintuck Christmas Carol
ex Ch. Wakefield's Fanny
Breeder-Owner: Mrs. W. J. S. Borie

"Danny" lived only five years, but in that time he scored 7 Bests in Show and 24 Group Firsts. He will always be remembered as one of the few Springer Spaniels to have won Best in Show at Westminster.

Ch. Rostherne Hunter, W.D.
(English import — Whelped 1957)
By Ch. Studley Major ex Ch. Rostherne Beauty
Breeder: J. Malarkey
Imported and owned by Mrs. R. Gilman Smith (Mrs. Frederick Brown).

175

Am. & Can. Ch. Geiger's Chief Geronimo, C.D., W.D.
Whelped 1959
By Ch. Geiger's Winaway Duke, UD ex Schwedekrest Lady Pamela
Breeder-Owner: Tillie Geiger.

Am. & Can. Ch. Magill's Patrick, C.D., C.D.X.
Whelped 1965
By Am. & Can. Ch. Geiger's Chief Geronimo ex Cindy's Delight
Breeder-Owner: Wayne D. Magill.

Ch. Gingerbread Boy of Hillcrest, C.D.
By Ch. Rostherne Hunter, WD ex Ch. Ginger Snap of Hillcrest
Breeder-Owner: Henriette Schmidt.

Ch. Tamridge Homestretch
Whelped 1966
By Willowbrook Make It Snappy ex Tamridge Away We Go
Breeder-Owner: Barbara Parker.

Dick Cooper, recognized as one of the country's top all-breed handlers, is pictured winning Best in Show with Ch. Salilyn's Hallmark. Dick handled five of the Ten Modern Greats listed in this book, four of which received the Quaker Oats Award for Top Sporting Dog of the Year. —*Ritter*

George Alston is noted for showing many top winning Springers. He is pictured here with Ch. Salilyn's Private Stock after winning Best in Show at Westchester Kennel Club, 1982—the only Springer ever to win this show. George guided Stock not only to being the nation's No. 1 Sporting Dog for 1982, but also to many other prestigious wins including Best in Show at the American Spaniel Club Specialty in 1983. —*Ashbey*

178

15

Ten Modern Greats

$\mathbf{T}$HERE HAVE BEEN many notable Springers in the show ring from the era of the 1970s to 1983. From this distinguished number, I have tried here—in view of the limited space—to select the ten that I believe were most outstanding in meeting the two-pronged qualification of having established great show records themselves, and of siring get that were likewise outstanding winners and producers. It is particularly interesting, in studying the pedigrees of the dogs that are dominant in the rings today, to note that almost without exception they stem from these dogs.

The ten, presented in chronological order, are:
- Ch. Inchidony Prince Charming
- Ch. Charlyle's Fair Warning
- Ch. Salilyn's Aristocrat
- Ch. Salilyn's Colonel's Overlord
- Ch. Chinoe's Adamant James
- Ch. Salilyn's Encore
- Ch. Salilyn's Classic
- Ch. Salilyn's Hallmark
- Ch. Telltale Author
- Ch. Salilyn's Private Stock

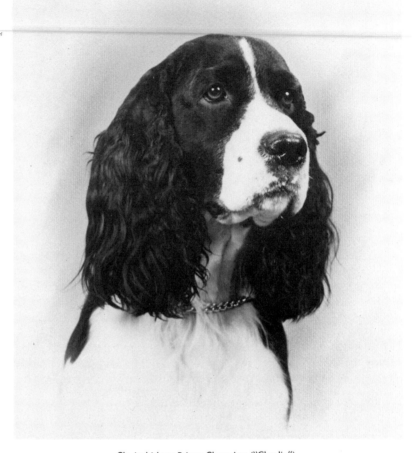

Ch. Inchidony Prince Charming ("Charlie").

CH. INCHIDONY PRINCE CHARMING
Whelped July 8, 1959

		A/C Ch. Frejax Royal Salute
	Ch. Frejax Royal Request	Frejax Apache Star
Ch. Salilyn's Sensation		Firebrand of Sandblown Acre, CDX
	Queen Victoria of Salilyn	Salutation of Salilyn
Ch. Salilyn's Citation II		Firebrand of Sandblown Acre, CDX
	Ch. King Peter of Salilyn	Salutation of Salilyn
Salilyn's Princess Meg		Ch. Salilyn's Speculation
	Ch. Salilyn's Animation	Salilyn's Lady Macbeth

CH. INCHIDONY PRINCE CHARMING

		Traveler of Sandblown Acre
	Firebrand of Sandblown Acre, CDX	Dawn's Elf of Sandblown Acre
Ch. King Peter of Salilyn		A/C Ch. Frejax Royal Salute
	Salutation of Salilyn	Nancy of Salilyn
Ch. Salilyn's Cinderella II		Ch. Co-Pilot of Sandblown Acre
	Ch. Chaltha's The Gainer	Ch. Chaltha's Hope
A/C Ch. Walpride Gay Beauty		Ch. Dormond's Dark Danger
	Walpride Sensation	Dormond Gypsy

Ch. Inchidony Prince Charming was bred by his owners, Becher and Dorothy Hungerford. Mr. Hungerford, a lawyer and later an American Kennel Club field representative, is now deceased. He was much loved and is sadly missed by all who knew him.

Among Prince Charming's 50 champion sons and daughters are: the two top winning Springers of their day, Ch. Charlyle's Fair Warning and Ch. Salilyn's Aristocrat; the rocketing littermates—Ch. Canarch Inchidony Sparkler and Ch. Canarch Yankee Patriot; and the National Specialty Best in Show winner, Ch. Ramsgate's Scotch Mist. Interestingly, Prince Charming produced six Best in Show winners out of six different bitches.

It is also interesting that although Prince Charming's sire, Ch. Salilyn's Citation, was to win 3 Bests in Show, 14 Groups, and 3 Specialties, he had not yet finished his championship when Mr. Hungerford elected to breed Ch. Salilyn's Cinderella to him. This was Citation's first mating, and Charlie was the only puppy in the litter. Both Citation and Cinderella were the result of linebreeding to Rodrique on their paternal and maternal sides.

Ch. Charlyle's Fair Warning.

CH. CHARLYLE'S FAIR WARNING
(black/white—whelped 1962)

```
                        Ch. Salilyn's Sensation, CD
                  A/C Ch. Salilyn's Citation II
                        Salilyn's Princess Meg
            Ch. Inchidony Prince Charming
                  Ch. King Peter of Salilyn
            Ch. Salilyn's Cinderella II
                  A/C Ch. Walpride Gay Beauty
CH. CHARLYLE'S FAIR WARNING
                  Ch. Ebony of Hillcrest
            Ch. Banneret's Regal Brigadier
                  Banneret's Gay Festival
      Charlyle's Nanette
                  Salilyn's Young Lochinvar
      Charlyle's Happy Choice
            Ch. Charlyle's Royal Heiress
```

Charlyle's Fair Warning was bred by Charles R. Clement, who handled him to his championship and then sold him to Ann Pope of Boston. "Sam" established himself as a winner and sire of winners. His show score included 4 Bests in Show, 5 independent Specialties and 43 Group Firsts. He won the National Specialty in 1966 and the parent club award for "Springer of the Year" for 1966 and 1968. And to date, he's the sire of 54 champions.

Sam is but one of the many fine Springers that have come from the Charlyle Kennels, named for Charlie Clement and his wife, Lyle. Starting in 1933 with a roan tri-colored bitch, their success really began with the breeding of a granddaughter of Ch. Co-Pilot of Sandblown Acre to Ch. Frejax Royal Minstrel, a breeding that gave them the excellent producer— Ch. Charlyle's Royal Flush.

Among many proud moments for the kennel, a highlight has to be the win of the National Specialty in 1962 by Charlyle's Holdout, from the Open class: Holdout was bred, owned and handled by Mr. Clement.

Charlie Clement still keeps his sincere interest in Springers and was present at our 1983 National Specialty at the age of 96; a dearly loved and highly respected breeder.

Ch. Salilyn's Aristocrat.

CH. SALILYN'S ARISTOCRAT
(liver/white—whelped 1964)

Ch. Salilyn's Sensation, CD
A/C Ch. Salilyn's Citation II
Salilyn's Princess Meg
Ch. Inchidony Prince Charming
Ch. King Peter of Salilyn
Ch. Salilyn's Cinderella II
A/C Ch. Walpride's Gay Beauty

Ch. Frejax Royal Request
Queen Victoria of Salilyn
Ch. King Peter of Salilyn
Ch. Salilyn's Animation II
Firebrand of Sandblown Acre, CDX
Salutation of Salilyn
Ch. Chaltha's The Gainer
Walpride Sensation

CH. SALILYN'S ARISTOCRAT

A/C Ch. Salilyn's Citation II
Salilyn's Royal Consort
Ch. Ascot's Estralita
Ch. Salilyn's Lily of the Valley
Ch. King William of Salilyn
Salilyn's Glenda
Ch. Salilyn's Good Omen

Ch. Salilyn's Sensation, CD
Salilyn's Princess Meg
Ch. Ascot's Ajax
Ascot's Diamond Lil
Firebrand of Sandblown Acre, CDX
Salutation of Salilyn
Ch. Cartref Bob Bobbin
Salilyn's Surprise

In the calendar year of 1967, before he had reached his third birthday, Ch. Salilyn's Aristocrat won a total of 45 Bests in Show and 71 Group Firsts to establish an all-time record for all breeds—a Phillips Rating total of 34,553 points for the year! This record stood just until 1971 when—in what must be the ultimate honor for any serious dog breeder—it was surpassed by Aristocrat's son, Ch. Chinoe's Adamant James.

Following his record-breaking year, Risto was removed from regular competition by his breeder-owner, Mrs. Julia Gasow, and was shown just four more times: at Westminster in 1968, where he placed second in the Sporting Group; at the annual National Specialty Shows in 1968 and 1969, where he was Best in Show each time; and then, at age of eight, again at Westminster 1973, where he spectacularly won the breed and third in the Group. This was his fourth Best of Breed win at Westminster.

Risto's winning had gotten off to an early start. He finished his championship at nine months of age from the Puppy Class, and from this class won his first Group. In all, he won 66 Bests in Show, 108 Sporting Groups and 5 Specialty Shows including Best in Show at the American Spaniel Club Specialty in 1967. He was handled throughout his career by Dick Cooper.

But outstanding as he had been as a winner, it is as a producer that Ch. Salilyn's Aristocrat most importantly will be remembered. To date, "Risto" has sired 188 champion get. He is the All-Time, All-Breed Top Producer with 10 Top Producing progeny and 11 Top Ten Winners. His bloodlines have carried down through each generation and are prominent in the current winners of today. His son, Ch. Telltale Author, a Best in Show and Specialty winner, is now most valuable to the breed as a Top Producing sire.

185

Ch. Salilyn's Colonel's Overlord.

CH. SALILYN'S COLONEL'S OVERLORD
(black/white—whelped 1967)

Ch. Salilyn's Citation II
Ch. Inchidony Prince Charming
Ch. Salilyn's Cinderella II
Ch. Salilyn's Aristocrat
Salilyn's Royal Consort
Ch. Salilyn's Lily of the Valley
Salilyn's Glenda
CH. SALILYN'S COLONEL'S OVERLORD
Ch. Salilyn's Cocktail Time
Salilyn's Good Fortune
Ch. Salilyn's Good Omen
Ch. Salilyn's Radiance
Ch. Salilyn's MacDuff
Ch. Randalane's Bright Chips
Ch. Ascot's Libby

Ch. Salilyn's Sensation, CD
Salilyn's Princess Meg
Ch. King Peter of Salilyn
A/C Ch. Walpride Gay Beauty
Ch. Salilyn's Citation II
Ch. Salilyn's Estralita
Ch. King William of Salilyn
Ch. Salilyn's Good Omen

Ch. Salilyn's MacDuff
Ch. Salilyn's Concerto
Ch. Cartref Bob Bobbin
Salilyn's Surprise
Ch. King William of Salilyn
Shercliff's Lady Debbie
Ch. Kaintuck Marc Anthony
Ch. Sunhi's Doody

Andy was Springer of the Year for 1969, also top Phillips' System winner in the breed and the only Springer to place in the Top Ten Sporting Dogs for that year. As a sire, he produced three Top Ten winners, including one "Modern Great", Ch. Salilyn's Encore. He has a total of 50 champion get.

Andy was co-owned by Forrest Andrews and Julia Gasow and handled by Dick Cooper.

Ch. Chinoe's Adamant James.

CH. CHINOE'S ADAMANT JAMES
(liver/white—whelped 1968)

A/C Ch. Salilyn's Citation II	Ch. Salilyn's Sensation, CD
Ch. Inchidony Prince Charming	Salilyn's Princess Meg
Ch. Salilyn's Cinderella II	Ch. King Peter of Salilyn
Ch. Salilyn's Aristocrat	A/C Ch. Walpride Gay Beauty
Salilyn's Royal Consort	Ch. Salilyn's Citation II
Ch. Salilyn's Lily of the Valley	Ch. Salilyn's Estralita
Salilyn's Glenda	Ch. King William of Salilyn
	Ch. Salilyn's Good Omen
CH. CHINOE'S ADAMANT JAMES	
	Ch. Salilyn's Sensation, CD
A/C Ch. Salilyn's Citation II	Salilyn's Princess Meg
Ch. Inchidony Prince Charming	Ch. King Peter of Salilyn
Ch. Salilyn's Cinderella II	A/C Ch. Walpride Gay Beauty
Ch. Canarch Inchidony Brook	Ch. Kaintuck Marc Anthony
Ch. Syringa Disc Jockey	Ch. Syringa Sue
Ch. Canarch Sunnyside, CD	Ch. Rostherne Hunter
Melilotus Hufty Tufty	Melilotus Princess Dona

In according him his win of Best in Show all-breeds at Westminster in 1971, the late judge O. C. Harriman dubbed Ch. Chinoe's Adamant James "super dog". The accolade seems no exaggeration. "D-J" (derived from his original nickname of Diamond Jim, which he acquired because of a white spot on his hip) held the record for the greatest number of Bests in Show and Group Firsts ever scored by an American show dog within one year— 48 Bests in Show and 86 Group Firsts in 1971, a record held to 1980 when it was broken by a Standard Poodle, Ch. Lou-Gin's Kiss Me Kate. Included in "D-J's" winning were such major events as Westminster, Chicago, Beverly Hills, Indianapolis, Western Reserve, Harrisburg, and a phenomenal streak of 30 consecutive Group Firsts.

Following his spectacular year, "D-J" was shown just three times in 1972, going Best in Show each time: first at the American Spaniel Club, then at Westminster in Madison Square Garden, where he became the first dog in two decades to win Best in Show back-to-back; and then in closing, his home town show at Louisville, Kentucky. This brought his career total to 61 Bests in Show, 107 Groups and 3 Specialties.

Adamant James was bred by Mrs. Ann Roberts of Lexington, Kentucky. Whelped June 30, 1968, he was purchased at the age of only ten weeks by the family of Dr. Milton E. Prickett, as a birthday gift for him (who had designated his choice of the litter two weeks earlier). "D-J" was shown throughout his career by Mrs. Roberts' brother, professional handler Clint Harris.

Ch. Salilyn's Encore.

CH. SALILYN'S ENCORE
(black/white—whelped 1970)

Ch. Inchidony Prince Charming
Ch. Salilyn's Aristocrat
Ch. Salilyn's Lily of the Valley
Ch. Salilyn's Colonel's Overlord
Salilyn Good Fortune
Ch. Salilyn's Radiance
Ch. Randalane's Bright Chips

A/C CH. SALILYN'S ENCORE

A/C Ch. Salilyn's Citation II
Ch. Inchidony Prince Charming
Ch. Salilyn's Cinderella II
Ch. Salilyn's Something Special
Salilyn's Royal Consort
Ch. Salilyn's Lily of the Valley
Salilyn's Glenda

A/C Ch. Salilyn's Citation II
Ch. Salilyn's Cinderella II
Salilyn's Royal Consort
Salilyn's Glenda
Ch. Salilyn's Cocktail Time
Ch. Salilyn's Good Omen
Ch. Salilyn's MacDuff
Ch. Ascot's Libby

Ch. Salilyn's Sensation, CD
Salilyn's Princess Meg
Ch. King Peter of Salilyn
A/C Ch. Walpride Gay Beauty
A/C Ch. Salilyn's Citation II
Ch. Ascot's Estralita
Ch. King William of Salilyn
Ch. Salilyn's Good Omen

Although a Best in Show dog, "Corey's" place in history will be as a sire of great importance. He has eight different Specialty winning get, including Top Winner and Top Producer Ch. Salilyn's Classic. His 40 champions have earned over 80 Bests in Show, and many have been Top Producers. "Corey" is owned by Edna Randolph and Don Snyder of Medford, New York.

Ch. Salilyn's Classic.

CH. SALILYN'S CLASSIC
(liver/white—whelped 1971)

Ch. Salilyn's Aristocrat
Ch. Salilyn's Colonel's Overlord
Ch. Salilyn's Radiance
Ch. Salilyn's Encore
    Ch. Inchidony Prince Charming
    Ch. Salilyn's Something Special
    Ch. Salilyn's Lily of the Valley

CH. SALILYN'S CLASSIC

    Ch. Inchidony Prince Charming
    Ch. Salilyn's Aristocrat
    Ch. Salilyn's Lily of the Valley
Salilyn's Arista
    Ch. Salilyn's Inchidony Banquo
    Ch. Valdarae's Pembroke Sea Mist, CD
    Ch. Phyliss Duchess of Pembroke, CD

Ch. Inchidony Prince Charming
Ch. Salilyn's Lily of the Valley
Salilyn's Good Fortune
Ch. Randalane's Bright Chips
A/C Ch. Salilyn's Citation II
Ch. Salilyn's Cinderella II
Salilyn's Royal Consort
Salilyn's Glenda

A/C Ch. Salilyn's Citation II
Ch. Salilyn's Cinderella II
Salilyn's Royal Consort
Salilyn's Glenda
Ch. Salilyn's MacDuff
Ch. Salilyn's Cinderella II
Ch. Salilyn's Santa Claus
Grande Pointe's First Lady

Classic's outstanding show record included 44 Bests in Show and 110 Group Firsts with 3 National Specialty Bests of Breed. In 1975 "Chip" received the Kennel Review Award for Top Sire for all breeds. He also won the Quaker Oats Award for Top Sporting Group Winner and tied with Aristocrat for Parent Club Sire of the Year. "Chip" has sired 100 champions, including 9 Top Ten Breed winners and 13 Top Producers. It is interesting to note that Classic's name appears frequently in the pedigrees of more current Top Winners and Producers than any other name.

He was bred and owned by Salilyn Kennels and handled by Dick Cooper.

Ch. Salilyn's Hallmark.

CH. SALILYN'S HALLMARK
(liver/white—whelped 1973)

Ch. Salilyn's Colonel's Overlord
Ch. Salilyn's Encore
Ch. Salilyn's Something Special
Ch. Salilyn's Classic
Ch. Salilyn's Aristocrat
Ch. Salilyn's Arista
Ch. Valdarae's Pembroke Sea Mist, CD

CH. SALILYN'S HALLMARK

Ch. Inchidony Prince Charming
Ch. Salilyn's Aristocrat
Ch. Salilyn's Lily of the Valley
Ch. Salilyn's Welcome Edition
Eng. Ch. Cleavehill Dandini
Ch. Kennersleigh Cleavehill Beliza Bee
Eng. Ch. Bella Bee of Kennersleigh

Ch. Salilyn's Aristocrat
Ch. Salilyn's Radiance
Ch. Inchidony Prince Charming
Ch. Salilyn's Lily of the Valley
Ch. Inchidony Prince Charming
Ch. Salilyn's Lily of the Valley
Ch. Salilyn's Inchidony Banquo
Ch. Phyllis Duchess of Pembroke, CD

A/C Ch. Salilyn's Citation II
Ch. Salilyn's Cinderella II
Salilyn's Royal Consort
Salilyn's Glenda
Glencora Shooting Star
Eng. Ch. Dulcie of Kennersleigh
Eng. Fld. Ch. Studley Major
Beliza of Bramhope

In 1976 "Nicky" won both the Great Lakes English Springer Spaniel Breeders Association Specialty and the National Specialty. Handled by Dick Cooper, he was also the Number One Sporting Dog in 1977—both systems, and winner of the Quaker Oats Award for that year. He was Parent Club Springer of the Year in 1976, 1977 and in 1978. He was named a Top Producer in 1979 and 1981 and has 30 champion progeny to date. "Nicky" was bred and is owned by Salilyn Kennels.

Ch. Telltale Author.

CH. TELLTALE AUTHOR
(liver/white—whelped 1974)

Ch. Salilyn's Citation II
Ch. Inchidony Prince Charming
Ch. Salilyn's Cinderella II
Ch. Salilyn's Aristocrat
Salilyn's Royal Consort
Ch. Salilyn's Lily of the Valley
Salilyn's Glenda

CH. TELLTALE AUTHOR

Ch. Salilyn Encore
Ch. Salilyn's Classic
Salilyn's Arista
Telltale Victoria
Ch. Inchidony Prince Charming
Canarch Triple Crown
Canarch Paddock, CD

Ch. Telltale Author was one of three champions sired by Aristocrat out of Telltale Victoria, a Classic daughter. His bid for the blue began at the 1975 GLESBA Specialty and history shows today that the Specialty ring would be his turf.

Author proved his merit among his peers earning 20 Specialty Bests of Breed, 13 independently held. Shown only twice in 1982, as a veteran, he defeated 350 Springer Spaniels by virtue of two Bests of Breed, the Eastern ESSC Specialty and the National Specialty. He retired the Wakefield Black Knight Memorial Trophy by having won the Eastern three times (1977, 1979 and 1982). He is the first to win the National from the Veterans Class and is also the first to win the ESSC of Michigan Fall Specialty three times (1977, 1978 and 1979). Twice awarded Best Springer Spaniel at Westminster, followed with a Group II, and in 1980 won the coveted Santa Barbara Sporting Group. He was the 1977 Parent Club Runner-Up Show Springer and the 1983 Parent Club Runner-Up Show Sire. Author was represented in the breed Top Ten in 1977, 1978, 1979 and 1980. In addition to his Specialty Awards, his all-breed record stands at 4 Bests in Show, 29 Group Firsts, 45 Group placements and 100 Bests of Breed. He has sired 24 champions—3 Best in Show sons, 11 Specialty winning get (three times sire of the National Specialties Winners Dog) and numerous sweepstakes winning progeny. Now retired, his lifetime record of breed points are an enviable 3, 181.

Author, an ageless, exhuberant showman, has demonstrated the greatness of his heart and the lasting quality of a fine dog. He was bred and is owned by Delores Streng. He was handled throughout his specials career by Karen Prickett and to his veteran wins by his owner.

197

Ch. Salilyn's Private Stock.

CH. SALILYN'S PRIVATE STOCK
(liver/white—whelped 1978)

Ch. Salilyn's Encore
Ch. Salilyn's Classic
Salilyn's Arista
Ch. Filicia's Bequest
   Ch. Charlyle's Fair Warning
Ch. Kaintuck Pixie
Kaintuck Sprite

CH. SALILYN'S PRIVATE STOCK
   Ch. Inchidony Prince Charming
Ch. Salilyn's Aristocrat
   Ch. Salilyn's Lily of the Valley
Ch. Salilyn's Sonnet
   Ch. Anglodale Mocha Bandit
Ch. Salilyn's Pirate Queen
   Ch. Salilyn's Something Special

Ch. Salilyn's Colonel's Overlord
Ch. Salilyn's Something Special
Ch. Salilyn's Aristocrat
Ch. Valdarae's Pembroke Sea Mist, CD
Ch. Inchidony Prince Charming
Charlyle's Nanette
Ch. Kaintuck Cupid
Ch. Cartref Spring Chime

Ch. Salilyn's Citation II
Ch. Salilyn's Cinderella II
Salilyn's Royal Consort
Salilyn's Glenda
Ch. Lorestra Gay Masquerade
Kenlor Mocha Minx
Ch. Inchidony Prince Charming
Ch. Salilyn's Lily of the Valley

"Stock's" show record includes 22 Bests in Show, 101 Group Firsts and 12 Specialty wins, including the 1981 National. "Stock" was Parent Club Springer of the Year in 1981 and 1982. He was Number One Sporting Dog in the Nation and Number One Springer Sire in 1982. He was Best of Breed at Westminster in 1982, 1983 and 1984 (GR 2 in '82 and '83, GR 3 in '84), and Best in Show at American Spaniel Club in 1983. As a producer, Stock has 18 champion progeny to date, including 5 Group winners and a Best in Show daughter. He was handled exclusively by George Alston for owners Julia Gasow (his breeder) and Robert Gough. Stock now resides at Salilyn Kennels in Troy, Michigan.

16

A Pictorial Gallery of
Notable Recent Springers

THIS CHAPTER strikingly shows how the dogs we have chosen as the "Ten Modern Greats" in Chapter 15 are the foundation for the notable winning dogs of today.

If you examine the pedigrees of these recent notables, you will see that each has stemmed from one of the "greats". We have identified the sire and dam of each dog, and for those marked with an asterisk a fuller pedigree is included on Pages 280 to 287. In addition, we have attempted to group them to show (as near as possible) their family relationship. This should prove an interesting and helpful guide to novices establishing themselves in the show sport.

Ch. El Toro's Scotch Flag

Ch. Salilyn's Signature ex Beryltown Gingershap of Toro
Whelped 1-69

Flag was the Top Winning Springer in the breed for 1973. In just over half of the year, he accumulated a Best in Show, 10 Group firsts and 3 Specialty Bests of Breed. Bred by Elva M. Taisey, he was owned by Earl Taisey and handled by George Alston. — *Ashbey.*

Ch. Vernon's Marco Polo

(Salilyn's Morning Breeze II
ex Salilyn's Dolly Vernon)
Whelped 7-13-70

Marco is the result of breeding sister to brother, those being a result of breeding mother (Ch. Salilyn's Lily of the Valley) to her son (Ch. Salilyn's Aristocrat). Marco retired after a brilliant show career undefeated from both the Veteran and Stud Dog Class. Today he lives on in his numerous progeny and his grandchildren. Marco was bred and owned by LaDaise Westlake of Milford, Michigan. — *Gilbert.*

Ch. Marjon's Miles Standish

(Ch. Marjon's Woodruff ex
Marjon's Priscilla Mullens)
Whelped 2-18-72

To our knowledge, "Miles" stands as the top winning tri-color to date in the breed. Winner of all-breed Bests in Show in both the United States and Mexico, his overall record included 4 all-breed Bests in Show, 2 Specialty Bests of Breed and 11 Group firsts. Miles is the sire of ten champions in both the United States and Canada. He was bred and owned by Peggy and Vern Johnson of Santa Ana, California.

Ch. Loujon Executor

(Ch. Chinoe's Adamant James
ex Ch. Loujon Jennifer)
Whelped 8-31-72

Ricky stood as #2 Springer in both 1975 and 1976. His show career included such outstanding wins as Group first at Westminster in 1976 and Best of Breed at the 1974 National Specialty. He is the sire of many champions, including Top Producer Ch. Loujon's Femininity. He is owned by Jo Ann Larsen and was handled by his breeder Karen Prickett. — *Booth*.

Ch. Salilyn's Exclusive*

(Ch. Salilyn's Colonel's Overload
ex Ch. Salilyn's Allure)
Whelped 8-11-76

Scoop was never seriously shown as a special but is best known for his accomplishments as a sire. He has produced many Specialty winning children, including Ch. Krystal's Exclusively Thomas and Ch. Salilyn's Tempo, both multiple Group and Specialty winners, and the Winners Bitch at the 1983 National Specialty (from the 6-9 Puppy Class), Mystic's Love-in-a-Mist. Scoop was bred and is owned by Salilyn Kennels. — *Booth*.

Ch. Krystal's Exclusively Thomas

(Ch. Salilyn's Exclusive
ex Laday Adamant Krystal)
Whelped 3-26-80

Thomas did top winning as a puppy, finishing at 14½ months old, including Best of Winners at two Specialties. His show career has many fine highlights with 2 Bests in Show, 11 Group firsts and 7 Specialty Bests of Breed. As a sire he has two American champions and three Canadian champions to date. Thomas was bred and is owned by John and Mary Grill and has been handled to all his wins by Cathy Prickett. — *Olson*.

Ch. Salilyn's Tempo

(Ch. Salilyn's Exclusive ex Ch. Salilyn's Limited Edition)
Whelped 6-9-77

Tempo was ranked #2 Springer in 1980 and 1981 and has multiple Group and Bests in Show wins to his credit. He was shown by the South's most prominent handler, Houston Clark of Chatanooga, Tennessee, for owners Alan and Sonnie Novick of Rustic Woods Kennels. — *Ritter.*

Ch. Kay'N Dee Geoffrey, Am. & Can. CD and WD

(Ch. Salilyn's Classic ex
Ch. Judge's Pride Jennifer, CD
Whelped 8-21-76

A multiple Group winner, Geoffrey has been awarded over 100 Bests of Breed and was ranked in the Top Ten in the breed in 1979 and 1980. He has produced 18 champion get, 10 alone in 1983. Geoffrey was bred by Dr. Mary Gibbs and is owned by Dr. Gibbs and Deborah Kirk. — *Ashbey.*

204

A/C & Bda. Ch. Kay'N Dee King of the Road, A/C CDX, WD

(Ch. Kay'N Dee Geoffrey ex Ch. Kay'N Dee Maginna's Gibson Girl, CD)
Whelped 11-21-80

Roady exemplifies the totally versatile dog, being a showdog, obedience dog and able to work in the field, with a Working Dog Certificate to his credit. Roady is owned by Deborah Kirk of Southbury, Connecticut.

Ch. Prelude's Echo*

(Ch. Salilyn's Colonel's Overlord
ex Ch. Salilyn's Debutante II)
Whelped 5-6-76

Co-owned by Julia Gasow and Jaqueline Tousley, "Floyd's" show record includes the Quaker Oats Award for Top Sporting Dog in 1979 and 1980. He won the National Specialty in 1979 and has over 20 Bests in Show to his credit, handled by Dick Cooper. He was a Top Producer in 1981 with over a dozen champion offspring that are multiple Group and Best in Show winners. He now resides with his owner Jaqueline Tousley in Zionsville, Indiana.

Ch. Salilyn's Headliner
at Marjon

(Ch. Prelude's Echo ex
Ch. Salilyn's Limited Edition)
Whelped 11-27-79

In 1982 "Troy" was #2 Springer and was awarded runner-up to Show Springer of the Year by the Parent Club. He has accumulated a total of 6 Bests in Show, 23 Group firsts and 2 Specialty Bests of Breed. He has three champion progeny to date, with several pointed towards their championships. Troy was bred by Salilyn Kennels and co-owned by Peggy and Vern Johnson with Gloria and Nat Reese. He is pictured here with his handler Corky Vroom. — *Bergman.*

Ch. Filicia's Rainmaker
of McDerry

(Ch. Salilyn's Encore ex
Ch. Filicia's Aliden Bisket)
Whelped 7-22-79

At this time, Rainmaker—a multiple Group winner—stands as the #3 Springer in the country. His progeny are not yet a year old but already have accounted for several major wins from the Puppy Class. Bred by Dr. Ann Pope, Rainmaker is owned by Arnold and Jane Goldie and Ann Pope. — *Ashbey.*

206

Ch. Filicia's Bequest*

(Ch. Salilyn's Classic ex
Ch. Kaintuck Pixie, CD)
Whelped 6-25-73

Sidney finished his championship in five shows, handled by his previous owner and breeder Ann Pope. He was then sold to Salilyn Kennels — to do his job as a top producer. His other littermates consisted of four champions, two of them Best in Show winners. Sidney is prominent in the pedigrees of many modern Springers and is the sire of the top winners — Ch. Salilyn's Private Stock, Ch. Kimet's Kristopher Robin and Ch. Telltale Gambit — and grandfather of Ch. Filicia's Dividend. He is owned by Salilyn Kennels. — *Klein*.

Ch. Filicia's Etching*

(Ch. Salilyn's Classic ex
Ch. Kaintuck Pixie, CD)
Whelped 6-25-73

A litter brother of "Bequest", Etching was the one to do the winning in the ring. During his show career, he accumulated a Best in Show, 33 Sporting Group firsts, and 5 Specialty Bests of Breed. "Max" was bred by Ann Pope and co-owned by Robert Gough with Ann Pope. He was handled throughout his career by George Alston — *Gilbert*.

A/C & Mex. Ch. Kimet's Kristopher Robin, Can. CD

(Ch. Filicia's Bequest ex
Salilyn's Radiant Taunya)
Whelped 9-8-79

Early into 1983, Kris is #1 in the breed. His many prestigious wins include Best in Show at Canada's Show of Shows (for only Best in Show winners) in 1982, Best in Show at the Kennel Club of Beverly Hills and Best of Breed at the 1983 National Specialty. In total, he has 8 Bests in Show and several fine Group wins. Kris has sired six litters to date, with progeny winning majors from the Puppy Class. Kris was bred and is owned by Nona F. Butts of Victoria, B.C. and handled by Gary Zayac. — Ludwig.

Ch. Bordalyn's Behold*

(Ch. Salilyn's Classic ex
Ch. Bordalyn's Begin Again)
Whelped 4-27-74

In 1979 "Rascal" was #4 in the breed with wins including the National Specialty and American Spaniel Club. As a sire, he has produced 16 champions, 7 Sweepstakes winners, and several of his progeny have been point winners at Specialty Shows. He was a Top Producer in 1978, having sired the Top Producers Ch. Salilyn's Limited Edition and Ch. Flintlock's Hope of Lear. Rascal was bred by Bonnie Bosley Christiano and owned by Debbie Ritter of Chesapeake, Virginia. — Ashbey.

Ch. Salilyn's Continental

(Ch. Salilyn's Classic ex
Ch. Salilyn's Sophistication)
Whelped 3-74

"Lincoln" captured the Quaker Oats
award for winning the most Sporting
Groups in 1978. To date, he has approximately 20 champion offspring.
Handled by Houston Clark, Lincoln was
bred by Salilyn Kennels and owned by
Patricia Cabot. — *Graham.*

A/C Ch. Winacko's Classic Replay, CD*

(Ch. Salilyn's Classic ex
Canarch Yankee Tea Party, CD)
Whelped 9-28-72

As a showdog, "Herbie" was a multiple
Group and Specialty winner and was
ranked in the Top Ten Springers in 1974
through 1976. He was Best of Breed at
the American Spaniel Club in 1980 from
the Veterans Class. Most importantly, he
has been most valuable as a producer.
To date, he has sired 38 champion offspring and was the Parent Club Sire of
the Year in 1981, and runner-up sire in
1978 and 1980. He has qualified five
times for the *Kennel Review* Top Producer award. Herbie was bred by David
Morman and is owned by Kathleen
Lorentzen of Saginaw, Michigan. — *Booth.*

Ch. Winacko's Editor's Choice, CD*

(Ch. Salilyn's Classic ex
Canarch Yankee Tea Party)
Whelped 9-28-72

Like his brother, Ch. Winacko's Classic Replay, "George" is also a Top Producer, with 27 champion progeny to his credit. Included in these are two Top Ten winners, Ch. Jester's Jack-in-the-Box and Ch. Chuzzlewit's Editorial. George was bred and is owned by David and Jan Morman of Winacko Springers. — Weston.

Ch. Jester's Jack-in-the-Box

(Ch. Winacko's Editor's Choice, CD
ex Ch. Venetian Jester's Jypsi)
Whelped 2-4-78

Bred and owned by Andrea Glassford, "Boxer" holds titles in Canada, Puerto Rico, Santa Domingo, Columbia and Uruguay, as well as in the United States. He is a multiple Best in Show and Specialty winner and was #3 in the breed and #7 Sporting Dog in 1981, always handled by Tom Glassford. He is the sire of many champions, some of whom are multiple Group winners. — Alverson.

A/C Ch. Donahan's Mark Twain*

(Ch. Telltale Author ex
Donahan's Vanna Brook, CD)
Whelped 6-4-77

Mark is credited with 8 Bests in Show, 32 Group firsts. He was awarded 5 Specialty Bests of Breed, including Best of Breed at the American Spaniel Club in 1981, Santa Clara Valley ESSA and Best of Breed over a large entry at the Puget Sound ESSA held the day before the 1982 National Specialty. Mark is the sire of 4 champions with numerous other pointed offspring. Now working towards his CD, Mark resides with his breeder-owners, Don and Carol Callahan.

Ch. Jester's Southwind Twister

(Ch. Jester's Jack-in-the-Box
ex Ch. Salilyn's Sugar N' Spice)
Whelped 7-7-80

Twister finished his championship from the Puppy Class and has since become a multiple Group winner. He is the sire of many champions, who in turn became Group winners. He was bred by Collette Bergeron and is owned by Andrea Glassford of Ashtabula, Ohio. — *Petrulis.*

211

Ch. Salilyn's Design*

(Ch. Salilyn's Classic
ex Ch. Salilyn's Applause)
Whelped 4-2-80

Desi started his show career by finishing his championship with five majors. He was used at stud for less than a year and eight of his progeny to date have finished their championships. Included in these are dogs which are doing outstanding Group and Specialty winning themselves. Desi was bred and owned by Salilyn Kennels. — *Booth.*

Ch. Loujon Black Label

(Ch. Salilyn's Design
ex Ch. Loujon Heritage)
Whelped 3-22-81

Just starting in his specials career, "Jack" has accumulated 3 Bests in Show, 13 Group firsts and 5 Specialty Bests of Breed. He was bred by Karen Prickett and is co-owned by Dr. and Mrs. Milton Prickett with Thomas Bradley III. — *Ashdey.*

Ch. Filicia's Dividend*

(Ch. Salilyn's Private Stock ex
Ch. Danaho's Lalique of Stanton)
Whelped 5-29-80

In just a short time of campaigning, "Zoot" has won 15 Bests in Show and 46 Group firsts, making him one of the Top Sporting Dogs for 1983. He is the sire of 4 champions to date, including one Specialty winner. Zoot is owned by Alan and Sonnie Novick and handled by Houston and Toddie Clark. — *Petrulis.*

213

Ch. Canamer Prime Time

(Ch. Telltale Author ex
Ch. Canamer Telltale High Life, TD)
Whelped 6-16-80

"Whitley" is currently rated as #5
Springer nationally, with a total of 3
Bests in Show and 30 Group firsts.
Having been campaigned only one
year, it is too soon to feel his impact as a
sire. Whitley was bred by Irene Eadie
and Delores Streng and lives with his
owner Irene Eadie of Canamer
Springers. — Olson.

Ch. Stepney's Advocate

(Ch. Salilyn's Private Stock
ex Ch. Salilyn's Delight)
Whelped 11-17-80

Bred and owned by Steve and Jane
Stewart, Jim has accumulated multiple
Group wins. He is the result of breeding
a Top Producing sire to a dam, and in
turn, making her a Top Producer. —
Ashbey.

Ch. Stepney's Standing Ovation

(Ch. Salilyn's Private Stock ex Ch. Salilyn's Delight)
Whelped 11-17-80

A litter brother of Advocate, "Bucky's" many wins include 5 Group firsts and Best of Breed at the 1983 Eastern English Springer Spaniel Specialty. Bred by the Stewarts, he is owned by Celie Valentine and Teresa Patton and handled by George Alston. — *Harkins*.

—Ludwig

—Ashbey

Ch. Aspengrove's Dubonnet*
(Ch. Goodwill Aspengrove Q.T. ex Salilyn's Lady Kaye)
Whelped 1-24-75

Dubah stands, without doubt, as the top winning Springer bitch of all time, with an outstanding record of 3 all-breed Bests in Show, 5 Specialty Bests of Breed and Best of Breed at the 1978 National Specialty. To date, she is the dam of 7 champions. Dubah is owned by Dr. and Mrs. Patrick Baymiller and handled exclusively by Ray McGinnis.

17

Important
Springer Bitches

Y OUR KENNEL is no better than the bitches in it. The wise breeder's greatest investment should be in a worthy bitch. She need not be the most glamorous show bitch, but should be selected for her lack of faults rather than her outstanding virtues. It is important that she be of true Springer Spaniel type, that she be sound of body and limb, that she be well balanced and have a loving, dependable disposition.

It is my personal opinion that the dog you decide to breed to your bitch must come from a line-bred family in which the characteristics you are looking for have been firmly established on both the paternal and maternal side.

Always, you must keep a vivid picture in your mind of the dog you would like to create, based upon the official breed standard (p. 267).

A Springer Spaniel female seldom wins Groups and Bests in Show. She is a bit softer in temperament, less aggressive and often lacks the fire and flash of the males. For this reason, most breeders feel as I do that it is a far greater thrill to win Groups with a bitch, having overcome the challenge of defeating striking males in the breed competition.

Approximately once a year, it must be remembered, the female has been home facing the ordeal of delivering and caring for a litter of puppies—hopefully our winners of tomorrow. Even if not bred, she is somewhat handicapped twice a year by her semi-annual heat cycles. This sometimes causes a coat loss and lack of energy, both badly needed in the show ring.

The sires and dams of each bitch pictured here has been noted, and for those marked with an asterisk, a fuller pedigree is included on Pages 280 to 287.

Ch. Salilyn's Lily
of the Valley*

Salilyn's Royal Consort
ex Salilyn's Glenda)
Whelped 4-11-62

Lily was most famous for producir.g the all-breed top producer and winner Ch. Salilyn's Aristocrat. She had a total of 8 champion get and was runner-up for Parent Club Dam of the Year in 1975.

Ch. Canarch Inchidony Brook*

(Ch. Inchidony Prince Charming
ex Ch. Canarch Suhmyside, CD)
Whelped 1964

Bred by Charles Hendee, Brook was the foundation bitch of Chinoe Kennels, owned by Ann Roberts, Lexington, Ky. Brook's 13 champions included the all-time record holder for the breed, Ch. Chinoe's Adamant James—twice Best in Show at Westminster, and Ch. Canarch Juniper Five, also a Best in Show winner.

Am. & Can. Ch. Nobility's Venetian
Dawn, Am. & Can. U.D.*

(Ch. Salilyn's Cocktail Time
ex Ch. Salilyn's Nobility Rose)
Whelped 1965

Dawn was winner of the *Kennel Review* Top Producer Award in 1970 and 1972. She was dam of 8 American champions, all of which also held Obedience titles. Seven of these were also Canadian champions, one with CD degree. Her daughter, Am. & Can. Ch. S. Cricket Venetian, CD, received the *Kennel Review* Award in 1971, a second generation Top Producer. One son, Ch. Venetian Count Ducat, was a Best in Show winner, and another — Am. & Can. Ch. Venetian Count Casanova, Am. & Can. CD, was No. 5 Springer in the U.S. in 1972, and No. 2 in Canada. Dawn was bred by George Kitto and owned by Marjorie and Gilbert Rollins.

218

Ch. Kaintuck Pixie, CD

(Ch. Charlyle's Fair Warning
ex Kaintuck Sprite)
Whelped 6-27-66

Pictured here upon going Best of Opposite Sex at the Keystone Specialty at the age of seven, Pixie also had many other Specialty wins, including Michigan and Eastern. Pixie was a Top Producer in 1974 and has 16 champion progeny, with 3 Best in Show winners. Bred by the late Mr. Stuart Johnson of Kaintuck Kennels, she was owned by Dr. Ann Pope of Filicia Springers. — *Gilbert.*

Ch. Salilyn's Sophistication*

(Ch. Salilyn's Aristocrat
ex Ch. Salilyn's Radiance)
Whelped 11-24-67

A litter sister to Ch. Salilyn's Colonel's Overlord, "Sophie" won 19 Bests of Breed, including 3 Group firsts and 11 other Group placements. In 1970 she was Parent Club Show Bitch of the Year; in 1975 she was a Top Producer and was named Show Dam of the Year by the Parent Club. Among her 7 champion get, there are 3 Best in Show winners, including Quaker Oats Award Winner Ch. Salilyn's Continental. Sophie was bred by Col. Forest Andrews and owned by Mrs. F. H. Gasow. — *Booth.*

Ch. Salilyn's Welcome Edition

(Ch. Salilyn's Aristocrat
ex Ch. Kennersleigh Cleavehill
Beliza Bee)
Whelped 10-13-68

Edie's most memorable win as a show dog came at the age of nine, when she was awarded Best of Opposite Sex at the 1977 National Specialty from the Veteran's class, defeating 26 champion bitches. As a producer, she is credited with 10 champion offspring including Top Winner and Producer, Ch. Salilyn's Hallmark, and her Top Producing daughter, Ch. Salilyn's Limited Edition. She was a top producer herself in 1974 and 1978 and was runner-up Show Dam of the Year in 1974. Edie was bred and owned by Salilyn Kennels.

Ch. Loujon Jennifer

(Ch. Salilyn's Captain's Table
ex Loujon Cameo's Caprice)
Whelped 4-20-69

Pictured winning Best of Winners and Best Puppy at American Spaniel Club in 1970. Jennifer was the dam of 5 champions, including Group and Specialty winner, Ch. Loujon Executor. Jennifer was bred by Loujon Kennels and owned by Karen Prickett.

Telltale Victoria

(Ch. Salilyn's Classic ex
Canarch Triple Crown)
Whelped 6-26-72

In 1975 Victoria was a *Kennel Review* Top Producer by virtue of her breeding by Ch. Salilyn's Aristocrat, producing 3 champions of her only litter. Included is one who is Top Producer and Specialty winner of today, Ch. Telltale Author. Victoria's littermates, Ch. Telltale Prime Minister and Ch. Telltale Rambling Heart have also been successful as winners and producers. Victoria was bred and owned by Delores Streng of Farmington Hills, Michigan.

Ch. Jahil's Angelica

(Ch. Chinoe's Adamant James
ex Salilyn's Rookie)
Whelped 9-4-71

During her show career, "Angel May" received the Parent Club Best of Opposite Sex Award in 1974. She was a Top Producer in 1976 and 1979 with 8 champion offspring, which earned her Parent Club Dam of the Year. Angel May was bred by Edward and Joanne Sellier and owned by James and Diane May.

Canarch Yankee Tea Party, CD*

(Ch. Canarch Yankee Patriot, CD ex Canarch Incandescent)
Whelped 11-28-69

Tina had produced 10 champions from three litters, all sired by Ch. Salilyn's Classic. Among those were dogs who became multiple Group and Specialty winners, as well as top producers. Pictured here winning the Brood Bitch class at the 1977 National Specialty with her sons Ch. Winacko's Classic Replay, CD and Ch. Winacko's Sequoia, who went Best of Winners that day. Tina was bred by Charles Hendee and owned by David Morman. — *Booth.*

Ch. Bordalyn's Begin Again, CD*

(Ch. Salilyn's Paramount ex Ch. Welcome Joie de Vivre)
Whelped 6-29-72

Angel was part of an all champion litter of three and later became the dam of an all champion litter of six herself. In the showring, she won the 1973 Eastern Futurity and many other fine wins but will be best remembered as a top producer. She had produced 11 champions until her untimely death in 1979. She was awarded Parent Club Dam of the Year in 1977 and was recognized twice as a *Kennel Review* Top Producer. Some of her offspring are credited with National Specialty wins and obedience awards. Angel was bred by Rhody and Bonita Bosley and owned by Bonita Bosley Christiano of Bordalyn Springers.

Am. & Can.
Ch. Telltale Valleybrook Secret,
C.D., C.D.X., T.D.

Ch. Telltale Prime Minister
ex Can. Ch. Valleybrook U.E. Loyalist)
Whelped 8-17-73

Heather has had her share of accomplishments with 8 titles to her name. She is a champion in the United States and in Canada and has a C.D. and C.D.X. in both countries along with 3 Tracking degrees. In 1981, Heather was awarded Dam of the Year by the Parent Club with 5 champion offspring including 2 National Specialty Futurity winners. She was bred by Howard Northey of Ontario, Canada and is owned by James and Irene Eadie of Park Ridge, Illinois, where she is a member of the Illini Search and Rescue Team.

Ch. Whitestar's West Wind

(Ch. Salilyn's Aristocrat ex
Sundance's Midnight Magic)
Whelped 11-18-73

Windy is the foundation bitch of Whitestar Kennels in Torrance, California. She is the dam of 3 champion progeny, all of whom have done Group and Specialty winning. Windy was bred and is owned by Arvilla White.

Ch. Loujon Heritage

(Ch. Chinoe's Adamant James
ex Ch. Loujon Jennifer)
Whelped 3-21-74

Susie is the dam of 7 champions, with several Group and Specialty winning progeny. She herself has had nice wins, pictured here going Best of Winners and Best Puppy at the American Spaniel Club show in 1975, repeating her mother's win. Bred and owned by Karen Prickett. — *Gilbert*.

Ch. Venetian Cricket's Cinnamon

(Ch. Salilyn's Classic ex
Ch. S. Cricket Venetian)
Whelped 8-24-74

Cinnamon has had Best of Breed and Group placements, and was a Best of Opposite Sex Specialty show winner. She has had four litters and has produced 8 champions by four different sires. Cinnamon was bred and owned by Patricia and Charles Gibson.

Ch. Telltale Stella

(Ch. Salilyn's Aristocrat
ex Telltale Victoria)
Whelped 9-2-74

Keeping in the family of Top Producers, like her brothers Ch. Telltale Author and Ch. Telltale Rambling Heart, Stella was runner-up Show Dam of the Year in 1982, having produced many fine progeny. Stella was bred by Delores Streng and is owned by Franz and Rosemarie Wagner.

Ch. Telltale Rambling Heart

(Ch. Salilyn's Aristocrat
ex Telltale Victoria)
Whelped 9-2-74

A litter sister to Ch. Telltale Author, Peggy distinguished herself early by winning a 5 point major and Best of Opposite Sex at the Michigan Specialty show. She is among the progeny that placed her mother, Telltale Victoria, on the *Kennel Review* Top Producers list. She is the dam of multiple Best in Show winner Ch. Telltale Gambit, who was bred and co-owned by Delores Streng and resides with his owner Fred Pierson.

Ch. Loujons Femininity*

(Ch. Loujon Executor ex
Varis Cinderella Star)
Whelped 8-4-75

Bred by David and Linda Slagle, Amy is the foundation bitch for Shinnecock Kennels of Maureen Brady and Patty Alston. She earned most of her championship points at Specialty shows, finishing at Westminster KC. Then specialed for ten months, she was Parent Club Springer Bitch of the Year for 1977 and was a Group winner. As a producer, she is credited with 16 champion progeny. All of her first litter by Ch. Salilyn's Exclusive went on to become champions. Her children are the recipients of 7 Sweepstakes wins and 9 Specialty wins. Amy was awarded Top Producer by the Parent Club in 1980 and 1982 and was runner-up Producer in 1981. *Kennel Review* also named her a Top Producer in 1980 and 1982. Definitely a bitch who achieved an outstanding show record and has carried on her qualities in her offspring.

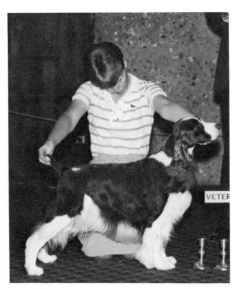

Ch. Venetian Jester's Jypsi

(Ch. Goodwill Copyright Reserved ex
Ch. Venetian Cricket's Shannon, CD)
Whelped 12-16-75

"Jypsi" has produced a total of 5 champions, with 2 Group winners included. She did most of her top winning as a Veteran, with a Best of Breed at the 1983 Michigan Specialty, Best of Opposite Sex at the Pittsburgh Specialty to her son, Ch. Jester's Jack-in-the-Box and Best of Opposite Sex at the 1983 National Specialty. Jypsi was bred by Marjorie Rollins and owned by Andrea Glassford.

Ch. Loujon Sarah

(Ch. Salilyn's Encore
ex Ch. Loujon Heritage)
Whelped 3-15-76

Sarah was Show Springer Bitch of the Year in 1981. During her career she became a multiple Group winner and Specialty Best of Breed winner. She was bred by M. E. DeGaris and owned by Karen Prickett of Loujon Kennels. — *Booth.*

Ch. Salilyn's Delight*

(Ch. Salilyn's Exclusive ex
Ch. Salilyn's Limited Edition)
Whelped 6-9-77

From a long string of Top Producers comes Ch. Salilyn's Delight. Her first litter by Ch. Salilyn's Private Stock put her on the top producers list in 1982 and was awarded Show Dam of the Year by the Parent Club. At this time, she is the dam of 5 champions with several almost finished. Delight was bred by Salilyn Kennels and is owned by Steve and Jane Stewart of Stepney Springers.

Ch. Danaho's Lalique of Stanton

(Ch. Filicia's Anlon Patriot
ex Ch. Danaho's Ballet Russe)

Rita was a Specialty winner with several Best of Breed wins to her credit. She produced two litters which resulted in four champions. Her litter by Ch. Salilyn's Private Stock produced Ch. Filicia's Dividend, one of the top winning dogs of today. Rita is owned by Dr. Ann Pope of Acton, Massachusetts.

Ch. Flintlock's
Hope of Lear*

(Ch. Bordalyn's Behold ex
Ch. Bordalyn's Once in Luv With Amy)
Whelped 6-21-75

Hope was recognized as Parent Club Dam of the Year in 1982, with a total of 6 champions to her credit. Hope finished her championship in 1978 along with two of her sisters, which earned her dam, Ch. Bordalyn's Once in Love With Amy, honor as runner-up dam of the year. Hope was bred by Betty and Ed Nudd and owned by Aida Angel and Joyce Goodson of Lear Springers in Stone Mountain, Georgia.

Ch. Salilyn's Lyra*

(Ch. Salilyn's Classic ex
Ch. Silverbow's December Dawn)
Whelped 11-1-76

During her show career, Lyra accumulated 12 Group firsts, plus 20 other group placements. In 1978 she was Best of Breed at the GLESBA Specialty, defeating 110 Springer Spaniels. In that same year, she was runner-up for Parent Club Show Springer of the Year. Bred by Nancy and Cecil Kemp, Lyra is owned by Salilyn Kennels.

Ch. Sylvan Classica

(Ch. Salilyn's Classic ex
Ch. Telltale Stella)
Whelped 9-77

Bred by Franz and Rosemarie Wagner, Classica has been awarded points twice at Westminster from the classes and once at the Long Island Specialty. She was bred and is owned by the Wagners of West Redding, Connecticut.

226

Am. & Can. Ch. Maginna's Royal Heiress*

(Ch. Chricket's Rhody Mac ex Ch. Loujon Maginna's Victoria)
Whelped 12-3-78

Princess finished her championship at 13 months of age with 3 majors. She had tied for runner-up Show Dam of the Year in both 1981 and 1982. She has 7 champion progeny from 2 litters and more pointed toward their championships. She was bred and is owned by Helen and David Maginnes of Maginna Springers.

Ch. Monogram's English Ivy

(Ch. Salilyn's Exclusive ex Joie's Venetian Jay Jay)
Whelped 1-19-79

Bred and owned by Maggie Madden, Ivy has produced 4 champion offspring, all sired by Ch. Salilyn's Private Stock. She was noted as a *Kennel Review* Top Producer in 1982, having an all champion litter of three, and has three other pointed get at this time. Her daughter, Ch. Monogram's English Garden is the top winning bitch for the 1982 and 1983 period. — *Booth.*

Ch. Canarch Lullabye

(Ch. Alamanac's Autograph ex Telltale Punctuation)
Whelped 5-8-79

Though Eva is still a young bitch, she already has 3 champions to her credit, with several youngsters coming up. One of her sons has some Specialty wins and several Bests of Breed early in his career. Bred by Marylee Hendee and Delores Streng and owned by Janice Johnson of Cambrian Kennels.

227

Ch. Kay'N Dee Maginna's
Gibson Girl, C.D.

(Ch. Vernon's Marco Polo ex
Ch. Loujon Maginna's Victoria)
Whelped 8-79

Gibson Girl was Winners Bitch at the 1980 National Specialty under Mr. Melbourne T. L. Downing. She has produced 12 puppies from two litters and all are champions. She was bred by Helen Maginnes and owned by Dr. Mary Gibbs.

Ch. Salilyn's Joy
of Phylwayne

(Ch. Prelude's Echo ex
Ch. Salilyn's Limited Edition)
Whelped 11-27-79

A litter sister to Ch. Salilyn's Headliner at Marjon, Joy has also accomplished quite a record. Completely owner-handled by Wayne Magill, she has 26 Bests of Breed, including one Specialty and 55 Bests of Opposite Sex, with 2 Specialties and 7 Group placements. She is pictured here in her win of Best of Breed at the Puget Sound ESSA under Mrs. Virginia Lynne, where she also won the Brood Bitch class. Having been bred but once, she has two champion daughters. Joy was bred by Salilyn Kennels and is owned by Wayne and Phyllis Magill of Kent, Washington.

Ch. Shinnecock's Simply Smashing

(Ch. Winako's Classic Replay, CD
ex Ch. Loujon's Femininity)
Whelped 4-8-80

Jessie is the result of breeding a top produc-
ing sire to a top producing dam. She has
lived up to her name with many impressive
Specialty Sweepstakes and Best of Opposite
Sex awards. She is ranked among the top
bitches in the ring today. Bred by Maureen
Brady and Patty Alston; owned by Christine
Miller and Maureen Brady.

Ch. Whitestar's Irish Lace*

(Whitestar's Wayward Wind
ex Lakme's Summer Star)
Whelped 7-5-80

"Kelly" finished her championship at the
1982 National Specialty by going Best of
Winners. In one year's time on the West
Coast, she has become a multiple Best of
Breed and Group placing bitch. She is currently ranked +3 bitch in the nation and has
been owner-handled by Arvilla Phite.

229

Ch. Stepney's Cinderella

(Ch. Salilyn's Private Stock
ex Ch. Salilyn's Delight)
Whelped 11-17-80

Bred and owned by Steve and Jane Stewart, Cindy finished in style with 4 majors, including Best of Winners at American Spaniel Club in 1982. Just starting out into motherhood, she has 2 champion sons, including the Winners Dog from the 1983 National Specialty, from the 9-12 Puppy class, Ch. Salilyn's Dynasty.

Ch. Monogram's English Garden*

(Ch. Salilyn's Private Stock ex
Ch. Monogram's English Ivy)
Whelped 12-16-80

During 1982, "Heather" completed her championship and then moved onto a Specials career which found her receiving the Parent Club award for Best of Opposite Sex Show Springer, defeating 1,198 Springers and ranked her #2 Springer by breed points behind her father, Ch. Salilyn's Private Stock. At not quite three, she continues a winning record with a Best in Show, 8 Group firsts and many other Group placements. Her Specialty winning record includes one Best of Breed, and 10 Bests of Opposite. At this writing, she stands as the top winning bitch of 1983. Heather was bred and is owned by Maggie Madden and has been handled throughout her career by Barbara Gamache.

230

18

Showing Your Springer

ALTHOUGH the main purpose of dog shows is to promote the breeding of purebred dogs, the showing of dogs has become a sport of major importance. It offers what is for many the opportunity of achievement as meaningful as the Olympics, and competition as exciting as the World Series.

Fundamentally, when you pay an entry fee at a dog show, you pay for the judge's opinion of your dog. His decision will be based upon how closely your dog conforms to the official standard of the breed, in comparison to the others in his ring. The American Kennel Club suggests a time allowance of less than three minutes for the judging of each dog, so it is essential that you have your entry looking his best and showing to advantage whenever the judge's glance happens to come his way.

This calls for homework. Ring manners can be taught fairly easily. For instance, any dog can learn to walk on a leash—but the important thing is how he does it. A top show dog loves the ring and therefore moves with style and spirit. To accomplish this end result you must have patience, and be willing to take things slowly, never making a "duty" of his lessons. The secret of making a showman is to keep the illusion, forever, that this is a "fun-game".

Training the Puppy for Show

A puppy's training can begin as soon as he is able to walk steadily. Stand him on a table and, while you hold his head up with your left hand, use your right hand to *very gently and slowly* distribute his weight evenly on all four legs. In a surprisingly short time, he will learn to hold this pose alone with merely a touch of your finger under his chin and his tail.

By the time he is seven weeks old, your puppy should be acquainted with a show lead. Use a soft 1/4-inch Resco variety. Children do well leash-breaking puppies. However, they must be emphatically cautioned never to pull or jerk the leash. The puppy must enjoy what he is doing and as soon as he begins to tire, the lesson must end.

I cannot emphasize too strongly the benefits of entering your dog in licensed matches and conformation classes, and of accustoming him to riding with you in the car, and to crowds and noises of all kinds. Last, but far from least, it is important to introduce him to a dog crate, for remember, at dog shows he must live in one.

Coat

To be able to build a strong, healthy coat, you must have the following:

1) *A healthy dog.* Coat is a mirror of the health and condition inside your dog.

2) *Proper diet.* Good food in adequate quantity is essential for prime condition, which is reflected in blemish-free skin and soft, shining hair—winter and summer.

3) *Sufficient exercise.* Also, it is necessary for your dog to have plenty of fresh air and sunshine. This calls for judgment under severe changes in the weather. For instance, the direct rays of the summer sun can be the ruination of a show coat. Not only will the liver dogs fade when subjected to constant sunlight, but the blacks, under the same conditions, will take on a henna hue that is most undesirable, and the body coat of both will become dry and harsh.

Bathing

"Cleanliness is next to Godliness". Contrary to some advice, we feel that frequent bathing with the best quality shampoos render health to a dog's skin and hair coat. Frequent applications of water, bathing once a week, livens the skin and removes scale. A good quality creme rinse, diluted with water, should follow every bath. It is suggested that a coat oil be applied to the coat through the week to prevent tangles and hair breakage. We use *"Pro-Gro",* manufactured by the Pro-Line Company.

It is essential to bathe and blanket our dog 24 hours before trimming.

Time Schedule for Show Trimming

If a dog is completely untrimmed, the work should be done in three stages, starting two full weeks before the show.

Otherwise, trim your Springer about 2 or 3 days before a show. The hair on his head and clippered areas will have grown out sufficiently to give him a natural look and to enable you to even out any marks or lines you may have left.

Ch. Telltale Author, English Springer Spaniel, owned by Delores Streng, with Ch. Oaktree's Irishtocrat, Irish Water Spaniel, owned by Anne Snelling, together before going into the Sporting Group to compete against each other.

TRIMMING THE SPRINGER FOR SHOW

It must be remembered that there has never been a "perfect" dog, but it is possible to greatly improve any dog with proper trimming. By studying the official standard you can form a picture of the Springer *you* like and trim accordingly, using the standard as your guide.

People who are skilled in show trimming have their own methods for obtaining their desired effects. As a matter of fact, a good trimmer can br recognized by the individual style he puts on a dog. We do not contend here that our way of trimming is the "right" way—only that it gives us the effect we like best.

In the past 15 years there have been changes in grooming. Better ways have been developed for getting that look or effect we want. But the overall picture remains the same. The real purpose is to cover up the bad spots and accentuate the good.

Tools Needed:

Straight scissors
Thinning shears (single bladed)
Resco medium tooth steel comb
Oster clipper with #10 blade
Stripping knives - fine, medium, coarse
Pin brush
Toenail clippers

Head (Photo #1)

This area is the most important part of trimming the Springer. The trimmer can accentuate the chiseling around the eyes and cheeks, thereby bringing out the dog's expression.

Ears

Start 1/3 of the way down. Trim against the grain up to the top of the ear. **(Photo #2).** Repeat the same procedure on the inside of the ear, allowing it to lay as close as possible to the head. **(Photo #3).**

1

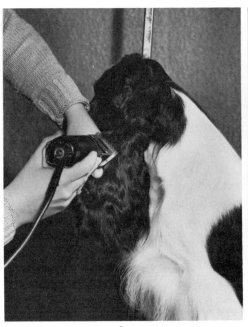

2

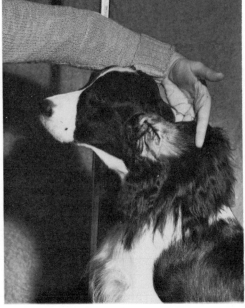

3

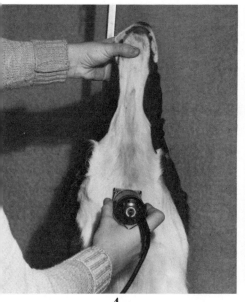

4

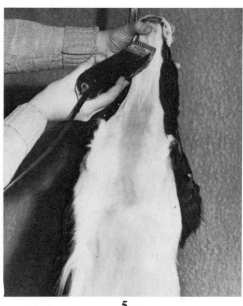

5

Throat—Start about 2 inches from the breastbone **(Photo #4),** trimming against the grain, up to under the chin. **(Photo #5).** Under the ear, with the grain, take the clippers down to your starting point. **(Photo #6).** Clean out the hair in between by going against the grain up under the lip. **(Photo #7).**

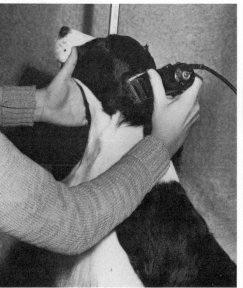

6

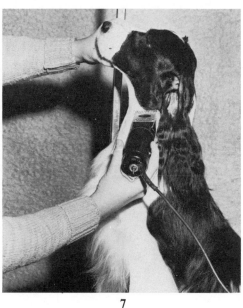

7

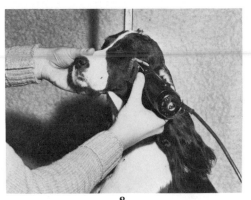

8

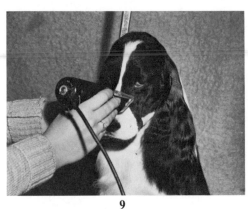

9

Lower face and cheeks—Clip closely against the grain to show chiseling around the eyes—all intending to bring out expression. **(Photo #8).**

The Stop—Using the corner of the clipper, go with the grain into the groove, and proceed over the skull, making it as flat as possible, to the occipital bone. **(Photo #9).** Then pull the skin forward with your thumb, and with the clippers smooth over the occipital bone. **(Photo #10).** Continue the clippers with the grain over the sides of the skull, being careful to leave the eyebrows. Blend the line that you made when the ear was finished. **(Photo #11).**

The whiskers should be removed with the straight scissors or lightly with the clippers. **(Photo #12).**

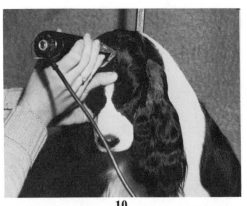

10

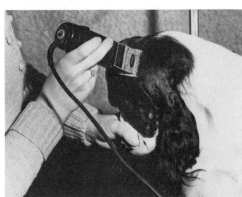

11

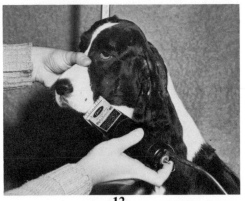

12

13

The Neck and Shoulder

With the dog's chin held upward in your left hand, trim the hair with the thinning shears to the line made by the clipper. **(Photo #14).**

Thinning Shears—Use of this tool requires practice for perfection. A medium weight, single-blade thinning shears gives best results and should be handled as if you were a barber trimming the back of a man's head.

Hold a "medium" tooth steel comb in your left hand and lift up the hair. As you move the comb upward against the grain, cut the ends of the hair above the comb. Comb the hair back down after each cutting. Repeat the procedure until the hair is the desired length. **(Photo #15).**

The hair on the top of the neck should be left longer so there is no apparent break to show where the neck ends. The hair should be left long enough on the neck to give the appearance of the neck blending into the shoulders.

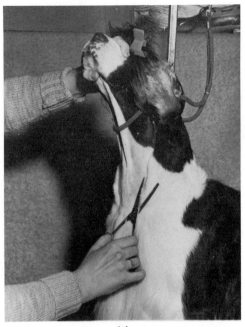

14

Blend in the clipper lines behind the ear at the occipital bone, into the neck. **(Photo #16).** Beward of the white hair—it can easily leave scissor marks.

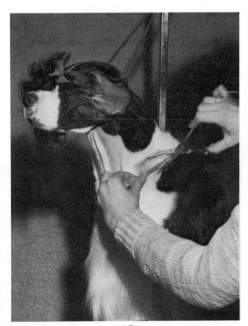

15

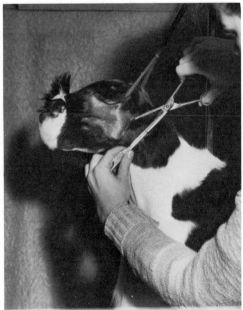

16

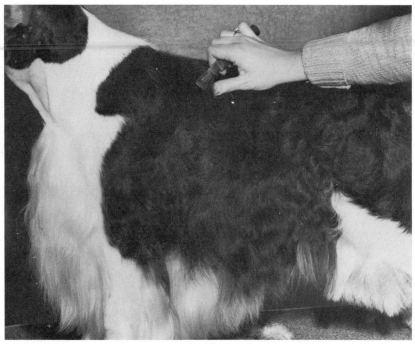

The Body Coat

The following procedure is used to give the coat a naturally flat look. In order to do this, you have to thin the undercoat by pulling it out with a stripping knife, as opposed to scissoring the top coat.

Hold the knife in your right hand. Keeping in mind it is the softer of the two coats you want to take out (*the undercoat*), gather a small amount of hair between your thumb and the blade and pull in the direction you want the hair to lay. **(Photo #17).**

It is important to be sure not to "pluck" the coat as with a Terrier, but to "pull" to avoid damaging the top coat.

We are thus able to improve the outline and the contour of the dog and at the same time keep the natural, unbarbered look as stated in the standard.

Trimming the Tail

This is the second and only area where the clippers must be used. Starting from under the tail, take your clipper with the grain of the hair to the tip of the tail—do *not* go over the tip. **(Photo #18).** Any hair on the tip may be carefully taken off with the thinning shears. **(Photo #19).**

Now, with the thinning shears, blend the hair into the upper thigh **(Photo #20).** Your stripping knife may be used here alternately with the thinning shears to blend for a more natural look. **(Photo #21).**

238

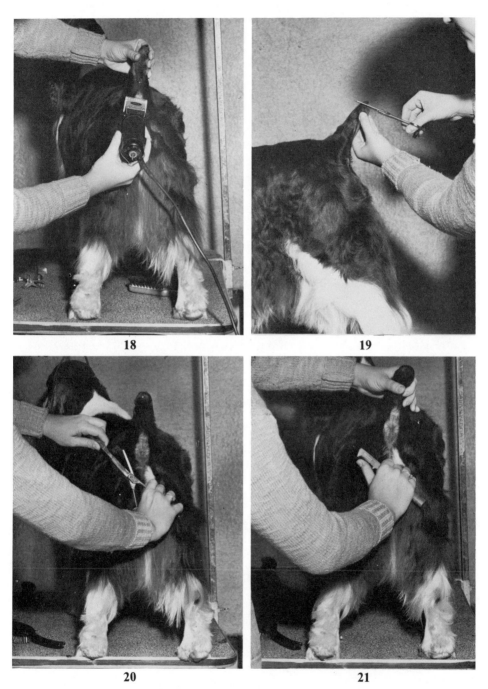

18

19

20

21

Stand back and look at your work frequently. If possible, trim in front of a mirror.

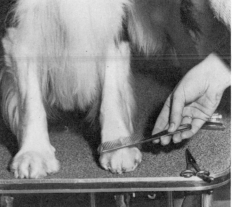

22   23

Trimming the Feet

Now to finish off that well-groomed appearance. Your goal is to make the foot appear as tight, compact and clean as possible. This is one area that calls for extensive use of the scissors.

With your straight scissors, pick up the foot and trim off the hair underneath and around the pads. **(Photo #22).**

Place the foot back on the table. Again, with straight scissors, trim around the foot to give a round outline.

After combing the hair up, on and in between the toes, **(Photo #23),** take your thinning shears and gradually scissor from the bottom up, to the arch. **(Photo #24).** Scissor only the hair you have combed up. Be careful not to remove any hair in between the toes. This helps give you your full compact look. **(Photo #25).**

To be penalized: Thin, open, or splayed feet (flat with spreading toes). Hare foot (long, rather narrow foot).

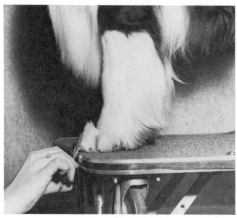
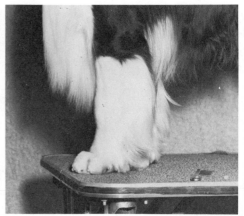

24   25

240

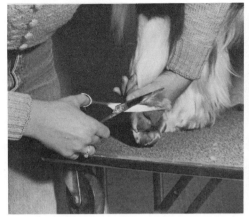

26

Pasterns

The pastern requires careful attention because if trimmed incorrectly, it can ruin the tight compact trim you have just finished on the front foot.

Comb out the feathering on the front leg. Gather the hair in your left hand and cut a straight line across. **(Photo #26).** In keeping with the neat appearance you have just given the foot, trim the feathering at an angle so that the hair isn't touching the ground. **(Photo #27).** It is important to be sure not to cut too far into the back of the foot, but softly blend it into the feathering to give it a natural, strong look, as stated in the standard.

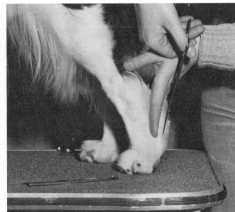

27

Hocks

The trim on the hocks can give the dog the effect of more or less angulation and more or less length of body.

Comb out the hair on the hock and, as done with the pastern, gather the hair down to the top of the pad and cut a straight line. **(Photo #28).**

Comb the hair up again. Now comes the time to determine whether your dog needs more or less angulation, leaving more or less hair at the top of the hock accordingly. **(Photo #29).** The point of the hock should be softened to make it less obvious to the eye—to take away from the sharp unattractive point. If possible, allow a small amount of feathering to fall softly over the top.

28

29

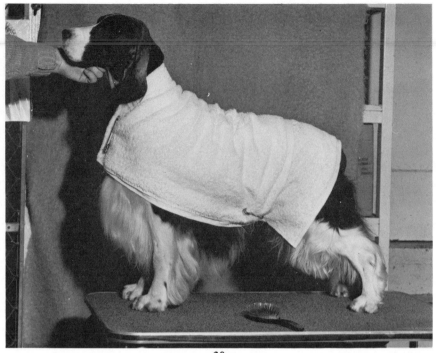

30

How to Blanket Your Dog

For blanketing our dog, we will need a bath towel and three blanket pins. The towel, or terry cloth jacket, should be of medium weight and wide enough to go around the dog's body. Some jackets fasten with tapes that cross underneath and tie on top; I do not care for these because they leave a line when the dog is dry.

Blanket pins are to be found at the notions counter in most department stores.

Fold the towel back, collar fashion, and pin under the neck. Carefully smooth hair once more on the back before laying towel down to tail. Pull snugly around rib cage and pin underneath. The last pin is used up under the loin to hold the towel tight over the back.

When the blanket is removed in the morning, your dog will have a smoothness and sparkling sheen that will delight you. **(Photo #30).**

The End Result!

"What is worth doing, is worth doing well" applies to show trimming a Springer Spaniel. We strive for a clean, natural, neat appearance that gives a stylish effect—without any signs of the scissors.

Marjon's Happy Thing, UD, High in Trial at the 1976 ESSFTA Nationals, "Utility Springer of the Year" and tied for "Obedience Springer of the Year". Whelped in October, 1970, "Happy" was bred by Peggy and Vern Johnson, and owned by Art and Sharon Stewart. She earned her CD in three straight shows in 1971 with an average of 194, and her CDX in 1972 with an average of 193. After a time out for puppies, she came back to attain her UD with a 192 average. "Happy" was a member of the top dog team in 1972, 1973 and 1976, representing the Santa Ana Valley Kennel Club.

19

The Springer
in Obedience

THE SPRINGER'S high intelligence and merry temperament make him a top-working Obedience dog. Obedience training offers many advantages not the least of which is making your dog a more enjoyable, well-behaved companion. It also holds tremendous appeal and fascination in that, if properly trained, you can enter him in the exciting competition of the Obedience trials. Before starting on an Obedience program, bear in mind that the English Springer Spaniel has an essentially soft temperament and, as a rule, will not take severe corrections. Avoid punishment, be lavish with praise. The techniques effective in training larger Working breeds are not applicable to the English Springer Spaniel.

Enroll in an Obedience training club or school, preferably one for Springers only. Today there is scarcely an area that does not have some group with the common objective of training dogs to be better behaved companions, or of working toward the coveted AKC Obedience degrees. These are: Companion Dog (C.D.), Companion Dog Excellent (C.D.X.) and the Utility Dog (U.D.).

The degrees are earned by receiving three "legs" (which are earned by qualifying scores of 170 to the perfect 200 points at each level) for each degree. The degrees must be earned in order, starting with the Novice Class (C.D.), which has the following exercises: heel on leash, stand for examination, heel free, recall, long sit (1 minute) and the long down (3 minutes). Next comes the Open Class (C.D.X.) and the exercises for this class are: heel free, drop on recall, retrieve on flat, retrieve over the high jump, broad jump, long sit (3 minutes) and the long down (5 minutes). Both the sit and down for the Open work are done with the handler out of the

O.T.Ch. Chuzzlewit's Favorite Son, the first English Springer Spaniel to earn the Obedience Trial Champion title. The parent club "Obedience Springer of the Year" for 1977, he carries a lifetime cumulative score of 195.966, and was a six-time High in Trial winner. Of his 36 Obedience class placements, 15 were first place wins. "Sonny" was bred by F. Nelson and Mr. and Mrs. G. Dahlberg, and owned by Clayton and Patricia Berglund. He was trained and handled throughout his career by Clayton.

—*Josinsky Studio*

dog's sight. Then we come to the Utility Class (U.D.) with the challenges of: hand signal exercises, two scent discrimination tests (leather articles and metal articles), directed retrieve, directed jumping and group examination (a long stand).

The ultimate title in Obedience is the Obedience Trial Champion (O.T.Ch.). Once you have obtained your U.D. degree then you may go out and try to win this new and exciting title. You must receive the required 100 points by wins which include a first place in Utility (or Utility B) with at least three dogs in competition; a first place in Open B, with at least five dogs in competition; and a third first place, in one or the other of these classes. The three first placements must have been under three different judges. The point schedule is based on how many dogs were in competition on the days that your dog won; usually either first or second in your class counts. If it is your intention to enter your Springer in Obedience trials, send for the booklet "Obedience Regulations", which will explain the necessary details and requirements as set down by the American Kennel Club. A copy may be obtained (single copies are free) by writing to the American Kennel Club, 51 Madison Avenue, New York, N.Y. 10010.

Of obvious assistance in the training of your dogs is a good book on the subject, and there are several that we recommend. One of the best is "Training You to Train Your Dog" by Blanche Saunders, founder of Obedience training as we know it in America today. An excellent book is

"The Pearsall Guide to Successful Dog Training" by Margaret E. Pearsall. The Pearsall methods are particularly interesting in that they are based on keeping in mind the dog's physical capabilities and limitations, and of what dog psychology has taught us of his behavior patterns. (Both of these books are available from the Howell Book House Inc., 230 Park Avenue, New York, N.Y. 10169). Another excellent book out very recently and geared to the reward, praise type of training is *Playtraining Your Dog* by Patricia Gail Burnham. Also recommended are *Training Your Spaniel* by Clarence Pfaffenberger and *Trials Without Tribulations* by Margo Ande.

Some knowledgeable people insist that Obedience training will interfere with showing your Springer in conformation. Rather, if properly trained, the dog will handle more confidently in a show ring with the other dogs. However, it is vital that prime consideration be given to the temperament. Too heavy a training hand will subdue the spirit so essential in a winning show dog, be it in the conformation or Obedience ring. Even the smartest, best performing Springer will leave a bad impression if he is dirty and untrimmed. Too often we hear, "Oh, he is only entered in Obedience." Never forget that there are often as many people watching the

Nancy's Fancy Lady, UD, "Obedience Springer of the Year" for 1972. Owned by Mr. and Mrs. Larry Libeau. Pictured here doing the Utility glove retrieve, she is the only Springer to earn the four Parent Club Obedience awards: "Novice Springer of the Year", "Open Springer of the Year", "Utility Springer of the Year" and "Obedience Springer of the Year".

O.T. Ch. Ruleon's Sir Dandy of Belmar, ESSFTA "Obedience Springer of the Year" for 1978 and 1980 (runner-up in 1979). Whelped in 1974, Dandy was bred by Billie and Elmer Marlin, and is owned and trained by Stephen G. Dreiseszun. (He was Steve's first dog, and the first he trained in Obedience.) Dandy became a UD at 2 years of age, completing his CD, CDX and UD within 12½ months. Only the second Springer to earn the O.T. Ch. title, Dandy consistently ranked in the top four Springers in the national Obedience rating systems, including 1st in the TSR Phillips and Schuman systems for 1978 and 1980. He has been "High in Trial" 8 times, including the 25th anniversary ESSFTA National Specialty, and had over 100 qualifying scores with 50% placements, including 24 1st placements.

Obedience ring at a show as the conformation ring. All Springers should be groomed before competition, and the handler demonstrate pride in his own appearance. These are psychological advantages. The English Springer Spaniel as a breed is being judged by the public in both rings, and should be well represented.

248

OBEDIENCE SPRINGER OF THE YEAR

Each year the English Springer Spaniel Field Trial Association, parent club of the breed, awards a Certificate of Merit to the "Obedience Springer of the Year", won by the dog with the highest average score for the preceding year.

To qualify for this prestigious award all dogs with five or more qualifying scores are considered. The average of the five best scores of each eligible dog is determined, and then the one with the highest average will be named "Obedience Springer of the Year". If one studies the breeding of these winners it is evident that they are from widely different areas and completely different breedings. Unlike the situation in conformation, the Obedience Springer competition is not dominated by a few big-name kennels. It would seem that no line has a monopoly on Springer intelligence.

Here are the dogs honored as "Springer of The Year" since inauguration of the award in 1959:

1959: Fleishman's Spectacular, U.D.
     owned by (Mr. and Mrs. A. Fleishman, Spokane, Wash.)
1960: Pussy Willow Sir Skeeter
     (R. G. Leonard, Adrian, Mich.)
1961: Bal Lakes Lady Patricia, U.D.
     (Edson Bahr, Edmonds, Wash.)
1962: Bal Lakes Lady Patricia, U.D.
1963: Bal Lakes Lady Patricia, U.D.
1964: Bal Lakes Lady Patricia, U.D.
1965: Tie: Loujon Deuce of Charlemar, C.D.X., W.D.
          (Kay Crisanti, New Richmond, Ohio)
     and La Belle Don Mitzi
          (Judy Lundbeck, Fargo, N.D.)
1966: Tie: Ch. Walpride Karrie of Charlemar, C.D.X., W.D.
          (Kay Crisanti, New Richmond, Ohio)
     and Loujon Deuce of Charlemar, C.D.X., W.D.
1967: La Belle Don Mitzi, C.D.X.
1968: La Belle Don Mitzi, U.D.
1969: Tigaria Pamper, U.D.
     (Ruth Wallace, Riverdale, Ill.)
1970: Loujon Lord Kelvin, U.D.
     (Theresa Luley, Indianapolis, Ind.)
1971: Ch. New Dawn of Marjon, U.D.
     (C. Thistel, Annapolis, Md.)
     Note: New Dawn won her C.D., C.D.X. and U.D. in one year.
1972: Nancy's Fancy Lady, U.D.
     (Laurence J. Libeu, Garden Grove, Calif.)
1973: Naia's Molly Malone, U.D.
     (Laurence J. Libeau, Garden Grove, Ca.)
1974: Naia's Molly Malone, U.D.
1975: Naia's Molly Malone, U.D.
1976: Tie: Marjon's Happy Thing, U.D.
          (Art and Sharon Stewart, Irvine, Ca.)
          Endeavor's White Frost, U.D.
          (Doris Peppers, Broomfield, Co.)

1977: Chuzzlewit's Favorite Son, U.D.
       (Patricia and Clayton Berglund, Bloomington, MN)
1978: Ruleon's Sir Dandy of Belmar, U.D.
       (Steve Dreiseszun, Phoenix, Az.)
1979: Jessica Imp of Whimsey, U.D.
       (Martha Leonard, Montclair, N.J.)
1980: O.T.Ch. Ruleon's Sir Dandy of Belmar
1981: O.T.Ch. Jessica Imp of Whimsy
1982: Ch. JD's Short-N-Sweet, U.D.
       (Jean Lucas, Renton, Wa.)

OBEDIENCE TRIAL CHAMPIONS

At this writing, three Springers have earned the Obedience Trial Champion title since it was established. They are listed in the order in which they earned the title.

1. O.T.Ch. Chuzzlewits Favorite Sun, U.D.
   (Clayton and Pat Berglund, Bloomington, Minnesota)
2. O.T.Ch. Ruleon's Sir Dandy of Belmar, U.D.
   (Steve Dreseszun, Phoenix, Arizona)
3. O.T.Ch. Jessica Imp of Whimsy, U.D.
   (Martha Leonard, Montclair, N.J.)

TRACKING and ENGLISH SPRINGER SPANIELS
by James M. Eadie,
AKC TD and TDX Judge

In reviewing the AKC Gazettes for the period January 1974 through October 1983 it is noted that 134 Springers have passed their TD test, and since the TDX test was approved in 1979, 9 Springers have accomplished this very difficult test to earn their TDX title.

In tracking, we acknowledge the dog's natural scenting abilities (which is well demonstrated when we see newborn puppies find their way to the dam's teat for nourishment) by training the dog to follow a track scent and find the article at the end of the track.

Not much equipment is needed in tracking considering the magnitude of this adventure. A non-restrictive harness, a 40-foot tracking lead, tracking stakes, articles, brush and comb, a field and a dog—preferably an English Springer Spaniel!

The AKC has published specific regulations regarding tracking tests. The dog only has to pass once to earn its title; however, a dog must be "certified" ready to take such a test by an AKC judge sometime prior to the dog being entered in a licensed test. This is to make sure that the dog is "ready" in the opinion of a judge and such certification must be attached to the entry form or the entry will not be accepted.

All AKC tracking tests are judged by two AKC approved judges who have plotted and laid out the tracks the day before the test for each individual dog entered. On the day of the test a tracklayer, a stranger to

A/C Ch. JD's Short-N-Sweet, UDT, WD, Can. CD. ESSFTA "Obedience Springer of the Year" for 1982, and High in Trial at the 1982 Specialty. ("Utility Dog of the Year" in 1981, with scores averaging 196 plus.) Whelped in 1976, "Shorty" was bred by Don and Jean Lucas, handled to championship by Don, and is Jean's first Obedience dog. He earned his American championship in 1980 with four majors and three BOBs from the classes. In Canada, he earned championship with a Group fourth from the classes, and his CD with wins including two Highs in Trial.

Canarch Madeira, CD, High Scoring Dog in Trial at the 1983 ESSFTA National Specialty, with a score of 199 from the Novice B class under judge Emma Brodzeller. Madeira was bred by Bill Davidson, and is owned and handled by Francie Nelson. Madeira achieved a Dog World Award of Canine Distinction for her Novice work; her average for her three CD legs was 197.5.

A distinguished Obedience trio, owned by Doris and Larry Peppers. At center is Endeavor's White Frost, UD, WDX. Whelped in 1971, bred by S. M. and M. L. Hite, "Susie" was handled to her CD by the Peppers' son Larry. Then mother Doris took over the training to take her to CDX in just 4 shows, and to UD in 7 shows. "Susie" earned the WDX at the tender age of nine in 1981. Ch. Ozark Princess Susanna, UD, achieved both her UD and conformation championship in 1979. Good-Will Happy Go Lucky, UD, WDX, (at right) completed his UD in 1982.

Canarch Contemplation, at left at age of nine, was the foundation bitch for Fanfare (formerly Chuzzlewit) Springers, owned by Frances Nelson. "Tempo" was dam of 3 champions, several Obedience/Tracking title holders, and of 3 Working Dog title holders. At center is her daughter, Ch. Chuzzlewit's Polonaise, and at right, her granddaughter, Canarch Madeira, CD, High Scoring Dog at the 1983 ESSFTA National Specialty.

Ch. Shieress Ember of
Springcrest, CD, TD

both the dog and handler, walks the individual test track leaving an article at the end of the track.

A TD test track is 440 to 500 yards in length, has two starting flags placed approximately 30 yards apart, at least two right angle turns and one article at the end of the track. The track is aged 30 minutes to 2 hours before the dog is run on the track. The dog must complete the track and retrieve or indicate the article at the end of the track.

Tracking is a non-competitive sport with dog and handler working as a team in the field. The handler is to make no corrections, give no directions, and neither scold nor chastise the dog while it is "working" a track. The only command the handler will give his dog is at the starting flag, when he downs or sits his dog for approximately 30 seconds to enable the dog to pick up the track scent and then commands the dog to "track" or "go find", or whatever starting command he may wish to use. When the dog has taken the direction of the track which is between the two starting flags, the handler will wait at the first flag while feeding out the tracking lead, always keeping tension on the lead.

After feeding out 30 to 40 feet of tracking lead, the handler will follow his tracking dog observing his actions, being able to read and understand them, knowing when he is investigating a turn or about to make one, when in trouble or off the track, patiently waiting for the dog to work out his problems. Remember, the terrain and track are new to all participants, except for the two judges who will pass or fail the tracking entry based upon the dog and handler performance.

The TDX test track is considerably more difficult being 800 to 1,000 yards in length. It has one starting flag, two cross tracks at various intervals walked by two tracklayers, and at least two obstacles must be overcome—road crossing, creek crossing, fence rows, embankments, etc. There should be changes in ground cover, at least three right angle turns, and four article drops—one at the start, two articles at intervals along the track and also

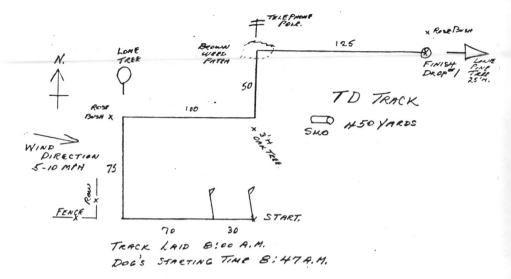

T.D. track — 450 yards.

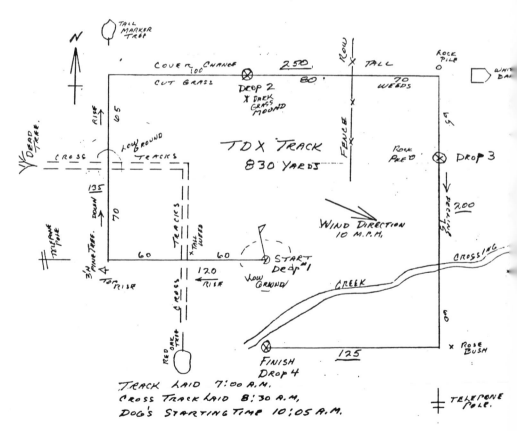

T.D.X. track — 830 yards.

Ch. Shieress Ember of Springcrest, CD, TD. "Eamy" is shown completing her 445-yard track in just 3 minutes at the David Dog Training Club test in California. Owner/Handler: Nyleen La Shier, Shieress Kennels.

one article at the end. The dog must indicate or retrieve all four articles which are to be presented to the judges upon completion of the track.

It is a great challenge to a dog and handler to successfully complete a TDX test with all the many variables. When passed, it is a very proud moment not only for the dog and handler, but for the judges, tracklayers and the spectators.

Springers who have attained their tracking titles have proved that they can be used very effectively on search teams, serving their communities when called upon to help locate children who may have wandered off in forest areas, or elderly people who have become confused and lost. Here, of course, they are trained to pick up human scent, working ahead of their handler and controlled by voice command and whistle.

The age of the Springer makes little difference in its tracking abilities, so long as the dog is healthy. An ideal time to start a Springer in tracking is at 4 months of age, as a puppy is very receptive to training.

In training your Springer to track you will develop a very close bond with him, for in tracking the dog is boss and you must learn how to read and understand him.

Recommended books on tracking—*Tracking Dog,* by Glenn Johnson; *Go Find,* by L. Wilson Davis; and *Scent,* by Milo D. Pearsall and Hugo Verbuggan, MD.

His

and Hers.

20

The Springer as a Pet

NOW PERHAPS you have no interest in field trials or dog shows, nor the patience to train a dog for Obedience. You might only be looking for a dog to be a member of your family—a pal—one that wants to please you, go wherever you go and do what you want to do. One, too, that will be good with the children and can be easily housebroken. You might also enjoy taking him hunting once or twice a year, though you have no time to actually train him for the field.

Then an English Springer Spaniel fills your bill. He is a natural in the field and can hunt all day with enthusiasm; yet, being of medium size, he is ideal in the home or car, and can easily adjust himself to any mode of living. Many Springers live in apartments, getting their exercise on leash or in the park.

This is a sturdy breed. Usually they are good eaters and can live indoors or out. But to thrive, a Springer must have human companionship. He is a happy fellow with a merry tail, eagerly anticipating your next move so that he can please you. Feed him well, love him, and he will repay you tenfold.

Buying a puppy is a thrilling and exciting experience, but for some it is a frightening responsibility as well. We have compiled some of the questions most frequently asked us by new owners, and perhaps answering them can help smooth the way for others.

But first, some general suggestions. Be prepared when you buy your Springer puppy to devote two or three days to properly orienting him. His habits must be established the first day you bring him home. It is far easier to *train* him than to *untrain* him.

Gentleness and repetition do the trick. No slapping, please. No newspapers. Just one word—"No!"—in a sturdy "I-mean-it" tone of voice.

A crate of suitable size is a wise investment, whether it is the folding wire variety or plywood. Feed and sleep him in it. This comes to be his own secure domain, greatly facilitates housebreaking him, prevents him from chewing or causing damage when left alone, and is the answer to rainy days when he comes in with muddy feet!

Play ball with your puppy from the beginning, coaxing him to bring the object back to you. He will love the "game" and be getting the best kind of exercise, particularly if he lives in an apartment. Moreover, this teaches him to "retrieve". He can soon be taught to "come" when called and, later, to "lie down". It is a pleasure to own a well-mannered house dog.

Don't give him bones. They cause too many kinds of trouble, much beyond their worth. But by all means give the puppy something to chew; any rawhide toys are good, particularly "Chew bars".

Now let us answer some of the questions most often asked by new puppy buyers:

How much do I feed my puppy? How often do I feed him? What do I feed him?

An 8-week-old Springer puppy should eat 1 1/2 to 2 lbs. of mixed food a day, divided into three meals, plus 1/2 to 1 can of evaporated milk.

2 parts dry food
1 part meat   Meat and
                  water weigh
1 part water   the same

Cover the dry food with very hot water and soak 15 minutes. Add meat and mix thoroughly. The consistency of the mixture is important. If too stiff or dry it will stick to the puppy's mouth, but if too sloppy it will have a laxative effect. The mixture should be soft and almost "fluffy".

When the puppy has finished his meal, or most of it, puncture a can of Pet or Carnation milk and pour some, *undiluted,* in the same pan.

Feeding time should be regular—as close as possible to the same time each day.

Between 9 weeks and 3 months, your puppy should consume 2 1/2 lbs. of mixed food a day. Shortly thereafter, 3 lbs. of food a day. As you increase his morning meal he will show less interest in his noon meal, at which time you may divide the full amount into two meals instead of three a day.

Never decrease the amount of food. Growing dogs need food more than adults. Some active young dogs at the ages of between 10 months and two years will eat 4 lbs. of wet food to satisfy their caloric requirement for show condition. Your puppy will love all table scraps and they may be added to his regular diet, particularly bits of fat and gravy. Cooked eggs and cottage cheese are excellent foods for him.

A candid shot of Ch. Chinoe's Eminent Judge, CDX.

How often should he have a bath?

Whenever you think he needs one. Use a "people's" shampoo, rinse him thoroughly, dry him well and keep him out of drafts.

What about distemper and other vaccines?

We can indeed boast about the effectiveness of our immunization program for canine distemper, hepatitis, leptospirosis, parainfluenza (kennel cough) and now the new P for parvovirus. The first vaccine should be given at age six weeks, followed by the same treatment three weeks later, and a third dosage in another thirty days. It is a mistake to bunch the injection at closer intervals because of maternal immunity. Mothers understand maternal immunity in their children. A long maternal immunity in puppies renders early vaccines to be less effective.

Parvovirus—Suddenly we have been confronted by this dreaded disease which is characterized by repeated vomiting over a period of five or six days, accompanied by watery diarrhea and bloody diarrhea. White blood counts drop from a normal of 10,000 to a WBC of 1,000 to 3,000. See your veterinarian and have intravenous fluids administered on a continuing basis.

Ask your veterinarian to issue a certificate and request him to remind you to return for yearly booster vaccines of distemper, hepatitis, leptospirosis, parainfluenza and parvo to keep high immunity against those diseases.

259

Has the puppy been wormed?

Yes, three times. At 5 weeks, 6 weeks, and 7 weeks of age. However, it is advisable to have your veterinarian run a fecal check in about 3 months. All worms (except tapeworms) produce characteristic eggs or ova readily detected under a microscope.

Tapeworm eggs are voided in small segments or packets passed on the outside of the stool. Sometimes the dried tapeworm packets are found on the hair underneath the tail.

Specific vermicides or vermifuges are available for each of the parasites we wish to eliminate. They must be administered with judgment. If used injudiciously they are capable of being toxic, causing dizziness, coma, diarrhea, kidney and liver damage. Use under the supervision of your veterinarian.

Should I take any precaution against heartworm?

Heartworm infestation in dogs is receiving increasing attention. Details concerning the life cycle and *spread* of this parasite are available from veterinarians and veterinary literature.

Heartworm infestation in years past was considered primarily a warm climate or tropical disease, but today, our Northern dogs are being infected with this parasite.

A blood examination by your veterinarian each Spring during the months of March or April is certainly to be recommended. In the Northern states, some areas show a very low incidence of heartworm. For example, possibly 1.5% of the dog population. The disease is endemic in other areas, and infestations of over 25% of the dog population are reported.

Administration of daily preventative medication must be decided between you, as the owner, and your veterinarian. Treatment of infected dogs is possible, and veterinarians approach these cases with care and consideration.

Is it true that Springers have ear problems?

Springers have pendant ears, and consequently less ventilation than in a short-eared or prick-eared dog. The ear canal of your puppy should be whitish-pink, free from debris and wax, and free from odor. The dark wax which sometimes accumulates in puppy ears, can be removed with Q-tips dipped in baby oil. Dogs have long ear canals and the eardrum is situated around the side of the ear canal. Consequently, the applicator can be inserted to its full length without causing injury. This point must be emphasized to mothers who, of course, use extreme care in cleaning their baby's ears. Ear infections are caused by bacteria, by parasites, and by fungus infections. Treatment of these more serious problems must be handled by a veterinarian.

What should I know about eye problems?

Retinal examinations must be made by a veterinary ophthalmologist on animals seven weeks of age and older. Here we are at the mercy of the examining specialist. Retinal dysplasia is said to show folds in the eye grounds or punched out areas. This condition usually does not cause complete blindness. Dogs do not have to read a newspaper and individuals so afflicted will make satisfactory pets. It probably would be best not to use for breeding. Dogs with detached retinas are blind and should be euthanized.

R   L

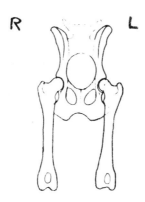

What is hip dysplasia?

Normal hip joints should show on a properly taken radiograph a deep, round cup for a socket or acetabulum and a round and closely or tightly fitting femoral head. There are varying deviations from this normal condition, classified from a taint to grade I through IV. Dysplastic dogs have shallow hip sockets appearing as saucers instead of deep cups. Laxity in hip joints results in abnormal wear, causing the femoral heads to remodel and to lose the round character; the femoral heads flatten. Laxity of hip joints also causes arthritic changes to be evident on the radiograph but not necessarily lameness. It is my opinion that some variations from the completely normal state may be tolerated. Radiographs taken at six months to eight months of age may give some clue as to hip conformation but a dependable judgment cannot be made until the animal is past one year old and, of course, the OFA requires a two year age limit.

I have observed cowhocked Springers, animals with poor rears showing perfect hip joints on x-ray. Conversely, I have seen show dogs with some degree of radiographic abnormalities with the most perfect angulation and leg placement and a gait that was ideal. Some tolerance is needed in the judgment of hip dysplasia.

Is it true that Springers shed a great deal?

Shedding is a problem that dog owners of all breeds experience to some degree. Hair growth in animals is not a constant process, but a phasic

261

At 3 months — well bred and well read.

one. In the first part of the phase, the hair is actively growing. In the second part, the growth stops and the hair goes into a resting stage. The resting hair is sooner or later shed and the follicle is left empty in preparation for the next growth phase.

Typically the dog goes through two growing and resting phases each year. The obvious is the resting phase associated with the spring shedding. Since dogs are now often kept inside most of the year, the cycles become less distinct until the animal sheds all year around.

Illness or stresses such as pregnancy may cause a dog's hair to go into a resting stage and shed. Regrowth will occur when the hair enters the next growth phase if the underlying stress is gone.

Excessive shedding may just be a variation of the normal, but should be checked for possible skin disease. Good health, a well-balanced diet and brushing all help.

We could not housebreak our last puppy because of constant diarrhea. Have you any suggestions?

We have different suggestions, depending upon the age of the puppy.

Diarrhea in puppies age two to three weeks:

Sometimes we have a different situation with younger puppies which is handled differently. This is a condition that occurs occasionally in our puppies. The stool is yellow and of watery consistency. Puppies are wet and greasy in appearance and this is usually caused by an infection. Coating agents such as Kaopectate and/or Peptobismol are *not* effective. Give

Tetracycline syrup, a few drops, approximately 20 mg., three times a day for two or three days.

Diarrhea in puppies six weeks old:
First eliminate parasites such as roundworm, hookworm and Coccidiossis. Treat with appropriate amount of broad spectrum antibiotic and feed a bland diet. Eliminate milk and heavy dog meal. Feed KD (Prescription Diet), one half can mushed with one quarter cupful of water and add one to two tablespoonfuls of ground beef. Other suggestions: several slices of whole wheat toast moistened with water to which raw beef has been added is helpful or try Shredded Wheat biscuit or shredded Ralston. Our Springers love scrambled eggs. Prepare a nice, big, well-cooked omelet.

When will my female have her first heat period?

There is a variation in heat cycles. Generally our Springers come in season for the first time at about 9 months (it can be as early as 6 or as late as 11 months). The heat period lasts about 18 days and occurs again at 6-month intervals for the remainder of her life. There is no menopause in a dog.

When should I breed her?

We suggest her second heat period unless the bitch has come in season late, is well developed and in excellent health. It is best to skip a season before breeding her again.

Interpreting vaginal smears: A bitch in estrus shows us and tells us that she is in heat. Her vulva is swollen and she has a discharge of a bloody secretion. When she twists and flags her tail and does not object to having us touch her at the rear, she is telling us she is in estrus and wishes to be bred. A vaginal smear is helpful in making a decision as to the stage of her heat cycle. A female in estrus shows red blood cells of varying amounts, from a few to loaded (90% to 100% cornified epithelial cells and no white blood cells, or at least very few). Breed her; she is ready.

Is it wrong to consider spaying her?

If you have no desire to raise a litter of puppies, or to ever show your female—if she is only to be your pet and companion, we urge you to have her unsexed. This is better than risking the likely possibility of a mismating to some roaming neighborhood male.

What is an acceptable age of a stud dog?

A prospective stud dog should be given his first opportunity at the age of eleven months. It is best to introduce him to an older bitch who is friendly and has had at least one litter of puppies. We should hold the bitch by the head and let him approach her and often, happily, we will notice him accomplishing his purpose very soon.

My dog came back from a boarding kennel yesterday and seems to have a bone caught in his throat. He is feeling fine—full of pep, eating well and his stools are good—but he sometimes raises a little mucus or liquid when he coughs. Do you think this is serious?

Your dog has symptoms of what we commonly call "kennel cough", properly *tracho-bronchitis* (an upper respiratory disease) or *parainfluenza*. Animals infected with this virus usually recover in about two weeks. I suggest you ask your veterinarian.

In answering the above questions, we have tried to pass on what we have learned as a long-time dog breeder and raiser. But in no way do we advocate the administering to your puppies and adult dogs as a do-it-yourself operation. Let your veterinarian be your dependable guide.

TAIL DOCKING and
THE REMOVAL OF DEWCLAWS

Tail docking, an important procedure, is best performed by a professional, namely, a veterinarian. The proper age is three to six days after birth but the most important consideration is the health of the puppies and the behavior of the mother dog. We wish to have the puppies warm and healthy with fully rounded bodies. The mother dog should be calm, happy, adjusted to caring for her litter and willing to leave them at intervals to relieve herself. Puppies are transported to the veterinarian in a box covered by a towel or blanket to maintain warmth and protect them from drafts. A hot water bottle or a heating pad may be used in the puppy bed to supply a degree of warmth in winter months. If the puppies are heated too much, they will protest loudly with distressing cries. In recognizing these sounds of discontent when a litter is brought to us, we remove the heat source and immediately there is silence or simply low sounds; all is serene. The mother should be brought to the veterinary office with the baby pups or conned into taking a breather in an outside pen during the puppies' absence.

The tails are clipped and cleansed with antiseptic soap routinely prior to docking. A ruler is used on each tail to insure uniformity. Some slight variation is allowed for a very small pup as opposed to a whopper but using the ruler is generally advisable. A dog has to live with his tail all of his life and a stubby tail detracts from his style. We use a tail docking instrument which cuts the tail in the shape of a V as shown in the accompanying illustration. The flaps of skin, top and bottom, are closed with three interrupted sutures of cotton or nylon thread #50. Cat-gut absorbable sutures will not do. The licking of the mother soon unties the knots or dissolves the sutures and we have an open end which must granulate to

one inch

three interrupted sutures

close. Suturing tails insures a proper skin covering over the amputation and also controls the bleeding which could result in a puppy's death.

Springer puppy tails are cut one inch from the body at age three to six days. If the age is ten or fourteen days, we cut them at one and one-quarter inches. Variation in size is, of course, taken into consideration.

The owners of Field Springers usually desire a long tail. Removal of only one-third of the tail pleases these owners. A consultation is held and a judgment made to the field trial man's wishes. A long tail and a flag on the end seems to be most desirable.

The front dewclaws on the Springer puppies are routinely removed at the time of tail docking. These extra toes are snipped with scissors and closed with one or two interrupted cotton sutures. The cut is deep enough to remove the entire toe and sutured securely to control the hemorrhaging. Now, rear dewclaws. Always examine the puppies for these extra appendages. They are present on 25 percent of the Springer puppies. You will note that there is a variation of these rear toes in size and position on the leg. Some are very tiny. Others are large or even double and extend almost to the level of the other four toes. When we encounter a rear foot like this, we count the four toes and then go about removing the dewclaw.

When the litter is returned to its home, puppies should be placed with the bitch immediately. She will be very busy licking and cleaning for a few minutes but within a short time nursing begins and the little ordeal has been accomplished.

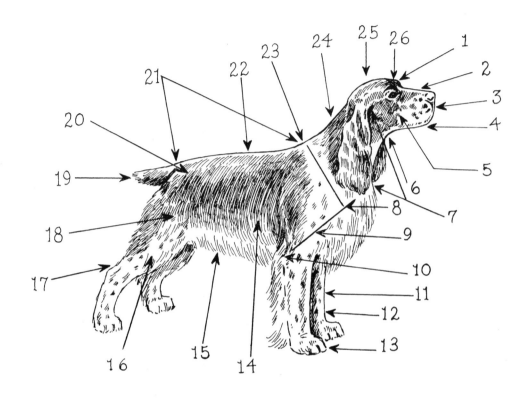

1—Stop, moderate; eyebrows, well developed
2—Nasal bone, straight
3—Muzzle, fairly square
4—Jaws, strong, even
5—Chiseling under eyes
6—Not too throaty
7—Ears, set low, falling close to head
8—Sloping shoulders
9—Brisket to elbow
10—Elbows, close to body
11—Forelegs, straight with good bone, slightly flattened
12—Pasterns, strong
13—Feet, strong, compact, toes arched, pads thick
14—Body, deep, ribs well sprung
15—Not tucked up
16—Stifle joint, strong, moderately bent
17—Hock joint, rounded, moderately bent, well let down
18—Thighs, broad, muscular
19—Tail, set low, carried horizontally with merry action
20—Hips, nicely rounded
21—Distance withers to base of tail, slightly less than shoulder height
22—Back, strong, no dip or roach
23—Shoulder blades, fairly close
24—Neck, arched
25—Occiput bone, rounded, inconspicuous
26—Eyes, dark, friendly, tight lids

21

Official AKC Standard for the English Springer Spaniel

(Approved by the Board of Directors, American Kennel Club, June 13, 1978.)

General Appearance and Type:

The English Springer Spaniel is a medium-size sporting dog with a neat, compact body, and a docked tail. His coat is moderately long and glossy, with feathering on his legs, ears, chest and brisket.

His pendulous ears, soft gentle expression, sturdy build and friendly wagging tail proclaim him unmistakably a member of the ancient family of spaniels. He is above all a well proportioned dog, free from exaggeration, nicely balanced in every part.

His carriage is proud and upstanding, body deep, legs strong and muscular with enough length to carry him with ease. His short level back, well developed thighs, good shoulders, excellent feet, suggest power, endurance, agility.

Taken as a whole he looks the part of a dog that can go and keep going under difficult hunting conditions, and moreover he enjoys what he is doing. At his best he is endowed with style, symmetry, balance, enthusiasm and is every inch a sporting dog of distinct spaniel character, combining beauty and utility.

To be penalized: Those lacking true English Springer type in conformation, expression, or behavior.

Temperament:

The typical Springer is friendly, eager to please, quick to learn, willing to obey. In the show ring he should exhibit poise, attentiveness, tractability, and should permit himself to be examined by the judge without resentment or cringing.

To be penalized: Excessive timidity, with due allowance for puppies and novice exhibits. But no dog to receive a ribbon if he behaves in vicious manner toward handler or judge. Aggressiveness toward other dogs in the ring NOT *to be construed as viciousness.*

Size and Proportion:

The Springer is built to cover rough ground with agility and reasonable speed. He should be kept to medium size—neither too small nor too large and heavy to do the work for which he is intended.

The ideal shoulder height for dogs is 20 inches; for bitches, 19 inches.

Length of topline (the distance from top of the shoulders to the root of the tail) should be approximately equal to the dog's shoulder height—never longer than his height—and not appreciably less. The dog too long in body, especially when long in loin, tires easily and lacks the compact outline characteristic of the breed.

Equally undesirable is the dog too short in body for the length of his legs, a condition that destroys his balance and restricts the gait.

Weight is dependent on the dog's other dimensions: a 20 inch dog, well proportioned, in good condition should weigh about 49-55 pounds. The resulting appearance is a well knit, sturdy dog with good but not too heavy bone, in no way coarse or ponderous.

To be penalized: Over-heavy specimens, cloddy in build. Leggy individuals, too tall for their length and substance. Over-size or under-size specimens (those more than one inch under or over the breed ideal).

Color:

May be black or liver with white markings or predominantly white with black or liver markings; tricolor; black and white or liver and white with tan markings (usually found on eyebrows, cheeks, inside of ears and under tail); blue or liver roan. Any white portions of coat may be flecked with ticking. All preceding combinations of colors and markings to be equally acceptable.

To be penalized: Off colors such as lemon, red or orange not to place.

Coat:

On ears, chest, legs and belly the Springer is nicely furnished with a fringe of feathering of moderate length and heaviness.

On head, front of forelegs, and below hocks on front of hindlegs the hair is short and fine.

The body coat is flat or wavy, of medium length, sufficiently dense to be water-proof, weather-proof and thorn-proof.

The texture fine, and the hair should have the clean, glossy, live appearance indicative of good health.

It is legitimate to trim about head, feet, ears; to remove dead hair; to thin and shorten excess feathering particularly from the hocks to the feet and elsewhere as required to give a smart, clean appearance.

To be penalized: Rough curly coat. Over-trimming, especially of the body coat. Any chopped, barbered, or artificial effect. Excessive feathering that destroys the clean outline desirable in a sporting dog. Off colors such as lemon, red, or orange not to place.

Head:

The head is impressive without being heavy. Its beauty lies in a combination of strength and refinement. It is important that the size and proportion be in balance with the rest of the dog. Viewed in profile the head should appear approximately the same length as the neck and should blend with the body in substance.

The skull (upper head) to be of medium length, fairly broad, flat on top, slightly rounded at the sides and back. The occiput bone inconspicuous, rounded rather than peaked or angular.

The foreface (head in front of the eyes) approximately the same length as the skull, and in harmony as to width and general character.

Looking down on the head, the muzzle to appear to be about one-half the width of the skull. As the skull rises from the foreface it makes a brow or "stop," divided by a groove or fluting between the eyes. This groove continues upward and gradually disappears as it reaches the middle of the forehead.

The amount of "stop" can best be described as moderate. It must not be a pronounced feature; rather it is a subtle rise where the muzzle blends into the upper head, further emphasized by the groove and by the position and shape of the eyebrows which should be well-developed. The stop, eyebrow and the chiseling of the bony structure around the eye sockets contribute to the Springer's beautiful and characteristic expression.

Viewed in profile, the topline of the skull and the muzzle lie in two approximately parallel planes. The nasal bone should be straight, with no inclination downward toward the tip of the nose which gives a down-faced look so undesirable in this breed. Neither should the nasal bone be concave resulting in a "dish-faced" profile; nor convex giving the dog a "Roman nose."

The jaws to be of sufficient length to allow the dog to carry game easily; fairly square, lean, strong, and even (neither undershot nor overshot).

The upper lip to come down full and rather square to cover the line of the lower jaw, but lips not to be pendulous nor exaggerated.

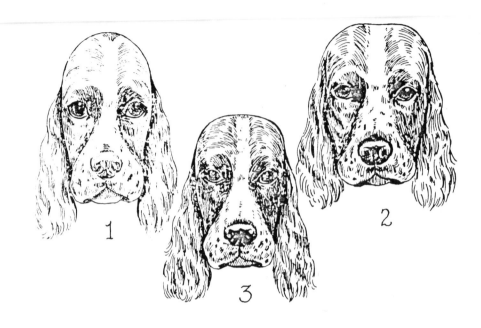

1. A bad head — Eyes too prominent — Narrow pointed skull.
2. Heavy skull — Cheeky — High set ears.
3. A well proportioned head.

The nostrils, well opened and broad, liver color or black depending on the color of the coat. Flesh-colored ("Dudley noses") or spotted ("butterfly noses") are undesirable. The cheeks to be flat (not rounded, full, or thick), with nice chiseling under the eyes.

To be penalized: Oval, pointed, or heavy skull. Cheeks prominently rounded, thick and protruding. Too much or too little stop. Over-heavy muzzle. Muzzle too short, too thin, too narrow. Pendulous, slobbery lips. Under- or over-shot jaws—a very serious fault, to be heavily penalized.

Teeth:

The teeth should be strong, clean, not too small; and when the mouth is closed the teeth should meet in an even bite or a close scissors bite (the lower incisors touching the inside of the upper incisors).

To be penalized: Any deviation from above description. Irregularities due to faulty jaw formation to be severely penalized.

270

Eyes:

More than any other feature the eyes contribute to the Springer's appeal. Color, placement, size influence expression and attractiveness. The eyes to be of medium size, neither small, round, full and prominent, nor bold and hard in expression. Set rather well apart and fairly deep in their sockets.

The color of the iris to harmonize with the color of the coat, preferably a good dark hazel in the liver dogs and black or deep brown in the black and white specimens.

The expression to be alert, kindly, trusting. The lids tight with little or no haw showing.

To be penalized: Eyes yellow or brassy in color or noticeably lighter than the coat. Sharp expression indicating unfriendly or suspicious nature. Loose droopy lids. Prominent haw (the third eyelid or membrane in the inside corner of the eye).

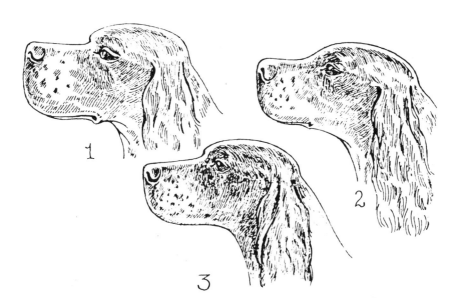

1. Too much stop — heavy lips — loose lidded eyes.
2. Too little stop — muzzle too short for skull.
3. A good head.

1. Sway-back.
2. Roach back.
3. Good topline.

Ears:

The correct ear-set is on a level with the line of the eye; on the side of the skull and not too far back. The flaps to be long and fairly wide, hanging close to the cheeks, with no tendency to stand up or out. The leather thin, approximately long enough to reach the tip of the nose.

To be penalized: Short round ears. Ears set too high or too low or too far back on the head.

Neck:

The neck to be moderately long, muscular, slightly arched at the crest, gradually blending into sloping shoulders. Not noticeably upright nor coming into the body at an abrupt angle.

To be penalized: Short neck, often the sequence to steep shoulders. Concave neck, sometimes called ewe neck or upside down neck (the opposite of arched). Excessive throatiness.

Body:

The body to be well coupled, strong, compact; the chest deep but not so wide or round as to interfere with the action of the front legs; the brisket sufficiently developed to reach to the level of the elbows.

The ribs fairly long, springing gradually to the middle of the body, then tapering as they approach the end of the ribbed section.

The back (section between the withers and loin) to be straight and strong, with no tendency to dip or roach.

The loins to be strong, short; a slight arch over loins and hip bones. Hips nicely rounded, blending smoothly into hind legs.

The resulting topline slopes *very gently* from withers to tail—the line from withers to back descending without a sharp drop; the back practically level; arch over hips somewhat lower than the withers; croup sloping gently to base of tail; tail carried to follow the natural line of the body.

The bottom line, starting on a level with the elbows, to continue backward with almost no up-curve until reaching the end of the ribbed section, then a more noticeable upcurve to the flank, but not enough to make the dog appear small waisted or "tucked up."

To be penalized: Body too shallow, indicating lack of brisket. Ribs too flat—sometimes due to immaturity. Ribs too round (barrel-shaped), hampering the gait. Sway-back (dip in back), indicating weakness or lack of muscular development, particularly to be seen when dog is in action and viewed from the side. Roach back (too much arch over loin and extending forward into middle section).

Croup falling away too sharply; or croup too high—unsightly faults, detrimental to outline and good movement.

Topline sloping sharply, indicating steep withers (straight shoulder placement) and a too low tail-set.

Tail:

The Springer's tail is an index both to his temperament and his conformation. Merry tail action is characteristic. The proper set is somewhat low, following the natural line of the croup. The carriage should be nearly horizontal, slightly elevated, when dog is excited. Carried straight up is untypical of the breed.

The tail should not be docked too short and should be well fringed with wavy feather. It is legitimate to shape and shorten the feathering but enough should be left to blend with the dog's other furnishings.

To be penalized: Tail habitually upright. Tail set too high or too low.

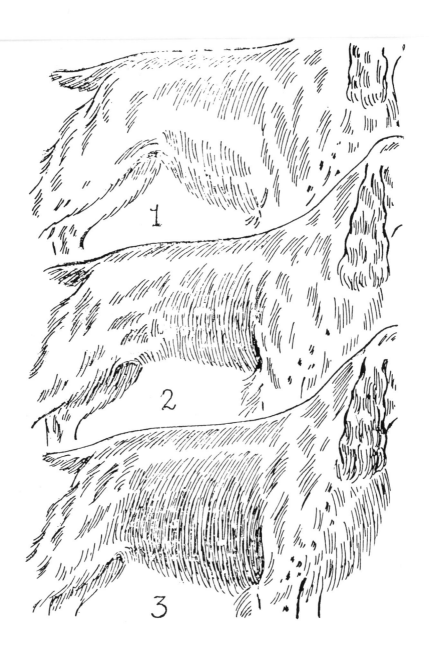

1. Too much tuck-up.
2. Narrow rib section — Shallow.
3. Good bottom line — No tuck-up.

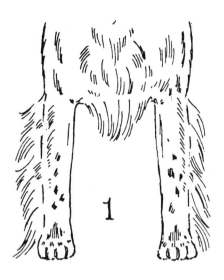

1. Too wide in front.

2. Bowed and pigeon-toed.

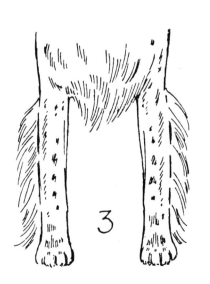

3. A good front.

Clamped down tail (indicating timidity or undependable temperament, even less to be desired than the tail carried too gaily).

Forequarters:

Efficient movement in front calls for proper shoulders, the blades sloping back to form an angle with the upper arm of approximately 90 degrees which permits the dog to swing his forelegs forward in an easy manner.

Shoulders (fairly close together at the tips) to lie flat and mold smoothly into the contour of the body.

The forelegs to be straight with the same degree of size to the foot. The bone, strong, slightly flattened, not too heavy or round. The knee straight, almost flat; the pasterns short, strong; elbows close to the body with free action from the shoulders.

To be penalized: Shoulders set at a steep angle limiting the stride. Loaded shoulders (the blades standing out from the body by overdevelopment of the muscles). Loose elbows, crooked legs. Bone too light or too coarse and heavy. Weak pasterns that let down the feet at a pronounced angle.

Hindquarters:

The Springer should be shown in hard muscular condition, well developed in hips and thighs and the whole rear assembly should suggest strength and driving power.

The hip joints to be set rather wide apart and the hips nicely rounded. The thighs broad and muscular; the stifle joint strong and moderately bent. The hock joint somewhat rounded, not small and sharp in contour, and moderately angulated. Leg from hock joint to foot pad, short and strong with good bone structure.

When viewed from the rear the hocks to be parallel whether the dog is standing or in motion.

To be penalized: Too little or too much angulation. Narrow, undeveloped thighs. Hocks too short or too long (a proportion of 1/3 the distance from hip joint to foot is ideal). Flabby muscles. Weakness of joints.

Feet:

The feet to be round, or slightly oval, compact, well arched, medium size with thick pads, well feathered between the toes. Excess hair to be removed to show the natural shape and size of the foot.

To be penalized: Thin, open, or splayed feet (flat with spreading toes). Hare foot (long, rather narrow foot).

276

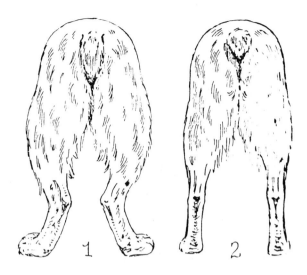

1. Cowhocks.
2. Good rear.

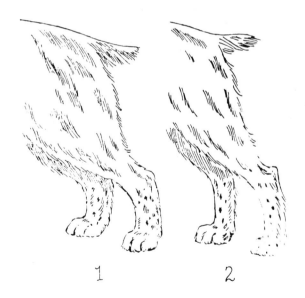

1. Good side rear.

2. Thigh too narrow — not enough angulation.
   Hocks too long and sharp.

277

Good Springer movement.

Movement:

In judging the Springer there should be emphasis on proper movement which is the final test of a dog's conformation and soundness. Prerequisite to good movement is balance of the front and rear assemblies. The two must match in angulation and muscular development if the gait is to be smooth and effortless.

Good shoulders laid back at an angle that permits a long stride are just as essential as the excellent rear quarters that provide the driving power.

When viewed from the front the dog's legs should appear to swing forward in a free and easy manner, with no tendency for the feet to cross over or interfere with each other. Viewed from the rear the hocks should drive well under the body following on a line with the forelegs, the rear legs parallel, neither too widely nor too closely spaced.

As speed increases there is a natural tendency for the legs to converge toward the center line of gravity or a single line of travel.

Seen from the side the Springer should exhibit a good long forward stride, without high-stepping or wasted motion.

To be penalized: Short choppy stride, mincing steps with up and down movement, hopping. Moving with forefeet wide, giving roll or swing to body. Weaving or crossing of forefeet or hind feet. Cowhocks—hocks turning in toward each other.

In judging the English Springer Spaniel, *the overall picture* is a primary consideration. It is urged that the judge look for *type* which includes general appearance, outline, and temperament, and also for *soundness,* especially as seen when the dog is in motion.

Inasmuch as the dog with a smooth easy gait must be reasonably sound and *well balanced* he is to be highly regarded in the show ring; however, not to the extent of forgiving him for not looking like an English Springer Spaniel.

A quite untypical dog, leggy, foreign in head and expression, may move well. But he should not be placed over a good all-round specimen that has a minor fault in movement.

It should be remembered that the English Springer Spaniel is first and foremost a sporting dog of the spaniel family and he must look and behave and move in character.

APPENDIX

*Pedigrees of some of the notable dogs and bitches
pictured in Chapters 16 and 17.*

Ch. Inchidony Prince Charming
Ch. Salilyn's Aristocrat
Ch. Salilyn's Lily of the Valley
Ch. Salilyn's Colonel's Overlord
Salilyn's Good Fortune
Ch. Salilyn's Radiance
Ch. Randalane's Bright Chips

Ch. Salilyn's Citation II
Ch. Salilyn's Cinderella II
Salilyn's Royal Consort
Salilyn's Glenda
Ch. Salilyn's Cocktail Time
Ch. Salilyn's Good Omen
Ch. Salilyn's MacDuff
Ch. Ascot's Libby

CH. SALILYN'S EXCLUSIVE *(P. 203)*

Ch. Salilyn's Encore
Ch. Salilyn's Classic
Salilyn's Arista
Ch. Salilyn's Allure
Ch. Salilyn's Aristocrat
Ch. Salilyn's Sophistication
Ch. Salilyn's Radiance

Ch. Salilyn's Colonel's Overlord
Ch. Salilyn's Something Special
Ch. Salilyn's Aristocrat
Ch. Valdarae's Pembroke Sea Mist, CD
Ch. Inchidony Prince Charming
Ch. Salilyn's Lily of the Valley
Salilyn's Good Fortune
Ch. Randalane's Bright Chips

Ch. Inchidony Prince Charming
Ch. Salilyn's Aristocrat
Ch. Salilyn's Lily of the Valley
Ch. Salilyn's Colonel's Overlord
Ch. Salilyn's Good Fortune
Ch. Salilyn's Radiance
Ch. Randalane's Bright Chips

A/C Ch. Salilyn's Citation II
Ch. Salilyn's Cinderella II
Salilyn's Royal Consort
Salilyn's Glenda
Ch. Salilyn's Cocktail Time
Ch. Salilyn's Good Omen
Ch. Salilyn's MacDuff
Ch. Ascot's Libby

CH. PRELUDE'S ECHO *(P. 205)*

Ch. Salilyn's Encore
Ch. Salilyn's Classic
Salilyn's Arista
Ch. Salilyn's Debutante II
Ch. Salilyn's Aristocrat
Ch. Salilyn's Sophistication
Ch. Salilyn's Radiance

Ch. Salilyn's Colonel's Overlord
Ch. Salilyn's Something Special
Ch. Salilyn's Aristocrat
Ch. Valdarae's Pembroke Sea Mist, CD
Ch. Inchidony Prince Charming
Ch. Salilyn's Lily of the Valley
Salilyn's Royal Consort
Salilyn's Glenda

Ch. Salilyn's Colonel's Overlord
Ch. Salilyn's Encore
Ch. Salilyn's Something Special
Ch. Salilyn's Classic
Ch. Salilyn's Aristocrat
Salilyn's Arista
Ch. Valdarae's Pembroke Sea Mist, CD

Ch. Salilyn's Aristocrat
Ch. Salilyn's Radiance
Ch. Inchidony Prince Charming
Ch. Salilyn's Lily of the Valley
Ch. Inchidony Prince Charming
Ch. Salilyn's Lily of the Valley
Ch. Salilyn's Inchidony Banquo
Ch. Phyllis Duchess of Pembroke, CD

CH. BORDALYN'S BEHOLD *(P. 208)*

Ch. Canarch Inchidony Sparkler
Ch. Salilyn's Paramount
Ch. Salilyn's Constellation
Ch. Bordalyn's Begin Again, CD
Ch. Welcome Great Day
Ch. Welcome Joie de Vivre
Ch. Welcome A Joy to Behold

Ch. Inchidony Prince Charming
Ch. Canarch Sunnyside
Ch. Salilyn's Inchidony Banquo
Ch. Phyllis Duchess of Pembroke, CD
Ch. Salilyn's Aristocrat
Ch. Salilyn's Bristol Cream, CDX
Ch. Welcome Great Day
A/C Ch. Flo-Bob's Me Too

Ch. Salilyn's Colonel's Overlord
Ch. Salilyn's Encore
   Ch. Salilyn's Something Special
Ch. Salilyn's Classic
   Ch. Salilyn's Aristocrat
Salilyn's Arista
   Ch. Valdarae's Pembroke Sea Mist, CD

Ch. Salilyn's Aristocrat
Ch. Salilyn's Radiance
Ch. Inchidony Prince Charming
Ch. Salilyn's Lily of the Valley
Ch. Inchidony Prince Charming
Ch. Salilyn's Lily of the Valley
Ch. Salilyn's Inchidony Banquo
Ch. Phyllis Duchess of Pembroke, CD

A/C CH. WINACKO'S CLASSIC REPLAY, CD (P. 209)
CH. WINACKO'S EDITOR'S CHOICE, CD (P. 210)

   Ch. Inchidony Prince Charming
A/C Ch. Canarch Yankee Patriot, CD
   Ch. Canarch Sunnyside, CD
Canarch Yankee Tea Party, CD
   A/C Canarch Inchidony Sparkler
Canarch Incadescent
   Canarch Sugar Pear

Ch. Salilyn's Citation II
Ch. Salilyn's Cinderella II
Ch. Syringa Disc Jockey
Melilotus Hufty Tufty
Ch. Inchidony Prince Charming
Ch. Canarch Sunnyside, CD
Frejax Model of Oak
Melilotus Hufty Tufty

Ch. Salilyn's Colonel's Overlord
Ch. Salilyn's Encore
   Ch. Salilyn's Something Special
Ch. Salilyn's Classic
   Ch. Salilyn's Aristocrat
Salilyn's Arista
   Ch. Valdarae's Pembroke Sea Mist, CD

Ch. Salilyn's Aristocrat
Ch. Salilyn's Radiance
Ch. Inchidony Prince Charming
Ch. Salilyn's Lily of the Valley
Ch. Inchidony Prince Charming
Ch. Salilyn's Lily of the Valley
Ch. Salilyn's Inchidony Banquo
Ch. Phyllis Duchess of Pembroke, CD

CH. FILICIA'S BEQUEST (P. 207)
CH. FILICIA'S ETCHING (P. 207)

   Ch. Inchidony Prince Charming
Ch. Charlyle's Fair Warning
   Charlyle's Nanette
Ch. Kaintuck Pixie, CD
   Ch. Kaintuck Cupid
Kaintuck Sprite
   Ch. Cartref Spring Chime

Ch. Salilyn's Citation II
Ch. Salilyn's Cinderella
Ch. Bannerett's Regal Brigadier
Charlyle's Happy Choice
Ch. Kaintuck Christmas Carol
Ch. Kaintuck Kate
Ch. Frejax King Peter
Cartref Coe of Bittersweet

Ch. Salilyn's Colonel's Overlord
Ch. Salilyn's Encore
   Ch. Salilyn's Something Special
Ch. Salilyn's Classic
   Ch. Salilyn's Aristocrat
Salilyn's Arista
   Ch. Valdarae's Pembroke Sea Mist, CD

Ch. Salilyn's Aristocrat
Ch. Salilyn's Radiance
Ch. Inchidony Prince Charming
Ch. Salilyn's Lily of the Valley
Ch. Inchidony Prince Charming
Ch. Salilyn's Lily of the Valley
Ch. Salilyn's Inchidony Banquo
Ch. Phyllis Duchess of Pembroke, CD

CH. SALILYN'S DESIGN (P. 212)

   Ch. Salilyn's Classic
Ch. Salilyn's Hallmark
   Ch. Salilyn's Welcome Edition
Ch. Salilyn's Applause
   Ch. Salilyn's Encore
Salilyn's Curtain Call
   Ch. Danaho's Ballet Russe

Ch. Salilyn's Encore
Salilyn's Arista
Ch. Salilyn's Aristocrat
Ch. Kennersleigh Cleavehill Beliza Bee
Ch. Salilyn's Colonel's Overlord
Ch. Salilyn's Something Special
Ch. Kaintuck Tolstoy
Spennymore's Noblesse Oblige

Ch. Inchidony Prince Charles
Ch. Salilyn's Aristocrat
Ch. Salilyn's Lily of the Valley
Ch. Telltale Author
Ch. Salilyn's Classic
Telltale Victoria
Canarch Triple Crown

CH. DONAHAN'S MARK TWAIN *(P. 211)*

Ch. Geiger's Chief Geronimo, CD, WDX
Ch. Magill's Patrick, CD, WDX
Cindy's Delight
Donahan's Vanna Brook, CD
Ch. Geiger's Chief Geronimo, CD, WDX
Ch. Lilley's Holiday Cheer, CDX
Ch. Lilley's Pheasant Quest, CD

Ch. Salilyn's Citation II
Ch. Salilyn's Cinderella II
Salilyn's Royal Consort
Salilyn's Glenda
Ch. Salilyn's Encore
Salilyn's Arista
Ch. Inchidony Prince Charming
Canarch Paddoch, CD

Ch. Geiger's Winaway Duke, UD
Ch. Schwedekrest Lady Pamela
Ch. Melilotus Little Acorn
Diamonds Duchess Delight
Ch. Geiger's Winaway Duke, UD
Ch. Schwedekrest Lady Pamela
Ch. King William of Salilyn
Ch. Sally Fetchitt

Ch. Salilyn's Classic
Ch. Filicia's Bequest
Ch. Kaintuck Pixie, CD
Ch. Salilyn's Private Stock
Ch. Salilyn's Aristocrat
Ch. Salilyn's Sonnet
Salilyn's Pirate Queen

CH. FILICIA'S DIVIDEND *(P. 213)*

Ch. Filicia's Etching
Ch. Filicia's Anlon Patriot
Ch. Filicia's Joy of Anlon
Ch. Donaho's Lalique of Stanton
Ch. Kaintuck Tolstoy
Ch. Donaho's Ballet Russe
Spennymore Noblisse Oblige

Ch. Salilyn's Encore
Salilyn's Arista
Ch. Charlyle's Fair Warning
Kaintuck Sprite
Ch. Inchidony Prince Charming
Ch. Salilyn's Lily of the Valley
Ch. Angledale's Moca Bandit
Ch. Salilyn's Something Special

Ch. Salilyn's Classic
Ch. Kaintuck Pixie, CD
Ch. Salilyn's Aristocrat
Ch. Kaintuck Pixie, CD
Ch. Charlyle's Fair Warning
Ch. Kaintuck Fortune Huntress
Ch. Spennymore Doc's Boy
Spennymore Billet Doux

Ch. Venetian Count Casanova, CD
Ch. Goodwill Copyright Reserve
Ch. Goodwill Persuasion, CDX
Ch. Goodwill Aspengrove, Q.T.
Ch. Inchidony Jack High
Ch. Goodwill Delightful Daisy, CD
Ch. Miss Becket's Delight, UD

CH. ASPENGROVE'S DUBONNET *(P. 216)*

Ch. Inchidony Prince Charming
Ch. Salilyn's Aristocrat
Ch. Salilyn's Lily of the Valley
Salilyn's Lady Kay
Ch. Anglodale's Mocha Bandit
Salilyn Pirate Queen
Ch. Salilyn's Something Special

Ch. Salilyn's Sensation
Ch. Salilyn's Citation II
Salilyn's Princess Meg
Salilyn's Royal Consort
Ch. Ascot's Ajax
Ch. Ascot's Estralita
Ascot's Diamond Lil
CH. SALILYN'S LILY OF THE VALLEY (P. 218)
Firebrand of Sandblown Acre, CDX
Ch. King William of Salilyn
Salutation of Salilyn
Salilyn's Glenda
Ch. Cartref Bob Bobbin
Ch. Salilyn's Good Omen
Salilyn's Surprise

Ch. Salilyn's Sensation, CD
A/C Ch. Salilyn's Citation II
Salilyn's Princess Meg
Ch. Inchidony Prince Charming
Ch. King Peter of Salilyn
Ch. Salilyn's Cinderella II
A/C Ch. Walpride Gay Beauty
CH. CANARCH INCHIDONY BROOK (P. 218)
Ch. Kaintuck Marc Anthony
Ch. Syringa Disc Jockey
Ch. Syringa Sue
Ch. Canarch Sunnyside, CD
Ch. Rostherne Hunter
Melilotus Hufty Tufty
Melilotus Princess Dona

A/C Ch. Salilyn's Citation II
Ch. Inchidony Prince Charming
Ch. Salilyn's Cinderella II
Ch. Salilyn's Aristocrat
Salilyn's Royal Consort
Ch. Salilyn's Lily of the Valley
Salilyn's Glenda

Ch. Salilyn's Sensation, CD
Salilyn's Princess Meg
Ch. King Peter of Salilyn
A/C Ch. Walpride Gay Beauty
Ch. Salilyn's Citation II
Ch. Salilyn's Estralita
Ch. King William of Salilyn
Ch. Salilyn's Good Omen

CH. SALILYN'S SOPHISTICATION (P. 219)

Ch. Salilyn's Cocktail Time
Salilyn's Good Fortune
Ch. Salilyn's Good Omen
Ch. Salilyn's Radiance
Ch. Salilyn's MacDuff
Ch. Randalane's Bright Chips
Ch. Ascot's Libby

Ch. Salilyn's MacDuff
Ch. Salilyn's Concerto
Ch. Cartref Bob Bobbin
Salilyn's Surprise
Ch. King William of Salilyn
Shercliff's Lady Debbie
Ch. Kaintuck Marc Anthony
Ch. Sunhi's Doody

Ch. Salilyn's Citation II
Ch. Inchidony Prince Charming
Ch. Salilyn's Cinderella II
A/C Canarch Yankee Patriot, CD
Ch. Syringa Disc Jockey
Ch. Canarch Sunnyside, CD
Melilotus Hufty Tufty

Ch. Salilyn's Sensation, CD
Salilyn's Princess Meg
Ch. King Peter of Salilyn
A/C Ch. Walpride's Gay Beauty
Ch. Kaintuck Marc Anthony
Ch. Syringa Sue
Ch. Rostherne Hunter
Melilotus Princess Dona

CANARCH YANKEE TEA PARTY, CD (P. 221)

Ch. Inchidony Prince Charming
Ch. Canarch Inchidony Sparkler
Ch. Canarch Sunnyside, CD
Canarch Incadescent
Frejax Model of Oak
Canarch Sugar Pear
Melilotus Hufty Tufty

Ch. Salilyn's Citation II
Ch. Salilyn's Cinderella II
Ch. Syringa Disc Jockey
Melilotus Hufty Tufty
Ch. Melilotus Royal Oak
Frejax Lilac Model
Ch. Rostherne Hunter
Melilotus Princess Dona

283

Ch. Inchidony Prince Charming
Ch. Canarch Inchidony Sparkler
Ch. Canarch Sunnyside, CD
Ch. Salilyn's Paramount
Ch. Salilyn's Inchidony Banquo
Ch. Salilyn's Constellation
Ch. Phyllis Duchess of Pembroke, CD

A/C Ch. Salilyn's Citation
Ch. Salilyn's Cinderella
Ch. Syringa Disc Jockey
Melilotus Hufty Tufty
Ch. Salilyn's MacDuff
Ch. Salilyn's Cinderella
Ch. Salilyn's Santa Claus
Grande Pointe's First Lady

CH. BORDALYN'S BEGIN AGAIN, CD (P. 221)

Ch. Salilyn's Aristocrat
Ch. Welcome Great Day
Ch. Salilyn's Bristol Cream, CDX
Ch. Welcome Joie de Vivre
Ch. Welcome Great Day
Ch. Welcome A Joy to Behold
Ch. Flo-Bob's Mee Too

Ch. Inchidony Prince Charming
Ch. Salilyn's Lily of the Valley
A/C Ch. Gay Beauty's Academy Award
Ch. Salilyn's Good Omen
Ch. Salilyn's Aristocrat
Ch. Salilyn's Bristol Cream, CDX
Ch. Geiger's Chief Geronimo
Ch. Belle of Schoodic

Ch. Salilyn's Encore
Ch. Salilyn's Classic
Ch. Salilyn's Something Special
Ch. Bordalyn's Behold
Ch. Salilyn's Paramount
Ch. Bordalyn's Begin Again
Ch. Welcome Joie de Vivre

Ch. Salilyn's Colonel's Overlord
Ch. Salilyn's Something Special
Ch. Salilyn's Aristocrat
Ch. Valdarae's Pembroke Sea Mist, CD
Ch. Canarch Inchidony Sparkler
Ch. Salilyn's Constellation
Ch. Welcome Great Day
Ch. Welcome A Joy To Behold

CH. FLINTLOCK'S HOPE OF LEAR (P. 226)

Ch. Salilyn's Paramount
A/C Ch. Bordalyn's Love Affair, CD
Ch. Welcome Joie de Vivre
Ch. Bordalyn's Once In Love With Amy
Ch. Beryltown Midnight Terror
Amanda Spaniels at the Bay
Lady Gertrude of Cherry Hill

Ch. Canarch Inchidony Sparkler
Ch. Salilyn's Constellation
Ch. Welcome Great Day
Ch. Welcome A Joy To Behold
Ch. Beryltown Brown
Ch. Beryltown Pocket Rocket
Rathwell of Arunel
Mab of Melilotus

Ch. Salilyn's Aristocrat
Ch. Chinoes Adamant James
Ch. Canarch Inchidony Brook
Ch. Loujon Executor
Ch. Salilyn's Captains Table
Ch. Loujon Jennifer
Loujon Cameo Caprice

Ch. Inchidony Prince Charming
Ch. Salilyn's Lily of the Valley
Ch. Inchidony Prince Charming
Ch. Canarch Sunnyside, CD
Ch. Salilyn's Aristocrat
Ch. Lin Bar's Black Beauty
Ch. Loujon Beau of Dewry Lane
Ch. Loujon Lightning Cameo

CH. LOUJON'S FEMININITY (P. 224)

A/C Ch. Salilyn's MacDuff
Ch. Salilyn's Inchidony Banquo
Ch. Salilyn's Cinderella II
Varis Cinderella Star
Ch. Salilyn's Aristocrat
Ch. Salilyn's Welcome Edition
Ch. Kennersleigh Cleavehill Beliza Bee

Ch. King William of Salilyn
Shercliffe's Lady Debbie
Ch. King Peter of Salilyn
A/C Ch. Walpride of Gay Beauty
Ch. Inchidony Prince Charming
Ch. Salilyn's Lily of the Valley
Eng. Ch. Cleavehill Dandini
Eng. Ch. Bella Bee of Kennersleigh

Ch. King William of Salilyn
  Ch. Salilyn's MacDuff
    Shercliff's Lady Debbie
  Ch. Salilyn's Cocktail Time
    Ch. King Peter of Salilyn
    Ch. Salilyn's Concerto
      Ch. Ascot's Estralita

A/C CH. NOBILITY'S VENETIAN DAWN, A/C UD *(P. 218)*

    Ch. Salilyn's Citation II
    Salilyn's Royal Consort
    Ch. Ascot's Estralita
  Ch. Salilyn's Nobility Rose
    Ch. King William of Salilyn
    Salilyn's Glenda
      Ch. Salilyn's Good Omen

Firebrand of Sandblown Acre, CDX
Salutation of Salilyn
Ch. Sir Lancelot of Salilyn
Candy Kisses of Kanona
Firebrand of Sandblown Acre, CDX
Salutation of Salilyn
Ch. Ascot's Ajax
Ascot's Diamond Lil
Ch. Salilyn's Sensation, CD
Salilyn's Princess Meg
Ch. Ascot's Ajax
Ascot's Diamond Lil
Firebrand of Sandblown Acre, CDX
Salutation of Salilyn
Ch. Cartref Bob Bobbin
Salilyn's Surprise

Ch. Salilyn's Aristocrat
Ch. Salilyn's Colonel's Overlord
Ch. Salilyn's Radiance
Ch. Salilyn's Exclusive
  Ch. Salilyn's Classic
  Ch. Salilyn's Allure
    Ch. Salilyn's Sophistication

CH. SALILYN'S DELIGHT *(P. 225)*

  Ch. Salilyn's Classic
  Ch. Bordalyn's Behold
    Ch. Bordalyn's Begin Again
Ch. Salilyn's Limited Edition
  Ch. Salilyn's Aristocrat
  Ch. Salilyn's Welcome Edition
    Ch. Kennersleigh Cleavehill Beliza Bee

Ch. Inchidony Prince Charming
Ch. Salilyn's Lily of the Valley
Ch. Salilyn's Good Fortune
Ch. Randalane's Bright Chips
Ch. Salilyn's Encore
Salilyn's Arista
Ch. Salilyn's Aristocrat
Ch. Salilyn's Radiance

Ch. Salilyn's Encore
Salilyn's Arista
Ch. Salilyn's Paramount
Ch. Welcome Joie de Vivre
Ch. Inchidony Prince Charming
Ch. Salilyn's Lily of the Valley
Eng. Sh. Ch. Cleavehill Dandini
Eng. Sh. Ch. Bella Bee of Kennersleigh

Ch. Salilyn's Colonel's Overlord
Ch. Salilyn's Encore
Ch. Salilyn's Something Special
Ch. Salilyn's Classic
  Ch. Salilyn's Aristocrat
  Salilyn's Arista
    Ch. Valdarae's Pembroke Sea Mist, CD

CH. SALILYN'S LYRA *(P. 226)*

  Ch. Inchidony Prince Charming
  Ch. Salilyn's Aristocrat
    Ch. Salilyn's Lily of the Valley
Ch. Silverbow's December Dawn
  Ch. Salilyn's Colonel's Overlord
  Ch. Salilyn's Touch of Mink
    Ch. Salilyn's Something Special

Ch. Salilyn's Aristocrat
Ch. Salilyn's Radiance
Ch. Inchidony Prince Charming
Ch. Salilyn's Lily of the Valley
Ch. Inchidony Prince Charming
Ch. Salilyn's Lily of the Valley
Ch. Salilyn's Inchidony Banquo
Ch. Phyllis Duchess of Pembroke, CD

A/C Ch. Salilyn's Citation II
Ch. Salilyn's Cinderella II
Salilyn's Royal Consort
Salilyn's Glenda
Ch. Salilyn's Aristocrat
Ch. Salilyn's Radiance
Ch. Inchidony Prince Charming
Ch. Salilyn's Lily of the Valley

Ch. Inchidony Prince Charming
Ch. Salilyn's Aristocrat
Ch. Salilyn's Lily of the Valley
Ch. Cricket's Rhody Mac
Ch. Salilyn's Classic
A/C Ch. Venetian Cricket's Cinnamon
A/C Ch. S. Cricket Venetian, CD

Ch. Salilyn's Citation II
Ch. Salilyn's Cinderella II
Salilyn's Royal Consort
Salilyn's Glenda
Ch. Salilyn's Encore
Salilyn's Arista
Ch. Inchidony Prince Charming
A/C Ch. Nobility's Venetian Dawn, A/C UD

A/C CH. MAGINNA'S ROYAL HEIRESS (P. 227)

Ch. Salilyn's Colonel's Overlord
Ch. Salilyn's Encore
Ch. Salilyn's Something Special
Ch. Loujon Maginna's Victoria
Ch. Chinoes Adamant James
Ch. Loujon Heritage
Ch. Loujon Jennifer

Ch. Salilyn's Aristocrat
Ch. Salilyn's Radiance
Ch. Inchidony Prince Charming
Ch. Salilyn's Lily of the Valley
Ch. Salilyn's Aristocrat
Ch. Canarch Inchidony Brook
Ch. Salilyn's Captain's Tabele
Loujon Cameo's Caprice

Ch. Marjons Black is Beautiful
Ch. Marjons Tumbleweed
Ch. Marjons M's Abigale Doolittle, CD, PC
Whitestar's Wayward Wind
Ch. Salilyn's Aristocrat
Ch. Whitestar's West Wind
Sundance Midnight Magic

A/C Ch. Canarch Inchidony Herald
Ch. Melilotus Beauty
Ch. Marjon's Woodruff
Ch. Marjon's Peppermint Patty
Ch. Inchidony Prince Charming
Ch. Salilyn's Lily of the Valley
Brilakents Prince Rudolph
Marjon's Candy

CH. WHITESTAR'S IRISH LACE (P. 229)

Ch. Goodwill Copyright
Ch. Lakme's Bicentennial Salute
Ch. Lakme's MS. Scorpio
Lakme's Summer Star
Ch. Kaintuck Tolstoy
Lakme's Librian Galaxy
Bonnie Belle of Merry-L

Ch. Venetian Count Casanova
Ch. Goodwill Persuasion, CDX
Ch. Salilyn's Aristocrat
Sundance's Midnight Magic
Ch. Charlyle's Fair Warning
Ch. Kaintuck Fortune Huntress
Prince Solo of Saxony
Sugar Belle of Merry-L

Ch. Salilyn's Classic
Ch. Filicia's Bequest
Ch. Kaintuck Pixie, CD
Ch. Salilyn's Private Stock
Ch. Salilyn's Aristocrat
Ch. Salilyn's Sonnet
Salilyn's Pirate Queen

Ch. Salilyn's Encore
·alilyn's Arista
Ch. Charlyle's Fair Warning
Kaintuck Sprite
Ch. Inchidony Prince Charming
Ch. Salilyn's Lily of the Valley
Ch. Anglodale Mocha Bandit
Ch. Salilyn's Something Special

CH. MONOGRAM'S ENGLISH GARDEN (P. 230)

Ch. Salilyn's Colonel's Overlord
Ch. Salilyn's Exclusive
Ch. Salilyn's Allure
Ch. Monogram's English Ivy
Ch. Salilyn's Aristocrat
Joies Venetian Jay Jay
Ch. Venetian Cricket's Dancer, CD

Ch. Salilyn's Aristocrat
Ch. Salilyn's Radiance
Ch. Salilyn's Classic
Ch. Salilyn's Sophistication
Ch. Inchidony Prince Charming
Ch. Salilyn's Lily of the Valley
Ch. Canarch Yankee Patriot, CD
Ch. S. Cricket Venetian, CD

Ch. Chinoe's Eminent Judge, C.D.X. and his son, Chuzzlewit's MacHeath. Eminent Judge is also the sire of the first O.T. Ch. Springer, Chuzzlewit's Favorite Son. Owner, Frances Nelson. —*Photo, Jean Jasinsky*

BIBLIOGRAPHY

ALL OWNERS of pure-bred dogs will benefit themselves and their dogs by enriching their knowledge of breeds and of canine care, training, breeding, psychology and other important aspects of dog management. The following list of books covers further reading recommended by judges, veterinarians, breeders, trainers and other authorities. Books may be obtained at the finer book stores and pet shops, or through Howell Book House Inc., publishers, New York.

Breed Books

AFGHAN HOUND, Complete	Miller & Gilbert
AIREDALE, New Complete	Edwards
AKITA, Complete	Linderman & Funk
ALASKAN MALAMUTE, Complete	Riddle & Seeley
BASSET HOUND, Complete	Braun
BEAGLE, New Complete	Noted Authorities
BLOODHOUND, Complete	Brey & Reed
BOXER, Complete	Denlinger
BRITTANY SPANIEL, Complete	Riddle
BULLDOG, New Complete	Hanes
BULL TERRIER, New Complete	Eberhard
CAIRN TERRIER, Complete	Marvin
CHESAPEAKE BAY RETRIEVER, Complete	Cherry
CHIHUAHUA, Complete	Noted Authorities
COCKER SPANIEL, New	Kraeuchi
COLLIE, New	Official Publication of Collie Club of America
DACHSHUND, The New	Meistrell
DALMATIAN, The	Treen
DOBERMAN PINSCHER, New	Walker
ENGLISH SETTER, New Complete	Tuck, Howell & Graef
ENGLISH SPRINGER SPANIEL, New	Goodall & Gasow
FOX TERRIER, New Complete	Silvernail
GERMAN SHEPHERD DOG, New Complete	Bennett
GERMAN SHORTHAIRED POINTER, New	Maxwell
GOLDEN RETRIEVER, New Complete	Fischer
GORDON SETTER, Complete	Look
GREAT DANE, New Complete	Noted Authorities
GREAT DANE, The—Dogdom's Apollo	Draper
GREAT PYRENEES, Complete	Strang & Giffin
IRISH SETTER, New Complete	Eldredge & Vanacore
IRISH WOLFHOUND, Complete	Starbuck
KEESHOND, Complete	Peterson
LABRADOR RETRIEVER, Complete	Warwick
LHASA APSO, Complete	Herbel
MINIATURE SCHNAUZER, Complete	Eskrigge
NEWFOUNDLAND, New Complete	Chern
NORWEGIAN ELKHOUND, New Complete	Wallo
OLD ENGLISH SHEEPDOG, Complete	Mandeville
PEKINGESE, Quigley Book of	Quigley
PEMBROKE WELSH CORGI, Complete	Sargent & Harper
POODLE, New Complete	Hopkins & Irick
POODLE CLIPPING AND GROOMING BOOK, Complete	Kalstone
ROTTWEILER, Complete	Freeman
SAMOYED, Complete	Ward
SCHIPPERKE, Official Book of	Root, Martin, Kent
SCOTTISH TERRIER, New Complete	Marvin
SHETLAND SHEEPDOG, The New	Riddle
SHIH TZU, Joy of Owning	Seranne
SHIH TZU, The (English)	Dadds
SIBERIAN HUSKY, Complete	Demidoff
TERRIERS, The Book of All	Marvin
WEST HIGHLAND WHITE TERRIER, Complete	Marvin
WHIPPET, Complete	Pegram
YORKSHIRE TERRIER, Complete	Gordon & Bennett

Breeding

ART OF BREEDING BETTER DOGS, New	Onstott
BREEDING YOUR OWN SHOW DOG	Seranne
HOW TO BREED DOGS	Whitney
HOW PUPPIES ARE BORN	Prine
INHERITANCE OF COAT COLOR IN DOGS	Little

Care and Training

DOG OBEDIENCE, Complete Book of	Saunders
NOVICE, OPEN AND UTILITY COURSES	Saunders
DOG CARE AND TRAINING FOR BOYS AND GIRLS	Saunders
DOG NUTRITION, Collins Guide to	Collins
DOG TRAINING FOR KIDS	Benjamin
DOG TRAINING, Koehler Method of	Koehler
DOG TRAINING Made Easy	Tucker
GO FIND! Training Your Dog to Track	Davis
GUARD DOG TRAINING, Koehler Method of	Koehler
OPEN OBEDIENCE FOR RING, HOME AND FIELD, Koehler Method of	Koehler
STONE GUIDE TO DOG GROOMING FOR ALL BREEDS	Stone
SUCCESSFUL DOG TRAINING, The Pearsall Guide to	Pearsall
TOY DOGS, Kalstone Guide to Grooming All	Kalstone
TRAINING THE RETRIEVER	Kersley
TRAINING YOUR DOG—Step by Step Manual	Volhard & Fisher
TRAINING YOUR DOG TO WIN OBEDIENCE TITLES	Morsell
TRAIN YOUR OWN GUN DOG, How to	Goodall
UTILITY DOG TRAINING, Koehler Method of	Koehler
VETERINARY HANDBOOK, Dog Owner's Home	Carlson & Giffin

General

AKC'S WORLD OF THE PURE-BRED DOG	American Kennel Club
CANINE TERMINOLOGY	Spira
COMPLETE DOG BOOK, The	Official Publication of American Kennel Club
DOG IN ACTION, The	Lyon
DOG BEHAVIOR, New Knowledge of	Pfaffenberger
DOG JUDGE'S HANDBOOK	Tietjen
DOG JUDGING, Nicholas Guide to	Nicholas
DOG PEOPLE ARE CRAZY	Riddle
DOG PSYCHOLOGY	Whitney
DOGSTEPS, Illustrated Gait at a Glance	Elliott
DOG TRICKS	Haggerty & Benjamin
ENCYCLOPEDIA OF DOGS, International	Dangerfield, Howell & Riddle
FROM RICHES TO BITCHES	Shattuck
IN STITCHES OVER BITCHES	Shattuck
JUNIOR SHOWMANSHIP HANDBOOK	Brown & Mason
MY TIMES WITH DOGS	Fletcher
OUR PUPPY'S BABY BOOK (blue or pink)	
SUCCESSFUL DOG SHOWING, Forsyth Guide to	Forsyth
TRIM, GROOM & SHOW YOUR DOG, How to	Saunders
WHY DOES YOUR DOG DO THAT?	Bergman
WILD DOGS in Life and Legend	Riddle
WORLD OF SLED DOGS, From Siberia to Sport Racing	Coppinger